# A BOOK OF
# DANISH
# BALLADS

SELECTED AND WITH AN INTRODUCTION BY
**AXEL OLRIK**

TRANSLATED BY
**E. M. SMITH-DAMPIER**

*Granger Index Reprint Series*

**BOOKS FOR LIBRARIES PRESS**
FREEPORT, NEW YORK

LIBRARY OF CONGRESS CATALOG CARD NUMBER:

68-57063

MANUFACTURED BY
HALLMARK LITHOGRAPHERS, INC.
IN THE U.S.A.

# CONTENTS

## *Volume I*

## Ballads of Chivalry

## Ballads of Satire

# Volume II

# EDITORIAL NOTE

AXEL OLRIK (1864-1917) was Professor of Folklore in the University of Copenhagen and founder of the Danish Folklore Collection. Denmark possesses a unique treasure in her wealth of ancient popular ballads, and it was natural that the world pioneer in Folk ballad research should be a Dane, Svend Grundtvig. He first introduced the practice of printing all variants of a ballad just as he found them. *Danmarks gamle Folkeviser*, publication of which began in 1853, became the model for Professor Francis James Child of Harvard University in his great work, *The English and Scottish Popular Ballads* (5 vols., 1882-1898). When Grundtvig died, in 1883, Axel Olrik, then in his twentieth year, took over the task of completing the gigantic collection of ballads which has been called "the greatest monument in the literature of Denmark."

Olrik was not satisfied, however, with a work that could be used only by scholars. He had an ardent desire to make the ancient folk songs and legends the property of the whole people. Therefore he selected fifty-one of the finest ballads and published them in collaboration with Ida Falbe-Hansen, without any learned apparatus but with an illuminating Introduction relating them to the life of the people. This volume, which was called *Danske Folkeviser i Udvalg* was published in 1899. It was followed in 1909 with another collection of thirty-two ballads entitled *Danske Folkeviser i Udvalg. Anden Samling*.

These two volumes still constitute the standard collection for popular use in Denmark and have been closely followed by

Miss Smith-Dampier, who had the benefit of Olrik's advice when she first began the work of ballad translation more than twenty-five years ago. Two of the ballads and a portion of the Notes, mainly those of philological content, have been omitted in accordance with his request. A few of the translations have been published before, but have been revised by Miss Smith-Dampier for the present edition.

THE COMMITTEE ON PUBLICATIONS

# DANISH BALLADS
## VOLUME I

---

# INTRODUCTION

# INTRODUCTION

៖

## THE DANCE AND THE DANCE BALLAD

O F THE DANISH BALLADS as we have them today, some were written down by ladies of quality during the sixteenth and seventeenth centuries; some, even till modern times, were still sung by the peasantry, in the communal work-rooms, or on festive occasions, or at home by mother to child. Long before they were put on paper, however, there was a period, that of their existence during the Middle Ages, when they were learnt solely by means of song, in totally different circumstances. They had not, in those days, any special association either with festivity or with handicraft, but were sung during the dance—a fact which requires more minute explanation.

The dance sprang up during the Age of Chivalry, and became a favourite accomplishment in every European nation. Men and women together formed a circle and danced the round. The music was supplied either by some instrument, or by one of the circle who sang a melody, improvising such words as occurred to him at the moment, an invitation to the dance, an outburst of joy, of longing, or of merriment. The Troubadours of Southern France and the later Minnesingers of Germany composed many of their minor poems as dance songs, and the dance found its way to every region on the wings of words and melody. It took the whole North by storm, from the Danish Court to the Icelandic farmstead. Indeed, it

· 3 ·

actually invaded the cloister. When the famous Absalon became Bishop of Sælland (1158), the monks of Eskilsö were in the habit of inviting their kinsfolk, both male and female, to feast and dance with them in the refectory. Where they were concerned, the Bishop soon put a stop to the pastime, but it flourished freely in other surroundings, and vainly did the great historian, Saxo Grammaticus, denounce such "mountebank antics" as unworthy of noblemen and warriors.

The dance is pictured in the ballads again and again. A mixed flock of men and women would take one another's hands, and dance in a chain or circle, on the floor of the hall, or preferably out-of-doors, in castle garth or meadow, or down by the waterside. Time and rhythm were regulated by a leader who either sang himself, or else (which was a more popular practice) had a woman dancing beside him to sing the ballad. The circle could be "broken" at any moment, when the dancers "stretched forth their hands" to bring in fresh partners. Dancing took place on any and every occasion; the King's men would dance together before the castle gate, the noble lady and her serving-maids would put down their work, and tread a dance on the floor of their chamber. Things went most merrily, however, when crowds flocked together to celebrate festal occasions, above all during the great popular feast-tides of the year, when the old games were superseded by the dance and dance ballad, on Midsummer Eve round the fires of St. John, or at the midwinter assemblies, the Yuletide feasts, with their Yule bucks, hart dances, and other mummeries. Even the solemnities of the church afforded occasion for the dance. The Eves of the greater festivals, the Vigils or watch nights, were hallowed with solemn worship; the people came thronging in multitudes to hear mass sung at the appointed hours of the night, and passed their time during the intervals with conversation and story-telling, with song and dance. Such was the intermingling during the Middle Ages of the earthly and the unearthly, the worldly and other-worldly. "Watch night" became the common term for all riotous youthful orgies by the watch-fire or under the maypole, orgies from which honest maidens held aloof. There were many varieties of dancing, however, from the wooing dance which might be too daring, to the sword dance of a more courtly description. At the bridal of Knight Stig he himself led the dance, a golden goblet in hand, from which he pledged the bride.

To the dance belonged the song, the words invented by the singer to fit the tune, preferably an expression of his own feelings, or an impression of the surrounding world. Now an incitement to gaiety, as in the little Icelandic verse:

> *Sweet the swan is singing*
> *All the summer night,*
> *Joy it is to dance and play,*
> *My lily white!*

Now an outburst of grief:

> *Heavy are my sorrows,*
> *A load of lead to bear,*
> *Burnt are all the castles*
> *Were builded new and fair.*[1]

Sometimes a brisk song for the warriors' weapon dance, like this Danish verse:

> *The King he rules the castle,*
> *And over all the land,*
> *And over many a gallant knight*
> *With shining sword in hand.*
> *(The King he rules the castle.)*

[1] This verse was sung by the Icelander Tord Andresson with evil forebodings, when he was taken captive by Earl Gissur (1264). On the following day the Earl broke his truce and had him hanged.

· 5 ·

> Now let the yeoman guide his farm,
> The knight his steed of power,
> But he that is King in Denmark
> Must rule o'er town and tower.
> (The King he rules the castle.)

"Spare not your shoon," runs a Faroëse verse, "tread hard on the floor; God knows alone if we meet at Yule once more."

All kinds of reference to the dancers' own circle may be found in the dance verses—a "love song" sung by a knight to a lady, and vice versa, or a jesting dialogue between a swain and a maiden, which might either have been committed to memory or improvised in the excitement of the occasion. This class of ballad might include satires on well known characters. "The dance by Ribe gate doth go, they mock at Swart Iver who is black as a crow," is a pithy example. Or proud Elselil, rising from her work, requests her maidens to dance with her, and sing a song of her wooers, the sons of Sir Lave of Lund:

> The one of them hight Sir Mogens,
> The other Sir Eske Hawk,
> In the royal court have they served
> so long,
> They can bear neither heat nor smoke.

> The third of them hight Sir Ove,
> A book-learned lord is he;
> There lies in my kist a clasp of gold
> Is worth them all the three.

This lyrical verse, in which is expressed the rich emotional life of the Middle Ages, became united as time went on with the narrative poem. In France little lyrical fables were used as dance poems, as undoubtedly were all English ballads in couplets, but in the North this union of lyric and narrative took place in an absolutely individual manner. Narrative poems were originally sung alone; they consisted of a series of two- or four-lined verses, each bound together with one single pair of rhymes. These end rhymes succeeded to the alliteration of the antique lays; and the rhymed poems were chanted by professional minstrels at the King's court, during journeys, or when armies marched to battle.[2] The Danish minstrel present at the battle of Graahede (1157) doubtless belonged to this class, as did the German singer who followed Knud Lavard to Haraldsted (1131). The new departure that took place (about 1200) consisted in the amalgamation of the long narrative ballad with the little dance lyric. The leader who set the dance going would begin with the customary expression of emotion, but would continue with a narrative ballad in an accordant mood; and, as the tune recurred with every verse, so also one or two of the lines were repeated which indicated the appropriate feeling. For example, we have quoted the little lyric of the King who rules the castle. From this the singer would proceed to a narrative dealing with the greatest King with the bravest of followers, the mighty King Didrik and his champions.

> *King Didrik sits in Brattingsborg,*
> *Both far and wide looks he:*
> *Oh, none know I in all the world*
> *That may my equal be!*

"The King he rules the castle," was repeated by the dancers, not only with the first verse, but with the whole series, as their common keynote. This line became the burden of the ballad. When the lyrical introductory stanza came to be looked on as a necessity for every narrative ballad, the composers of new ones would add their own introductions in a

[2] Thus Taillefer, William the Conqueror's minstrel, is said to have inspired the Norman army by singing the Song of Roland at the battle of Hastings (1066). (Translator's note)

corresponding key, often with some hint at the events of the story.

> I saw a sail fare o'er the Sound,
> (So many a pennon of gold)
> There sailed the Knight Strange with
> Dagmar the Queen.

> The King and Sir Strange they sat at
> the board,
> (So many a pennon of gold)
> There spake they so many a jesting word.
> There sailed the Knight Strange with
> Dagmar the Queen.

> Lithe now and listen, Sir Strange, to me,
> (So many a pennon of gold)
> Thou shalt fare to Bejerland and woo a
> maid for me.
> There sailed Sir Strange with
> Dagmar the Queen.

In course of time, burden and introductory stanza lost their connection. The burden is invariably found with the ballad, but the introduction has sometimes fallen away, or expresses something quite alien to the ballad itself.

### BALLADS IN GENERAL

From the artistic point of view, the ballads must be considered as in many respects conditioned by the life which gave birth to them, by the dance itself, and by the landscape which was so frequently its setting. The dance brought a richer vein of sentiment in its train, a strengthening of vitality, the budding of desire, and the blossoming of love. A wealth of emotion was liberated; even the outcry of despair was woven into the tissue of poetry. The actual band of singers and dancers is often pictured in the ballads. Again and again they hark back to similar scenes—the dialogue between Queen Sophy and Tove during the dance in the castle yard, or the dance of the Danish maidens which makes their fortune with the King of the Wends. When foreign ballads were imported, the dance lent them a native touch. Sir Oluf's meeting with the elf maid derives its real character from the maddening, alluring dance of the elves. And even the robust Ballad of King Didrik (No. 4), the adaptation of a Netherlandish warrior ballad, had to follow the custom of the country, and conclude with a merry jig, the wild Sivord Snarensvend dancing with the uprooted oak tree in his belt. The ballad as a whole might well be called a eulogy of the dance—the dance which opens the path for love, not to mention envy and hatred in the outcasts who stand and look on.

The burden had a remarkable part to play. With its constant repetition it may be compared to a gateway opening between the ballad itself and the circle of songsters. Now it is an invitation to high-born gentlemen to dance on, since day has not dawned as yet; now an outburst of the feeling whence the ballad sprang, of time which is long and grief so sore, or a cry of longing: "Could I but win me one of the fairest!" Sometimes it pictures the open-air setting, the unfolding leaves, or the "summer and the meadow that mate so well together." Or: "Now falleth and fadeth the leaf in the greenwood." Sometimes we see the sun shining red over the holy shrine, or the storm driving along the white strand to northward. The burden of "The Elfin Shaft" (No. 7), "gay goes the dance by the greenwood tree," is wonderfully interwoven with the narrative, depicting at one and the same time the circle of dancers beside the darkening wood, whose depths conceal all manner of sinister powers, and the actual dance of the elf maids, as it beguiles the unsuspecting knight. Such pictures of Nature as abound in modern poetry are not to be found in the ballad. The linden is beloved because of its "gilded leaves," when it blossoms in summer before the castle gate; the maiden may be likened to rose or lily, growing in the garden of castle and cloister; but oak and beech are mentioned merely as fuel or timber for building. Attention may be drawn to hart and roe as they sport among the forest trees, but the life of Nature as a whole is no subject of contemplation. It is seen only through the half-conscious emotions and impulses of man, and is shown in a variety of forms, from the youthful powers of growth to the fall and fading of the leaf, from sunshine to gathering storm and the cold cutting of the sea wind. The boat song, the leap of the hart, the charger's hoof-beat, the far-away sound of dancing beyond the fjord—all these have set their fugitive imprint on the burden.

The commencement of a ballad loses no time in plunging the listener into the action. The introductory verse must be sufficiently powerful to arouse the attention of the dancers. It must present a picture which instantaneously leaps into life before them all, which both conveys the atmosphere, and presents a situation peculiar to the character of the ballad itself.

> The smack lies up on the lee-land,
> And under her grows the grass,
> Oh never so rash a steersman
> As Sir John Remorssen was!

After this introduction the story proceeds to describe Sir John's luckless sea voyage.

At times this verse is purely lyrical.

> We were so many sisters small,
> (On the lea)
> So early did our father fall.
> The day it dawneth and the dew
>                     driveth so free.

Then the ballad relates the death of Sir Torben, and the meeting between his orphan daughter and his slayer (No. 35).

Sometimes, as in No. 44, the verse introduces the chief characters of the narrative.

> *Skammel he dwells up North in Ty,*
> *And Skammel is rich and gay,*
> *Five sons had he both fair and tall,*
> *But two went an evil way.*
> *And therefore treads Ebbe Skammelson*
> > *so wild a way alone.*

Finally, the introductory stanza (possibly because the original lyrical one has been lost) may present the opening scene of the story. "Gay goes the dance in the castle garth"— "Iver and Esbern both were merry, they sat a-drinking at the Ferry." Such quiet, vivid scenes lead us into the story. It seems a ballad rule never to plunge into violent passion or action, nor even into dialogue, until we have learnt to know the actors. But just because the conventions governing the opening scene are so rigid, we find occasion to observe the ever rich variety of the pictures in question. Knight and lady sit at dice in her bower, the mother instructs her daughter, "Queen Dagmar lies in Ribe sick," the knight rides out a-wooing, the chieftains sit drinking in the hall, the nobles ride out to buy garments in Ribe, Marsken awakes and tells his dream, "all on a Thursday evening they scoured both spear and sword," and so forth. From such simple everyday doings the ballad passes with astonishing ease to the fiercer conflicts of life. Often a brief dialogue places action and opposition clearly before us.

Daughter asks of mother:

> "Had I ne'er a brother?"
> "Yea, thou hast a brother bold,
> But captive he lies in the Count's
> stronghold."

This kind of lucidity can be found in every scene of a true ballad, which deals only with essential features, few though they may be. The action is compressed, with no superfluous word-painting or digression; all leads up to a single issue which is directly placed before us. Hence the ballad form has the capability of dealing with weighty and fateful happenings, and bringing them clearly home to the listener, even in the case of such complex situations as that of proud Adelus, between her love for Ebbe Skammelson and her sense of duty towards his brother (No. 44).

This directness is echoed by the complete simplicity of ballad versification. A great number, usually the most ancient, are composed in two-lined verses, which only allow space (so to speak) for what is absolutely essential. Others have a simple four-lined type of stanza. A slight variation may be found in the "Aage and Else" (No. 3) metre, the second and fourth lines of which have only two stresses.

> Three maidens sit in a bower,
> Two broider with gold,
> The third she weeps her own true-love
> Under darksome mould.

Such simply built verse, however, was enlivened by the changeful tunes, and by the burdens, often most artistically woven in between the lines (No. 37, "Lovel and John"). From this the versification derived its character, and the brief, unadorned narrative its emotional content.

The plain mode of expression was borrowed from everyday speech, and the rhythm handled with great freedom to follow its variations. If certain expressions appear far-fetched or artificial, it is merely because our language has altered considerably in course of time, and the ballads were naturally behindhand in adapting themselves to the change. The forms of speech adapted in the present selection were in current use during the sixteenth and seventeenth centuries. It has not been thought necessary to retain either special dialect forms, or such archaic words and expressions as occur very rarely, only those common to ballad poetry in general. Very few of these are derived from poetical sources. The "brown brand," for instance, is a relic of ancient heroic lays, and "rose" and "lily-wand," as descriptive of fair ladies, have a more modern poetical origin. For the most part the ballads were composed in the plain Danish of the thirteenth century, freely handled, and enriched with many technical expressions of chivalry, newly imported from foreign countries, Germany especially.

The imagery of the ballads is sparse and simple, borrowed, not from poetic tradition, but from everyday life, with a preference for agricultural interests. The arrows stick thick as hay in Knight Stig's kirtle (No. 19); Engelbret overthrows the Swedes as a farmer reaps his corn (No. 21). The minstrel does not shrink from comparing the burning Tove to a roast goose at Yuletide. Nothing was thought undignified, because the ballad from the first was independent of literary convention, and any image was approved which seized the essential qualities of the object described. This origin from the daily life and speech of the people gave the ballad a great advantage, by enabling it to survive changes in speech and taste, and (despite medieval German invasions and modern romanticism) to preserve an antique form of expression to which poets in every century have harked back, from those of the Renaissance to Oehlenschläger and Jacobsen.

These forms of expression were the common heritage of the people. Their preservation in the ballad was largely a matter of accepted convention, since, as the forms were so plain and straightforward, scenes of frequent recurrence would naturally be related in the same words—for example, how men drew swords to fight, how they greeted strangers, the dawning and darkening of the day, and so forth. Thus were developed the standard terms of the ballad, which stylized itself without deliberate intention of doing so.

### THE KNIGHTS' HOMESTEAD

Those men who most frequently play the part of hero, whose life as a whole forms its basic material, bear the name of knights in the ballad. This name must be taken in its earlier significance as applied to all who served in war as cavalry, and so were exempted from taxation. The distinction of rank between knights and squires, as recognized after the close of the thirteenth century, comes up incidentally with the mention of "knight and swain." The women of this class were called "ladies" and "damsels." All bore in common the name of "nobles," or "noble dames and damsels," and constituted a society which, on account of its good birth, good breeding, and warlike, adventurous life, considered itself somewhat superior to the neighbouring yeomanry.

It must not be pictured, however, as a ruling class dwelling in stately castles, and supported entirely by other men's labour. Sir Torben went out in person to plough his own land by the greenwood when his enemies fell upon and slew him (No. 35). Ingelille invited the elegant courtier to sit in the waggon beside her, and learn a farmer's ways from her, both harrowing and sowing (No. 40). A knight out a-riding might be accompanied by five, ten, or twenty swains (squires), but they had work enough in between times to get their daily bread.

> Oh some are out in good greenwood
> A-chasing the deer so free,
> And some are bridling the billows blue,
> Afar on the salt, salt sea.

The noble dame might enjoy appearing in public with a train of attendant maidens, but we may also get a glimpse of her alone in the house, because the squires have ridden off, and the maids are busy in the fields reaping the corn.

The hero of the ballad, then, was usually a knight; and in the second place, mostly as subordinate characters, appear those persons with whom he associated and was best acquainted. The chieftain is not always to be found at the plough or in the byre—such work, from the ballad point of view, afforded small opportunity for sensational happenings, and a certain contempt for rusticity gradually crept into the later ballads. There are more frequent references to the gatherings which brought the knight into contact with the world—the chase in good greenwood, the ride to the general meetings and conferences, to the church, or the district council, the Yeomen's Thing as it was called in distinction from the councils of the nobility, and the Land's Thing, or general council of the realm. At these councils the gentry of the neighbourhood met one another, bargains were struck, and all kinds of business settled; many a marriageable daughter would go with fast-beating heart to meet her father on his return, and ask news of the Thing. Occasionally longer expeditions were undertaken, sea voyages and so on. Forays against national enemies find frequent mention, mostly because of the disturbance brought about in home life. Pilgrimages too are spoken of, and trading journeys were by no means unknown to the gentry of the period.

The setting of the ballad is usually the native soil. No place is described in greater detail than the knights' "garth" or homestead. Only in the rarest instances must it be conceived of as a fortified castle; it would usually rather resemble a modern farm. The "castle gate" which gave entrance to it played no part whatever in the defences. There the knight and his lady would stand "wrapped in vair" (the cloak trimmed with marten fur), or the daughter plaiting her long tresses, or the serving-lad keeping an eye on the passers-by. On either side there would be a rampart, moat, or palisade, which seldom prevented unexpected enemies from effecting an entrance. Round the yard within stood a number of different buildings, thatched with straw or the "slender reed," built mostly of timber or wattle-and-daub. In the midst of the garth stood a linden, that favourite tree of medieval times, "bending its boughs" to the ground, and helping to conceal many a secret tryst of an evening between swain and serving-maid. The new arrival would take care to arrange the folds of his cloak in the yard before entering the hall, which formed the lower storey of what may be called the principal building. Thatched though it might be, this building would have a dignified aspect with its richly decorative woodwork, and the carved beams project-ing from the gable, precursors of the later weather vanes. An outer gallery ran the whole length of the building, either level with the ground floor, or a storey higher, giving access to the various rooms in the "loft" or "high-loft"—the bedrooms and parlours for husband and wife, guest chambers and others. This gallery played an important part in the everyday life of the household. It was there that Sverkel wooed Kirsteen after the dance, there that Queen Sophy spied on the King's talk with Signild, the dancing maiden; and along this gallery that Ebbe Skammelson lighted Adelus to the bridal bower.

Two other buildings played their part in the knights' life, from the poetical point of view. The one was the "maiden's bower," prettily adorned and, more important still, strongly locked, lest the "bower be broken" by an importunate lover. The ballads censure the man as "inexperienced" who built his daughter's bower too far out of the way, but we also have stories of maidens who scented mischief afoot, and secured themselves against danger. The second was the "stone house," or "stone hall," built as a place of refuge from attack, and a source of pride to its possessor.

> *A house have I walled round with stone*
> *That stands my garth within,*
> *I wot when I take refuge there*
> *I fear not a hundred men.*

We learn from the ballads, however, that it was none too easy at a pinch to get into the prison-like building. When no stone house was available, recourse would be had to the church tower, but this could generally be set on fire without much difficulty, as we see by the sad fate of young Engel (No. 33).

The expression "stone hall," however, varies in meaning, since it is sometimes applied indiscriminately to any stone building, quite frequently, for instance, to the "hall" or main dwelling house, if it differed in material from the usual construction of wattle-and-daub or timber. In a few exceptional cases the knight's dwelling had the character of a castle, with a dungeon and well locked gate, like that through which Sir Verner made his escape, after singing the ladies to sleep, and hanging up the bunch of keys on the drawbridge by way of farewell (No. 47). But that even such a castle could be remarkably insecure appears in the lively ballad telling how Kirsteen freed her captive brother. After a little chat at the castle gate with the Count's mistress, she proceeds to the prison tower without the slightest opposition, kicks the door open, and takes the prisoner home. The open homestead, however, was the usual thing, where, as the ballads tell us, the courtyard runs out into home field and garden. The whole scene was animated by frolicsome animal life and bright-coloured costume; it was there that the squires trod the sword dance, and the lady "bore up the burden" for the dance of her maids.

The class of society depicted in the Danish and other Northern ballads differs totally from that which produced the picturesque ballad of chivalry in other countries. Denmark had no Troubadours or Minnesingers, who earned their bread at one castle or another by the delivery of long narratives of knightly adventure. Nor did it possess those minor courts of princes or nobles where such minstrels found most congenial quarters. The one exception, the Ducal Court of Gottorp in Slesvik, was hardly adequate, and its intellectual value was early lessened by the powerful influence of the Holstein nobility. The Danish court itself was no centre of native poetical culture, its national character being destroyed by its numerous German marriages and other ties with foreign countries. The names of the German minstrels are known on whom Erik Menved and Valdemar Atterdag lavished their gold, but no Danish name appears among them. The patrons of Danish song were the Danish gentry in general, not the small number of noble families who built lordly castles, and united their estates through worldly-wise marriages. The class in question were scattered in a thousand gentleman's seats, great and small, in every parish all over the country, not to mention a number of farms whose owners handed on their armorial bearings and freedom from taxation to the son who inherited the homestead—a minor "nobility" which degenerated in time to peasant status, notably after participation in the Peasants' Revolt of 1534. From this class, corresponding to our modern squires, landowners, and the more independent type of yeoman, the ballad derived its vigorous, straightforward mode of expression, and its love of reality. It mirrors their outlook and their life.

Other magnates of the community appear mostly in the background, the King's figure less distantly than others. A large cycle of ballads commemorates the intimates of Valdemar the Great and Valdemar the Victorious; and in the earliest historical ballads we are told of devotion to the King, and of patriotism as personified in the King. Later on, however, we find only fugitive glimpses of this loyalty, such as the words of the page in the Finderup Ballad (No. 25), and all personal interest in the royal family disappears. The King mostly appears as a chieftain with greater power than the rest, a power which he exercises according to his own whim, often in a most egotistical and tyrannical fashion. He wishes to deprive Nils Strangeson of his new-built castle; he imprisons another knight till he gives up his true-love—though, it must be mentioned, for a wealthier match. The King in his wrath murders Knud of Borg on his bridal day, and in his jealousy has Valraven hurled into the sea (No. 46). As a friendly power, he is less active and very arbitrary. He may appear on occasion at the Thing as upholder of justice and defender of the helpless, but it is not his conduct with which the minstrel is chiefly concerned (No. 40).

The King is surrounded and served by a circle of noblemen or courtiers. The King and "all his merry men" tread the dance by the castle gate, and in so doing play their part for the ballad minstrel. Probably many new chivalrous customs came in through the Court, the cult of good breeding, and of magnificence in externals, together with that of the dance itself and the dance lyric. All these foreign fashions spread with remarkable speed all over the country. Poetry ceased to seek inspiration in the life of the Court, which was looked at askance by the ordinary singer. As against the unruly flock of young bachelor courtiers, the latter looked on himself as the home-dweller, the spokesman of the settled community. The refined customs at Court furnished fine subjects for mockery. "So long have they served in the royal court, they can bear neither heat nor smoke," jeers the countrified songstress, whose own hearthside was doubtless not without such little eccentricities. In a serio-comic ballad we find Svend Felding set up as a champion of Danish plainness and frugality against Queen Jutte and her German courtiers. This point of view found its wittiest expression in the little ballad of "The Maiden at the Thing" (No. 40).

> Young was Inge the maid,
> Yet she rode to the Thing unafraid.

It is hard to say which is the more admirable, the wit and economy of method with which the poet keeps his principal personages in hand—even his heroine is touched in rather ironically—or the advanced conception of the community which exalts bodily labour and sees no use in a class of idlers, a standpoint hardly to be found in any other ballad of chivalry. This one, indeed, takes a point of view opposed to the whole tendency of the age.

The Church, which formed part of the medieval community, stands somewhat aside from the special world of the ballad. The churchman's way of life was rather problematical in the eyes of the Danish gentleman—whose ideal was freedom, and who had no notion of binding himself down "as a monk to his cowl of grey" (No. 29). The whole relationship was too remote, though the gentleman might enjoy listening outside the convent, "where nuns did read and sing." Only through the convent school where young damsels were educated, was a somewhat closer relationship established; and by this channel some notion of religious teachings filtered through in course of time amongst the nobility.

Relations with the townsfolk were equally distant. The ballads speak only of the town, not its inhabitants—Ribe with its merchandise, fine clothes, and jewellery, Middelfart with its ferry, and so forth. Not till the fifteenth century do the rich burghers come on the scene, they who build houses "midway in Randers street," with lofty storeys and gilded ornaments, shining over wall and mead to the discomfiture of the gentry whose houses are put to shame. By that time, however, the best period of the ballad was a thing of the past.

Much closer was the contact between gentleman and yeoman. The knight, indeed, originally rose from the latter class; and the ballad is fond of describing well born youths as "noble yeomen's sons," just as it places Tove, the yeoman's daughter, as a rival to the anointed Queen. The knight was involved with the yeoman in any number of business transactions, sometimes in the ownership of common land, which all made for a good neighbourly spirit. "Here are rich franklins dwelling in town, swords will they lend us and byrnies brown." When occasion requires, the ballads depict the farmer's prosperity, with hawk and hound, oxen and kine; the farmer's son rides a good horse, and "every maid hath her crown of gold." Nobody except wicked Queen Bengerd wishes the peasant to content himself with one ox and one cow, and a wattled hurdle by way of a door. Ill will between knight and peasant is unheard of, and the former is always protector against robbers or profligate chieftains. For all that, the monotonous course of farm life lacked poetic value in the eyes of the warrior, just as the "kirtle grey" looked mean beside the gay garments of captain and page. In very exceptional cases the yeoman's wife may appear as heroine of a ballad—and in the jocular specimens she and her husband are special favourites, but by no means to their honour.

There was, finally, a class of person who must be considered if we are to obtain a comprehensive picture of medieval life. These were the swains or squires, who liked to call themselves "courtiers" when they served in the royal household—served, that is to say, for a salary and military training. We may see them following their liege on his journeys, with lance heads shining above them—"their glaives go glimmering up aloft"—and when they take a hand in hunting, fishing, and ordinary farm work. Young nobles were to be met with amongst them, younger sons who owned no lands, but some were peasant-born—conditions which also obtained among the noble lady's "maidens." Marriage sometimes meant a return to the peasant-class—"Then must I doff the scarlet red and don the wadmal grey." Nevertheless, participation in "gentle" life set its stamp on them; they were part of the public that kept the ballad dance going, and are continually mentioned in the ballads—although, since they are always praised or blamed according to their measure of fidelity, we see them only from the liege lord's point of view. There are splendid examples of this quality to be found, but the individual life of even the finest type of squire is only a side issue. The "Trusty Swain" whose valour saves the life of his master, young Danneved, turns out (in one version) to be no ordinary retainer, but the actual son of the lady Mettelil; and the same sort of promotion is bestowed on the little horse-boy who wins the damsel's hand at dice (No. 39):

> For I am ne'er a horse-boy
> Altho' it be thy word,
> My father is the noblest King
> That ever walked abroad.

Only a small number of ballads have a squire as hero, a couple dealing with poachers, and the well known "Elfin Howe."

> So now, I bid ye, all gentle swains
> That to the Court would fare,
> Tarry ye not by the Elfin Howe,
> Nor lie down to slumber there.

These particular ballads are late ones, often wanting in life and lucidity, but at least they bear testimony as to the manner in which the knight's follower tackled life on his own account when the higher class of gentry began to withdraw itself from contact with the retainers, and a definite distinction was established between the squire in the castle hall and the knightly family in the ladies' bower.

This development furnishes the subject of "King Erik and the Scornful Maid" (No. 48), wherein we make acquaintance with the more fastidious type of gentry. The noble damsel who wears golden rings and ties up her sleeves with silken ribbons refuses to take the squire's toil-hardened hand in the dance—a change indeed from the times when Sir Torben and Ove Stigson stood at the plough themselves. This ballad, however, does not concern itself with those who dwelt in high-loft and bower, but with the "poor swains" in the hall, whose hands were coarsened with the building of fences and wielding of pitchforks, who had at times to rove the country in search of a job, though taking part, on the other hand, in the warlike feats of chivalry, in feast, tournament, and foray. Their preference, very naturally, turned to the unproductive activities of their lords, and in this ballad they take their revenge for the undignified situation which the nobility wished to assign them.

### THE LEADING THEMES OF THE BALLADS

No other work was in a position to give so detailed a picture of medieval life as the ballad. It follows the life of man from the cradle to the grave—the birth of the child, with lights burning in every corner as a defence against the elves—the little tot "playing with apples and pears"—the young lad whose father wishes to send him out to "service," while his mother thinks him too young to bear the heavy coat of mail. It depicts the young girl with her sharp tongue and heavy sleep of a morning, and shows her in every stage of life, till the white-haired woman has completed her sum of emotional experience. Nevertheless, the ballads show a marked preference for the prime of life, the strength of youth and manhood, and there again, they select those events which are all-decisive in the life of the individual. At that period, the outlines of human existence were clearly defined, and the ballad chooses action rather than lyrical or picturesque effect.

Amongst its outstanding themes, love and the blood feud stand first and foremost.

The feud between man and man, a feature of medieval life, was a heritage from antiquity, and the gentry took a pride in the pursuit of these private quarrels, which emphasized their distinction from the more peaceful part of the population. It was natural, therefore, that the feud should furnish a subject for minstrelsy. The lays of olden times were in one way or another mostly concerned with combat, which now took a lesser, but by no means insignificant place. Some of the feud ballads glorify the heroes of the combat, the young avengers of their father, or the bold fighter whose sword wins him promotion; but there are others which dwell, not on the victor, but on the sorrow following after the strife, and two of these rank amongst our best medieval ballads.

"Torben's Daughter" (No. 35) tells how Sir Torben is slain in a blood feud at his plough stilts, how his young daughter, all unknowing, welcomes his slayer to the house, and how, seized with compassion, he sets her on his horse and carries her off to a new happiness hinted at in the burden. Here the ballad touches the apex of condensed narrative power. A mere thirty lines suffice to show the development of two persons' destinies, by means of sensational changes both in the inner and outer life. Indeed, the minstrel makes so straight for his goal that he has no time to tell us the names of his principal characters.

No less striking is "Nilus and Hillelille" (No. 32). Here again the action takes place on the dark heathland of the stern West Jutland landscape, but without morning dew or bright hope of dawn. The ballad opens with an experience very natural in those wild, wind-swept regions, when a bridal train crossing the heath is overtaken by a storm, and this tempestuous scene gives the minstrel the keynote of his story. The whole treatment has the same "weather-bitten" stamp; there is no lingering over the emotions, no images nor verbal decoration. All is in keeping with the dour character of the actors. The squires who die for their lord without a moment's hesitation—Sir Peter with his quenchless thirst for revenge, though bearing no personal ill will towards his new kinsman, whom, indeed, he would willingly have spared for Hillelille's sake. This temperament, however, makes itself most clearly manifest in the woman's figure which only appears towards the end of the ballad, with her intense devotion to her blood relations, and equally intense hatred of all who injure them. Sir Nilus, himself with the same steely temper, develops into a grand warlike figure when, after long hesitation, he throws himself into the fray.

> Oh, I have sworn by the holy Cross
> Whereon Our Lord did bleed,
> No sword to draw on the Sabbath day
> Save in the direst need.

This Christian virtue of his and, from first to last, his tender care for his young bride, are features which individualize and ennoble his portrait, though it springs nevertheless from the same root as the others. Just as in the ballad's birthplace every tree and thicket is deformed by the same biting west wind, so all the characters are stamped by the same harsh circumstances of life. Their bearing is that of the sturdy oak, their minds have the iron toughness of the twisted heather stems. One frail blossom grows, by ill luck, among the hardened moorland vegetation—the young bride Hillelille. The first scene shows her bowed by the fierce wind over the heath, the last how she withers in the clash of violent wills which she has vainly tried to soften.

And so we come to the all-inclusive theme of love, which is treated from many angles in the ballads.

There is a great predilection for the bold, impetuous knight who carries off his lady love despite her family's opposition, or tears her from the arms of a rival. Their merit in modern eyes is not always proportionate to the favour they enjoyed in the Middle Ages, but in "Lovel and John" (No. 37) we find a heroic figure unique in its briskness and boldness. At that period a special delight was found in the joust, which worthily concludes Sir John's adventure. No other ballad is so imbued with the tone of that rough, somewhat brutal sport of the chivalrous age. The introductory verse resembles a challenge to the joust, and in the burden (Be ye well boun, or: Put your armour on) there is a constant reminder of the weapon play which finally decides who is to possess the maiden. A similar conception of love finds expression in the fine humorous Ballad of Tyge Hermanson: "All on a Thursday morning it rained both far and wide." Sir Tyge, who dares not cross the swollen river to fetch his bride, despatches Nilaus Bendikson in his place; and, since Tyge cannot, as time goes on, pluck up his courage to attend his own wedding, his friend takes his place as bridegroom. And when the laggard at last arrives, Ingelille merely answers:

> Now hadst thou been a lady's knight,
> And plighted me thy word,
> Then hadst thou broken the billows blue
> All with thy naked sword.

In the expression "lady's knight" or "squire of dames" is comprised a whole volume of the medieval outlook on life. It describes the youth whose passions are full of vitality, who is capable of captivating a damsel with his talk and his dancing, and has the strength to win her against all opposition.

There are ballads of love besides with a woman as principal character, a woman of beauty, wits, and courage to grasp the joy of life. If they do not penetrate deeply under the surface, they are lively in characterization, and have their own special elusive fairy-tale atmosphere, where luck in love coincides with luck in outward circumstance, with "bearing gold crown and the name of a Queen." To this class belongs "The Stolen Bride" (Vol. II, No. 15), which tells how the alluring song of young Kirsteen and proud Karen transformed the Wendish royal sea-rover to a wooer. Thus the ballad echoes the old, unhappy, far-off things in the memories of Denmark. The ballad best beloved all over the North, however, is "The Maiden's Morning Dream" (No. 38), with its child-maiden heroine, who foresees her good fortune, and will not be talked out of belief in her prophetic dream. This story too is linked up with the Wendish invasions of Denmark, or, properly speaking, the figure of the King was borrowed from "The Stolen Bride," or some similar ballad; the historical background has been forgotten, and he is merely the Prince of fairy tale. The burden, "When the Wends are marching to the castle," awakes no reminiscence of sack and pillage; it merely prophesies approaching happiness.

Those that may be called genuine love ballads lay greater stress on the actual relationship between man and woman. They have a remarkable power of beautifying everyday circumstances with the glamour of love. Esbern Snare's courtship of young Kirsteen (No. 20) centres round the question as to whether the damsel has learnt enough tailor-craft to be married—just as the story of Inge (No. 40) tells of a girl who hands over her lands to the King rather than submit to the unlawful usurpation of her relatives. Cupid sports merrily, however, with the kirtle sewn by little Kirsteen; though Sir Esbern utters no word of courtship, the very request for the garment is a declaration, the shaping of it a solemn duty, the adornment a pastime, and all her solicitude over it a confession of love. Bolder, yet full of charm, is Inge, the country girl, who knows how to speak up before the men at the Thing, and win the dandified Sir Ove. And the half-grown girl, youngest of all the Queen's maidens (No. 41) delights us no less with her cheeky tongue and housewifely diligence.

These and many similar ballads represent woman as the Danish gentleman of quality was most frequently pleased to picture her. She was by no means a being of supernatural beauty, object of the knights' reverential devotion, after the fashion of chivalrous love as we imagine it, of whom so many examples abounded in countries farther south. The woman of the ballads played much more of a part in everyday life, was intrepid, quick of tongue, and strong in action when occasion required, and those ages of unrest and lawlessness furnished plenty of occasions when women had to defend themselves. They were, so to speak, descendants of the self-reliant women of olden times; the memory of the Shield Maidens was still alive in the ballad period, and the minstrels admired the damsel whose unpractised feminine hand could draw the sword and deal a manly blow with it. Diligence and pluck, in jest or in earnest, were the essential characteristics of these medieval women; but the minstrel never fails to let a breath of youth and maidenliness lend its charm to his favourite figures.

The ballads chiefly favoured that sort of love, both in men and women, which was combined with courage to seize its desire, but many other aspects are touched on by the way. In "Torben's Daughter" the chief emphasis is on the remorse which gave birth to tenderness; and self-sacrifice forms the theme of the pretty little ballad of "The Wounded Maiden" (No. 42). The opening scene depicts such a sword dance as is familiar in old pictures, with knight and maiden taking hands, surrounded by knights bearing drawn swords, who crossed blades incessantly during the dance. The maiden, accidentally injured, refuses to betray the culprit, and, in answer to the King's question, invents an excuse. Whereupon the knight in question, realizing her secret motive for shielding him, comes forward and asks her hand in marriage. The story ends with a little dialogue very characteristic of the period. What, asks the father, can a man want with a cripple who can neither sew nor dress herself?—thus expressing the contempt felt by the Middle Ages, with their fresh, strong sense of life, for any maimed human being. The knight's answer, " 'Tis by my fault the mischance befell And therefore I love the maiden well," sets up a higher standard, showing the impulse of true love to make good what was ill done, and bring a return offering to her whose silence had saved him.

It is not always a celebration of happy love, however; the tragic side has its singers, as in "Ebbe Skammelson" (No. 44) which ranks among the finest of medieval ballads. The subject is one of those bloody dramas so frequent in olden times—the winning of Ebbe's betrothed through a lie on the part of his treacherous brother, the return of the cozened suitor on the bridal day, and his slaying both of bride and bridegroom. In this wild setting we witness the collision between two powerful personalities, Ebbe himself and proud Adelus. She is a gentlewoman through and through, noble, steadfast, tender "as any mother," but not specially passionate. Significantly enough, she does not bear the usual generic name for a mistress, "little Kirsteen," but the less common "proud Adelus" (in some versions "Lucielil"). We are shown her serene trust in Ebbe's love, her acquiescence in the second betrothal after the false news of his death, and her high-minded conviction after his return where her duty lies. When Ebbe proposes to kill his brother and carry her off, she turns on him in anger:

> And wilt thou strike thy brother down,
> Ne'er will I be thine, I vow,
> And thou shalt sorrow thyself to death
> Like lone bird on the bough.

This same loftiness characterized the group of noble Danish ladies, "strong of will and true of troth," whose names are preserved in history. Ebbe's picture is no less finely developed, with his noble frankness as against the craft of his brother, his chivalry towards women, the affectionate relations between him and his sisters, and single-hearted love which turns when opposed to the madness of despair. "And therefore treads Ebbe Skammelson so wild a way alone"— the burden depicts the outlaw's lot, severed by his own action from kith and kin. Even the minor characters are drawn to the life in a few words—Skammel, the prosperous magnate, with no suspicion of the treachery brewing in his own house, so taken up with the wedding guests that he has hardly time to give his returning son "a goblet of gold to pledge the bridal pair." The mother is well characterized with her own cunning, and her preference for her wily son Sir Peter. Finally we have Sir Peter himself in all his meanness, staying at home in order to win his brother's betrothed by a lie, and cowardly enough to renounce her if by so doing he can save his own life. And yet—this is part of the ballad minstrel's art—the narrator himself never utters a disparaging word of him.

Many places in Denmark and Sweden claim to be the scene of the ballad; but the truth is that Skammel dwelt

"North in Ty," the northern part of Jutland, where the home-stead of Nordentoft has for centuries been pointed out as its setting. The great clan of the Strangesons names Ebbe as the founder. The latest researches place the period as round about 1300, when the power and independence of the nobility first became notable, and the troubles in Denmark set their stamp of gravity on the people and their poetry alike.

The conditions of existence native to the ballad world were rife in wild and harrowing scenes. Men's stormy passions drove them to deeds which ruined their happiness. Moreover, the order of society tended to bring a tragic element into love. A woman was not permitted to guide her own destiny—her father, brother, or sometimes more distant kinsmen, had that matter in their hands. Only in one exceptional circumstance had she a legal right to go to the Thing, and choose her husband herself; that is to say, when her family kept her single in order to enjoy her inheritance. A woman had no escape from a marriage forced on her by her relatives, other than an elopement with "her own true-love"—in which case it remained to be seen whether her kinsfolk could eventually be talked over.

Concubinage was another source of strife and unhappiness. By ancient custom, a man was permitted to take a wife without the solemnity of marriage, and the exchange of the bridal gift on the one side and the dowry on the other. She had no status of conjugal equality with him as his lawful wife; she was only his leman or light-o'-love, and the association could be broken off when either party wearied of it. This custom was often practised when the knight did not consider his sweetheart as his equal in birth or wealth, and wished to keep a free hand for a more suitable marriage, but sometimes the reason lay in the suitor's having carried off the damsel from her bower without the consent of her family. The Church tried its best to abolish this relationship, but the ballads are less definite in their judgment. Sometimes the superior type of woman is mentioned as fit for a wife, and the inferior for a mistress, but their chief concern is with the fateful conflicts to which the looser relationship gave rise. The knight, returning from a journey, slays the unfaithful mistress who has plighted troth with another, or, more frequently, the knight chooses a new bride, irrespective of the fact that his mistress in birth, beauty, and devotion is perfectly worthy of him. Thus Sir Peter (No. 45) conceals his new matrimonial projects from young Kirsteen, who nevertheless attends the wedding, rouses the bride's suspicions with her good looks and fine array, follows them to the bridal bower so as to feel the full depths of her sorrow, and then burns them in their bed.[3] Once and once only did concubinage give occasion to a ballad so light and charming as "Sir Peter's Harp" (No. 43), where the knight thinks of making the damsel his mistress, but, touched by her deep and humble love, repents his resolution, and has their bridal celebrated "with honour."

### THE HISTORICAL BALLAD

Ballads on historical subjects played a prominent part in Danish medieval poetry. In an age lacking books and newspapers, people crowded round the minstrel, to discuss any great event, examine what had occurred in all its bearings, and take sides in praise or blame with the principal actors. Thus the memory was preserved of important happenings of the past. It was not, however, the mere relation of current news or bygone history which created the historical ballad. Whereas modern poetry for the most part creates imaginary persons, the medieval singer would take some well known

[3] There are different endings to this ballad, but the fire-raising is best authenticated as the original. In one version she stabs Sir Peter. In another she hangs herself in the orchard, and Sir Peter, overcome by despair, takes his own life.

character and invest it with new life. No demand that a work should in every detail be the creation of its author existed at that period, and just as one ballad would borrow phrases or verses from another, so were scenes and characters borrowed, now from earlier sources, now from recollection of events in real life.

The earliest historical portraits which appear in the ballads are those of a series of great men living about the middle of the twelfth century. The ballads usually betray the fact that they were composed, not by contemporaries, but an admiring posterity. The most remarkable portrait is that of Stig Hvide. The little story of his heroic death under the royal standard (No. 19) is, to be sure, no novel or striking composition, but we find the noblest virtues of chivalry—fidelity towards his liege lord, and honour for his lady—united in Stig's steadfast valour. "Ne'er shall my true-love learn in the land Stig let the King's banner be loosed from his hand." Equally vivid is the minstrel's joy in life and colour (we see the hero under the banner striped red, gold, and blue, with red sleeves pierced by the arrows, and wounded in the lily-white hand) and in fresh, simple similes from Nature—the arrows flying thick as hay, the sword that bites like a burning brand. Stig Hvide was an historical personage, a Jutland chieftain married to the sister of Duke Valdemar (later on Valdemar the Great), and he was killed in the civil war under Valdemar and Svend at the battle of Viborg (1151). The patriotic sentiment which glorifies his fall belongs, not to the period when the ballad was composed, but to that of Valdemar, with its devotion to King and Fatherland. Another ballad, undoubtedly later, described Stig's marriage to the King's sister, whom he wins through the eerie power of the Runes (Vol. II, No. 14).

The Ballad of Esbern Snare is still looser in its relation to history; possibly the minstrel knew little more than the name of the bold fighter in the civil and Wendish wars. But a young hero of that kind was well adapted to figure in a love story, and its liveliness is in keeping with his memory (No. 20).

With the Ballads of King Valdemar, Queen Sophia, and Tove we reach firmer ground. History tells us that Tove was Valdemar's mistress, and had borne him a son named Christopher before the King was forced through political considerations to conciliate his opponent Knud Magnusson by marrying his beautiful half-sister Sophia. Tove, in all probability, was sent back to her native place. The King's love for her was proved by his affection for her son, till the latter died at an early age. Of Tove's later fortunes nothing is known; it is very doubtful whether, as the ballad relates, she was done to death in the heated bathroom—such a deed on the part of the jealous wife would have broken up the good understanding between Valdemar and herself. Possibly even her contemporaries knew little that was definite of Tove's fate, but the blank was filled up by ballads on the relations between the rivals.

We have two of these, or rather one and the same—in the original version A, as preserved in Iceland, and B, a later adaptation as sung in Denmark. The earlier selects the occasion of Valdemar's marriage (1157). Tove, at her lover's request, is ready to welcome the royal bride, but Sophia shows her no mercy (Nos. 17 and 18). In Tove the poet painted his ideal woman. Her beauty (as often in the earlier ballads) is suggested through the luxurious splendour of her attire, her lovable nature by her amiability to her lover's lawful wife, as contrasted with the unmixed hatred of the latter. The leading idea is that only the evil woman feels jealousy, while the nobler nature can include her lord's beloved in her affection. This was a favourite theme of European literature during the thirteenth century. There is, besides, an imaginative sympathy for the ease with which men fall into temptation; a wistful lament over Valdemar's attempt to make vows to two women at once resounds in the burden.

The later ballad has superior poetic value. Instead of the simple dialogue and account of the journey we have scenes full of life—Tove dancing among the Queen's maidens, or going to church with silken train "swimming" after her. The dialogues have disappeared, and the two women confront each other in varying situations. Whereas the earlier poet describes Tove's appearance in a series of verses, her charm is shown here more vividly in a single line. The conception of the character has altered. Tove is no unearthly ideal, merely a much loved young woman whose beauty gains radiance from her happiness, who never asks whether others have a claim on what she so securely possesses. The Queen is not inordinately jealous; Tove has a place amongst her ladies, but her joy wakens resentment, which is increased by the King's gratitude to her, and the grudge breaks out when the Queen sees the mistress parading in all her glory. The idea of sharing love is not for them—each desires it all, and so the story ends in hate and destruction. This desire of having love all to oneself harks back to primitive human feeling, and the situation pictured by antiquity in the quarrel between Brynhild and Gudrun over the love of Sigurd. A whole series of ballads take the same line, all combating the idea that love can content itself with a half-love in return.

This second Tove Ballad is recognizably later than the events it relates, probably by a century at least. It omits mention of Valdemar's marriage to Sophia, and represents Sophia's eldest son Knud (later King of Denmark) as a son of Tove's.

The thirteenth century ballads were in closer touch with their subject matter, and composed by contemporaries or the next generation; some indeed on the impulse of the moment. It was not always the greatest personality, nor (to our way of thinking) the most important event which set the poet to work, but some sudden striking occurrence which sent a thrill of joy or grief through the entire population. None of Valdemar's victories which enlarged the boundaries of his country made sufficient impression to be commemorated in a ballad, but his solitary defeat furnished subject for "The Battle of Lena" (No. 21) inspired by the loss of the fallen nobles.

Sverker, last but one of the many medieval Kings who fought for the Crown of Sweden, reigned long in peace, but after he had caused some of his predecessor's sons to be executed, their only survivor, Erik Knudsen, rebelled and drove him from the country. Coming to Denmark, he asked help of Valdemar the Victorious, and his father-in-law Ebbe Suneson, the Sælland chieftain of the White family. With a Danish army under Ebbe's command, he invaded West Gothland, and encountered Erik's Swedish forces on January 31, 1208. The Danes were severely defeated; of the four Sunesons who took part in the battle Erik and his brother Laurentius were killed; Sverker himself escaped, only to fall two years later in another attempt to regain the Crown. The Swedish chroniclers rejoiced over the victory; the Danes contented themselves with mentioning the time, place, and overthrow. The impression made by the great slaughter on the contemporary Danish mind may be seen in the tragic conclusion of the ballad. The picture of the women waiting, only to see their men's horses come riderless home, is the best thing in it, which probably kept it alive on men's tongues throughout the ages. We cannot feel certain as to its original content. One verse mentions "young Engelbret"—the German-born Count of that name who married Ebbe Suneson's youngest daughter; but this mention is due, less to any specially momentous part played by him in the battle, than to the capital verse comparing his doughty strokes to those of the farmer reaping corn. If such praise is given to one member of the family, there must surely have been other verses dealing with Ebbe himself, the leader who fell in battle, with Laurentius his brother, Bishop Peter and other survivors of the family, not to mention various other prominent men—those contemporary chieftains who also took part in the fray and obviously belong to the picture. In course of time the ballad singers replaced the missing names by substituting those of King Didrik's champions, while still later on Vedel and other literary men inserted the historical names. We prefer to present the ballad as it stands, the remnant of a much longer poem, rather than borrow from the more modern amplifications.[4]

Of Valdemar's actions as a ruler, his short-lived expansion of the kingdom, and his many years' labour over its internal organization, the ballads have nothing to say. They preserve, however, the portraits of two women, Dagmar and Bengerd, who represent the double aspect of the Crown's relation to its subjects, the mild and peaceable, the stern and exacting. Many a minstrel sung of them, and one figure stands out in all the ballads, more wondrously attractive than the people could ever previously have conceived, or were ever again in a position to imagine.

The Princess who was brought to Denmark in 1205 as bride of Valdemar the Victorious had spent a youth of trial. Born in the royal castle of Bohemia, she followed her exiled mother to the abode of the Count of Meissen, where she and her sisters took part in the mother's battle for her rights, as well as in her piety and good works. Denmark greeted the Princess with acclamation; her Slav folk-name of Dragomir

[4] The numbers assigned to the Danish army vary greatly in different versions of the ballad. It is impossible to tell what was given in its original form.

was changed to Dagmar (Maid of Day, or Light-Bringer). "Margareta was her true name," writes a chronicler, "but she was called Dagmar because of her beauty." Her life was but a brief one; she bore her husband a son (Valdemar), and died two years later, possibly in childbirth, cut off in the bloom of her youth, and the first freshness of her subjects' devotion.

Two years later, in 1214, Valdemar wedded the Portuguese Princess Berengaria. Nothing certain is known of her, except that she too was handsome. There is no mention of her character except in the ballads, though we have a species of indirect testimony from the next generation, in the fact that not one of her sons named a daughter after her. The royal line she came of was strong in action, but greedy and quarrelsome. Her name in Danish was turned to Berngerd (later Bengerd), a name of no evil significance, though of a harsh and alien sound.

We have three ballads with Dagmar as heroine, and one with Bengerd. How far any one of them reflects contemporary impression is difficult to say. If any does so, it must be the satire or "spite-song" making Bengerd responsible for certain unpopular forms of taxation. It is worked up from a scene often treated by the ballads in a more or less facetious manner. Bengerd demands the "morning-gift" after the bridal night, and her demands are unlimited. She wants to tax every man, woman, and child in the kingdom, to "bind the whole land in iron," to lay chains across all harbours, and claim tribute from all incoming vessels. King Valdemar, in popular opinion, was just the man to oppose shameless tyranny of this kind, and he has the last say in the matter.

> Now Bengerd in mirk and mould abides,
> And the peasant hath oxen and kine besides.

One minstrel (hardly the original author) treated this satisfactory conclusion in a fantastic and by no means historically accurate form. When the King goes to the wars, his dead Queen warns him in a dream not to let Bengerd rule the realm during his absence; he consequently takes her with him, and she is killed by the first arrow which is loosed in the combat.

The Dagmar Ballads date from the same period.

The year 1205 witnessed two notable events, the coming of Dagmar herself, and the decision to release Bishop Valdemar from prison. A member of the reigning family, he had lain for thirteen years in the prison of Söborg, since the discovery of his conspiracy with various foreign princes to usurp the throne as vassal of the German Emperor. Meanwhile the great Pope Innocent had made strong representations to the King to effect the Bishop's release from the secular arm; the King, after long delay, at last consented to do so, and in 1206 the Bishop went off to plead his cause before the Papal Tribunal. He subsequently fanned the flames of strife between Valdemar and the German princes, and kept North Germany in a state of constant warfare till all his plans were frustrated by the victorious Danish King. It is difficult, looking backwards, to imagine who could have induced Valdemar to release his bitterest foe. The Pope's urgent demands are known through contemporary letters; it may be read in a monkish chronicle that the release came about through "the loving remonstrances of Bishop Andreas and others"; but the eyes of the people turned to the new-come Queen as peacemaker, and certainly not without reason.

The ballads set all these persons and circumstances before us in living pictures. We see the young Queen, whose mother had taught her compassion for all the afflicted, tender and loving, yet strong of will and quick of tongue where her acts of charity were concerned—the scene is brilliantly

drawn where she sets down her crown on the table and refuses to be Queen unless her first request is granted. The
minor characters stand out vividly, the Bishop thirsting for
revenge, and the King with his statesmanlike point of view.
The ballad is not historically accurate (the Bishop is called
the Queen's maternal uncle, whereas he was son of a similar
relative on the King's side) and can scarcely be contemporary work. It has much artistic interest, however, inasmuch
as it served as a model copied and repeated in the other
Dagmar Ballads, and set up an ideal figure for Danish queens
which prevailed for many a long year.

A second ballad, composed in honour of Dagmar's bridal,
gaily relates how Junker Strange courted her by proxy, and
brought her home as his master's bride.

Latest and finest of all is the ballad of Queen Dagmar's
death, with its burden: "In Ringsted rested she, Queen
Dagmar." It was not sung by the generation who had seen,
known, and mourned for her, but by descendants for whom
her memory was associated with her tomb in Ringsted Cathe-
dral by the side of King Valdemar. Meanwhile, her image
had developed still greater beauty; its connection with the
events of its own period had grown dim, and even the idea of
Bengerd's wickedness had sunk into the background. The
minstrel sang only of the love between the most winsome of
queens and the greatest of kings. In her last words we find
a detail easily misunderstood in modern times—the confession that, had she not tied up her sleeves so gaudily, and "set
stripes" (a gay headdress) on her head, she need not have
burnt in the flames of Purgatory. This must not be understood merely as the acknowledgment by a pure spirit of its
venial errors. When a departing soul was called back to the
body from the verge of the other world, it returned in a
moment of the profoundest solemnity; and this scene must
be compared with other similar ones in medieval literature,

where queens and other dignitaries reveal what they must suffer for their pride and luxurious living. Gaudy attire was not looked on as an innocent weakness; to the ascetic Middle Ages it was worldliness of the most arrant type, and here the spirit of the age throws a fugitive gleam over the lives of Dagmar and Valdemar. At that period the sound of church bells was mingled with that of the Trump of Doom—that is to say, during the age of. the Crusaders and Mendicant Friars. It is curious, not that this circumstance should affect Danish literature, but that only a hint of it should tinge the tender piety of the Dagmar Ballad.

Thus did Denmark produce two historical ballad cycles, the one dealing with Valdemar the Great, Tove, and Queen Sophia, the second and later, which has more concern with the condition of the populace, commemorating the consorts of Valdemar the Victorious. Scarcely were these more or less completed than a new one appeared, which in poetical value far outshone its predecessors. It treats of the turbulent doings that took place after the death of King Erik Klipping, and Marsk (Marshal) Stig came in course of time to take the place of hero. Six ballads are in existence dealing with the principal actors of that unrestful period. They were regarded by some later editors (Vedel and Svend Grundtvig) as a regular series, connected with and continuing one another. Modern investigators, however, believe them to be a collection of original and independent accounts of isolated events, which were afterwards amalgamated to form longer poems. We have in all four short ballads, which are more or less first-hand stories, and two longer composite works.

The impulse for these ballads was given by the regicide of 1286. During the greater part of his reign Erik was at feud with his self-willed nobles; they forced him into giving assurances safeguarding the influence of the aristocracy and the freedom of the people (a species of Danish Magna

Carta), but the King would not keep his word. One late autumn night—the Eve of St. Cecilia, November 22—he was murdered in his bed at the village of Finderup. The perpetrators of the deed were unknown, and only the fifty-six wounds on his body bore witness to their numbers. The King's page, Rane, was present, and, according to his own account and that of his friends, "he naked and weaponless warded his master," but later on, apparently, sufficient evidence came to light that he was in league with the murderers. Suspicion pointed towards the nobles who had been the King's chief opponents, and the general feeling against them was very strong, though they and their friends maintained their innocence. These suspicions finally came to a head at the Court held at Whitsuntide 1287, when nine noblemen, belonging for the most part to the same family, were condemned to outlawry. Of these the most prominent were Count Jacob of Halland, and the Royal Marshal, Stig Anderson.

The first burst of anguish, unrest and anger against the as yet undiscovered murderers gave rise to the first ballad, "The King-Slaying in Finderup" (No. 25), with its striking burden: "And therefore the land lies in peril." The minstrel sums up the political situation in a couple of lines: "So many dwell in Denmark would all be masters there"—independence and royal power confronting each other. The slaying is briefly treated, with the details that were known to be authentic. Rane's defence of the King is mentioned, but treated as a mere pretence. The ballad concludes with the powerful scene, real or imaginary, of the page who comes riding the King's horse, announces the sad tidings, and calls on the Queen to save kingdom and subjects from danger.

The outlaws fled to Norway, and took refuge with Erik Priest-Hater. They persisted in maintaining their innocence, and their many adherents and relatives in Denmark kept up friendly relations with them. What dangerous enemies they could be was shown in 1289, when they joined in a foray on Denmark with the Norwegians, and still more plainly the following year, when Stig built his fortress on the island of Hjœlm, and harried coast and country as a pirate.

The second and third ballads commemorate this state of affairs. The first, very imperfectly preserved, tells how the dejected outlaws assembled to leave the country, and how Marsk Stig commands the building of his island fortress. The second (No. 26) carries on the story up to the situation they had to face in exile. Stig's ominous dream, his ride to the Thing where the assassins were to be named, his coarse retort to the Queen regarding her love for Ove the Seneschal—the rage of the young King who condemns him to outlawry—the building of the fortress, and the terror of the plain farmer when the towers rise up like horns over the neck of the Isle—in all this we have a poetical version of what took place at Nyborg, and what followed three years later.

Finally we have the fourth ballad. The years have gone by, the political situation of former times has been forgotten; the other outlaws have faded into the background, and nothing remains but the memory of the King's death and the bitter enmity of Marsk Stig. A rumour which existed even in his own day that some love affair was at bottom of the murder, came to be associated with the outlawed chieftain, and Marsk Stig was shown as taking action to avenge the King's relations with his wife. This idea is finely treated in a short ballad (No. 27). The preceding events are merely hinted at (the manuscripts use the expression "he [the King] enticed," or "he ravished"); the story begins with Stig's return home, his wife's refusal to greet him, and the breaking of her silence when, in an agony of despair, she calls herself Queen of Denmark—that is to say, the King's mistress—and demands revenge. Her husband rides to the Thing, calls the criminal to account, and, refusing the

King's ingratiating offers of reparation, defies him to the death. So runs the ballad, which seems more or less of an introduction to the story of the Finderup murder. It has small pretension to historical accuracy, especially as the action throughout is supposed to take place in Sælland.

At last an impulse was felt to amalgamate the contents of all these ballads in one single narrative. The earliest attempt to do so resembles the general run of ballads, but obscures or omits most of the characteristics peculiar to the cycle. Then came a fresh attempt, "The Long Ballad of Marsk Stig" (No. 28), which takes up all the scenes of the others, frequently word for word, and weaves them into a poem which is possibly the most notable produced in Denmark during the Middle Ages. Its peculiar method of creation, every episode having been previously handled in a little ballad of its own, lends the whole narrative life, variety, and a sense of the changefulness of human existence which is to be found in no other ballad. Scene after scene is given which the earlier ballads only indicate in a single line. The denunciation at the Thing is repeated in greater detail, with a special insistence on the righteousness of Stig's revenge. By this means the story is linked up with the Finderup Ballad, since Rane makes his appearance as the son of Ingeborg's sister, and conspires with Ingeborg to bring the King's death about by enticing him to Finderup. The murder is preceded by an uncanny warning which is found only in the Long Ballad, but may well have been derived from some more ancient folk song.[5] The account of the murder follows that of the older ballad, but lays still more emphasis on Rane's treachery. The little page's announcement is slightly touched in; it could only be shown in the background before we see the swiftly

[5] The elf maid's mocking words, when the King enquires as to his fate, are rather obscure. Possibly they may be interpreted: Thy life hangs on nothing more secure than the little hook by which thy sword is attached to thy belt.

following scenes of Stig's ride to Skanderborg, his angry exchange of insults with the Queen and Prince, and the gentler picture of his home-coming, when his wife promises to go with him into exile. The whole concludes with his haughty exaltation in his hold at Hjœlm, and the repetition of the last verse of the "Outlaw" Ballad— an ending essential to his representation as "my noble lord, the young Sir Marstig."

This Long Ballad, with its well defined figures appearing in a series of fascinating scenes, must be regarded as a sort of culminating point in ballad poetry. No other, Ebbe Skammelson excepted, shows such power in characterization, and such mastery over a mass of detail. We are, nevertheless, approaching the period of the decline of the ballad. The very power with which it makes literal use of its predecessors is a sign of lessening capacity for the creation of new scenes. This narrative in over a hundred verses with its succession of brilliant pictures is on the very verge of forsaking the ancient simplicity of the ballad form, and passing over into the more complicated art of the poetical romance, rich in sentiment and reflection, as it was developed towards the close of the Middle Ages.

Half a century after Erik Klipping's death, another political assassination took place, of still greater significance in Danish history. It was commemorated in a ballad perhaps more celebrated in its home country than any other—the Ballad of Niels Ebbeson (No. 29).

Niels came on the scene as a heroic deliverer when his country was actually in the throes of dissolution. King Christopher had died in 1332, his young son Valdemar was abroad, and various parts of the country were held in pledge by the Holstein nobles. The worst of these tyrants was a certain Count Gert, or Gerhardt, who had Fyn and Jutland at his mercy. Early in 1340 he entered North Jutland with a considerable army. The appearance of Prince Valdemar and a rebellion among the Jutes made it obvious that strong measures were necessary to strengthen his dominion. With the great part of his forces he secured himself in Randers, where he suddenly met his death.

What actually happened during that memorable night of April 1, 1340, was hotly disputed at the time. The Holstein party represented it as an act of treachery on the part of the Count's sworn vassals, the Danes as a valiant deed of arms. The truth seems to have been something of this kind: In the dark of night, when the new moon had set, the warriors who were in the secret (forty-seven all told) entered Randers together, pretending to be the Watch. They assembled in a burgher's house, and soon after midnight, when the town was asleep, they attacked the Count's bodyguard, broke in his door, and, after a brief resistance, killed him and his page. Immediately afterwards they beat their drums; a house was fired to divert the enemies' attention, and, amidst the confusion, the little band slipped through the streaming crowds with the loss of only one man, crossed the bridge over the Gudenaa, which they had previously loosened, and broke it down behind them. That the ringleader in this great feat was Niels Ebbeson soon became known to all. He inevitably became leader in the war for freedom against Holstein, till he fell at the battle of Skanderborg, on the 1st of November that same year.

Those seven months comprise the whole of Niels Ebbeson's history. Apart from that period, very little is known of him. Three distinguished families vied with each other in claiming him as a relative, but he rightfully belonged to the Strangesons, the great family in Ty, which played its part during the first half of the fourteenth century, and had ancestors commemorated in the Ballad of Ebbe Skammelson. The most prominent of them were the numerous children of Ebbe Strangeson, three of whom (Niels and his two brothers) fell at Skanderborg. They could always get support from other members of the clan, and their good friends and distant cousins, the Frosts, besides being allied by marriage to Ove Haas and the

Globes of Vendsyssel, and more distantly to Niels Bugge, the most powerful chief in Jutland. The ballad mentions all these as taking part in the war of independence, Ove Haas excepted, who stood by the Count and was killed in Randers. Niels is the one among the sons of Ebbe of whom least is known. His homestead, called Noringsris in one version, cannot be identified with certainty. His body, together with those of his brothers, was carried home from Skanderborg to the monastic church of Vestervig, where the family had its burial place.

The support of his kinsmen and the help given in the critical hour by steadfast friends and true patriots was not much talked of at the time. His great deed was honoured by all, was fully described in the chronicles of the period, which are usually so terse, and even found its panegyric in the dry Latin Annals. Richest of all, however, was the ballad composed in the people's own native speech. It was not a mere eulogy but a narrative of what actually occurred. This is the more obvious because it lacked a burden, and was therefore not meant for a dance ballad, but was passed on from one man to another, or carried from place to place by wandering minstrels. The story follows history, though not in every particular—the poet knew much that was true, but had to draw on his imagination where history was silent. He uses the clear, simple form of the folk ballad, follows his hero through scene after scene to the crucial point, and brings out the opinions of his principal characters by means of dialogue. Niels Ebbeson's defiance of the Count and the latter's death are the two principal episodes (possibly modelled to some extent on the Marsk Stig Ballads), and the wider historical connections are indicated in the great dialogue where Niels renounces his fealty.

This is the most noteworthy thing in the ballad, the clearest possible exposition of the views held by the gentry of the ballad world. The whole community is pictured in the introductory verses, with the class distinctions which had now become standardized, knight and squire over against yeoman and burgher, all alike terrorized and threatened by the neighbourhood of the common enemy. The political situation is laid bare in the dialogue, which relates how some of the Jutland chieftains, formerly the Count's vassals, have "renounced" him, that is to say, renounced their fealty. In the Count's furious declaration that no man may leave his liege lord's service while the latter desires to retain him, we see the feudal system from the German point of view, which regarded the vassal as bound by the mere fact of his birth in a bond only to be broken with the master's consent. Niels, however, knew only the Danish law, which was of a very different import:

> For this is the Danish custom,
> And hath been since days of yore,
> If a swain would change his service
> He should have leave therefor.

This feudal custom originated with the King's house-carles or bodyguard, and the ancient Law of Commutation, which gave every man the right to "take his leave" every twelvemonth and find service with a new lord. This right was specially cherished as the basis of liberty in the Danish State, the monastic life forming the only exception.

> Oh, none is bound with a holy vow
> Save a monk to his cowl of grey,
> Let chieftains come and chieftains go,
> Men serve them as best they may!

So ancient a heritage of freedom was a source of much embarrassment to the Danish Kings, not least for Valdemar Atterdag when dealing with the nobles of Jutland at the period when the first versions of the ballad were composed. Count Gert regards this curtailment of his rights as rebellion against his authority, and proceeds to declare Niels Ebbeson an outlaw. In the interview which follows between Niels and his retainers, he puts in practice the doctrine he had previously explained to the Count, and the test proves successful, since none of them refuse to risk their lives for him. Once more emphasis is laid on the matter, just before the attack, when Niels for the second time gives them the choice of following him or "taking leave"; his little page takes the latter course, but only in order to "serve him best of all," by saving him at the worst pinch from the superior power of the enemy. Thus the law of free will service scores its most brilliant victory.

Attempts have been made to provide this little "Swain Trust" with an historical origin, but in the ballad as sung by the people we can discover no pretext for doing so. In one version he is called "little Swain Trust" (the little trusty lad), in another the son of Niels Ebbeson's sister, without mentioning his name, just as in "Nilus and Hillelille" the two faithful squires are given the same relationship to Nilus. He is, in a word, only one among the many little pages of the ballad world, who follow their masters to danger or death. Not till Vedel collated the original texts in his publication of 1591 did the page reveal his own name and family. In later days a novel of Ingemann's established his position still more definitely, and the historians (so far in vain) have ransacked ancient documents for any mention of him. We must therefore erase his name from the authentic history of Denmark, which has thus one character the less, and pay attention to the significant fact that a Danish minstrel could not conceive of any daring enterprise without a little trusty swain to play his own bold and quick-witted part in its execution. Perhaps this evidence of the reliance placed on him by Niels Ebbeson's minstrel and the Middle Ages in general is better worth having than any historical name and lineage.

In the two concluding verses of the ballad mention is made of the poor woman who gives Niels her last two loaves of bread, and of his flight to Noringsris, or, as another version has it, to Norway. This may be a later addition, but may, on the other hand, be genuine. The woman who hails Niels as a deliverer takes a prominent place in the motley procession of figures great and small, pictured by the minstrel as taking part in the fight for freedom—the independent chieftain, the wise wife, the clever little page, and the rough "swarthy swain." Thus with a rare artistic power is the sentiment evoked of a whole nation united in the casting off of an alien yoke.

There is another version of the ballad differing from this one, with its quiet emphasis on wisdom and fellowship, and its patriotism which only appears incidentally. This second ballad was the work of a contemporary poet full of enthusiasm for Niels Ebbeson's work as a gallant feat of arms done in the full light of day. In this we find his vigorous speech to his squires, and the failure of the trick by which access was to be gained to the Count in his bedchamber. The door is burst open with glaive and spear, and at that very moment the dawn breaks. From this, despite all the controversy over his memory, a heroic portrait emerges of the actual slayer of the Count. The historical details may undergo correction by posterity, but the superb folk-power of the ballad will live on.[6]

Round about the year 1400, the historical ballads declined both in number and poetical merit. The Ballad of Queen Margaret's victory over King Albrecht, composed some time after the battle of Falköping, smacks more of the chronicle, as

[6] Besides the "Night" version, and the "Day," which was rather later, we possess one still earlier, but in very imperfect preservation. In this Esge Frost appears (with historical accuracy) as the vassal who swore fealty to the Count and subsequently failed him (his son Anders was erroneously substituted) and Niels has recourse to his brother Knud of Bygholm for help in his enterprise. The interview with the house-carles and the doings of Swain Trust seem as yet not to have been invented. The death of Ove Haas, on the other hand, originated apparently in this more historically accurate form of the ballad.

do the ballads dealing with the warlike feats of the fifteenth century. One fresh note sings out among all this decadent verse—the poem on Christian II, known as the Bird Ballad. Here the King figures as the old eagle, whom the hawks (nobility) conspire against and drive away, so that they alone may bear rule in the forest, and a lament is sung by the luckless small birds who were vainly relying on his help. The sentiment, genuine enough, wells up from the lowest class of the people—it is the first poem to make out a case against the nobility—but the artistic form seems to have been borrowed from literary models. Animal fables were employed everywhere during the Middle Ages as a means of impressing political opinions on contemporary thought, but rarely with such singlehearted feeling for the significance of the picture.

### BALLADS OF MAGIC

The ballads of chivalry and historical ballads give the fullest picture of ordinary medieval existence, but much of the deepest thought of the period on human life, together with some of its finest poetry, are to be found amongst the pictures of the supernatural world, the ballads of magic. Their content consists, first and foremost, of such pictures of unearthly beings as were derived from tradition, and of unearthly powers, or magic, as they were reshaped by a newly Christianized people.

It would be a great mistake to regard these ballads as close translations from the lays of antiquity. These dealt chiefly with the long-drawn-out strife between the Æsir and the Giants, but when the altars of the Gods were overthrown, the root of this poetry was hewn away. Only one merry adventure of Thor's, who disguised himself in Freyja's raiment and became the Giant King's bride (Lay of Thrym) passed over from Eddic poetry into a ballad, Norwegian by origin, which travelled later to Sweden and Denmark.

The actual worship of the Gods was abolished, and in the case of Denmark wiped out with remarkable completeness early in medieval times. Nevertheless, in addition to the great divine figures, popular fancy was familiar with a number of lesser ones, peopling hill and dale, forest and fen, stream and sea. These beings were conceived of as living powers which operated the workings of Nature, and their characters shaped in accordance with the impression made by Nature on man. Their ways and doings were handed down by oral tradition in little fairy tales; and now when the old Gods had vanished, and before the Christian God was definitely apprehended in the personal sense, a wealth of poetry sprang up dealing with the Nature spirits.

Sea and river in those days did not particularly impress people with the beauty and ever-changeful motion so familiar to modern poets. The sea was a grim power which demanded victims; its depths concealed a monster who delighted in the devouring of men, a mighty dragon who awoke tempest with his wing-beats. The river was but a treacherous friend; many a man and woman who heedlessly approached its brink was dragged down by the Kelpie, and only found again as a pale and bloodless corpse.

"Germand Gladensvend" (No. 6) tells of the insatiable greed of the sea. The child dedicated by his parents, though all-unknowing, to the troll of the deep, cannot escape his fate, even though he seeks refuge with his true-love in "Engeland," the fabulous, half-fairy realm of Danish tradition. Fleeing with him in the "feather-fell," she defends him against all the other birds of the air, but her powers fail before the sea Troll which takes on the disguise of a grisly vulture. There are powers of evil and inevitable destiny which are able to defeat the noblest love.

We meet with a similar grisly water Kelpie in "The Mighty Harp" (No. 8), though in this case the hero, by force of his magical music, forces the Kelpie to give up the maiden whom he captured as she rode over Blide Bridge to her bridal. This ballad recalls the Greek myth of Orpheus and Eurydice, which, according to modern research, got to the North via England and Brittany, and lost its original less happy conclusion on the way.

The same theme in a simpler, it may be said coarser, form reappears in "Saint Olaf and the Trolls" (No. 9). This was originally a Norwegian ballad associated with the mountain of Hornelen (distorted in Danish to Hornelummer), on the west coast of Norway, north of Bergen. So popular was the story in Denmark and Sweden that it often formed the subject of frescoes in the churches, that of Vallensbœk in Copenhagen amongst others. The story of the trolls petrified and shut up in the mountain by command of the hero King was partly a saintly legend, partly the repetition of the Old Norse tale of the hero who befooled the trolls into being surprised by the sunshine and turned to stone. Their picture as given here differs from that usually found in Danish ballads, and smacks more of Norwegian popular humour.

"The Mermaid's Spaeing" (No. 10) has a deeper traditional foundation. A story well known of old tells of a sea creature held captive by the King till it shall reveal where the treasures of the deep are hidden, but it makes no reply, and prophesies disaster to the royal family by way of farewell. This folk story forms the theme of the ballad, but has a different conclusion. The young Queen weeps over the coming misfortune, but the pitying Mermaid comforts her: "Now weep not for words thou didst hear from me, the gates of Heaven stand open for thee!" This strikes a note more definitely Christian than is often to be found in the ballads. It conveys the hope of mankind for salvation, and on the other hand, the vain yearning of Nature, the "groaning and travailing" spoken of by St. Paul, and frequently dwelt on by later poets. A change has come over the sentiments of ancient times; the former fear and hatred evolves into a pitying sympathy with the whole of creation.

Something of this more kindly feeling appears in "Agnes and the Merman" (No. 11), the latest of the sea troll ballads, which originated among the populace after the close of the Middle Ages. To describe it as a Danish ballad would only be true in a certain sense, since the power of creating completely original poems hardly existed at that late period in that particular class. It is an adaptation of the German "Schöne Agnete," which in its turn was originally Slav, but the representation of the Nature power is completely transformed. Instead of the treacherous wooer, who drags Agnes into the depths from the bridge (cf. No. 8), we have the beautiful, wistful Merman, who woos her only by virtue of his love, while she follows him of her own free will. For all that, the ballad retains a hint of the old terror; Agnes returns to the world of God and man, and with biting words renounces her husband from the sea.[7]

During the time when fear of Nature dominated the ballad, the same feeling prevailed for the kingdom of Elfland. A few latish ballads have a certain liking for it, but in "The Elfin Shaft" (No. 7), the best known of these poems, Elfland is a region of eerie powers, which can entice and kill the man who trespasses on its boundaries. The main lines of this ballad can be traced through one country after another, from its birthplace in Brittany or Northern France to its diffusion over the greater part of Europe. Its Northern form, however, gets its distinctive stamp from the native folk-belief in the elfin dance and the elfin bolt, which make a new ballad of it. Where the white mists rise from the fens near the greenwood, weaving round tree and hill, there is the fairy

[7] This idea was elaborated by Matthew Arnold with the rich orchestration of his "Forsaken Merman." (Translator's note)

dance, or where the sunbeams have thrown a rainbow, or still more frequently in the gloaming of the "white nights" of summer. This dance was known to all, and would present the most natural of subjects to the circle of singers down by the river of an evening. As for the elfin shaft, the other essential trait in the conception of the elf-folk, it was originally believed that any person (or animal) who suddenly fell dead, or was seized with sudden pain, had been struck by the invisible arrow of the fairies. A slightly more advanced train of thought regarded a "fairy blow" between the shoulders as the magical means of inducing a painful or fatal sickness.

This dark horror is not to be found in all the elfin ballads. The same theme finds gayer treatment in the little ballad of the squire who lies down to sleep on the Elfin Howe, and is just saved by cockcrow from being borne off underground. A few ballads, indeed, depict the captive as returning to earth again, but this idea is rarer and springs from a shallower type of feeling.

The second large group of magical ballads is that which treats of "shape-changing" or transformation—a subject not peculiar to the ballads, but treated still more frequently in folk tales. These little stories of exciting and perilous adventure went roaming for centuries from parlour to nursery, from alehouse to hunter's watch-fire, through one country after another, constantly becoming citizens of new cities. More and more definitely a favourite theme came to the fore, that of the wicked stepmother who changed her stepchild to a troll, an animal, or the like, after which the story proceeded to show how the unlucky victim regained human form. Meanwhile medieval poetry was working on the same themes, which even penetrated into the higher class of literature, the compositions of individual authors. The fantastic French romances of chivalry are full of such scenes. They passed over from Brittany into the English folk ballads, and we have our rich share of them here in the North.

A little ballad called "The Maiden Hind" (No. 12) can be traced from England and France to Denmark and Sweden. Despite his mother's warning, the youth shoots the hind which is his own enchanted sister, and the ballad ends with a little mournful after-song which gives a couple of pictures of the falling dew and the far-flying cranes. There is no definite connection with the story, only a subdued lament over happiness that is so hard to win, and trouble that is so hard to escape—the complaint of a tormented soul in the quiet of eventide.

Generally, however, these ballads strike a happier note. The fairy tale is the expression of man's unconquerable hope despite all odds. The chief point of these stories, deliverance from the ugly disguise which enshrouds the human form, is the great subject—the other colourful pictures proper to the fairy tale are cast out as superfluous.

We have a whole series of these scenes of deliverance. Now the knight kisses the little snake in the grass, now he fights the mighty bear; now proud Ingelil, weeping and wringing her hands, follows the awful dragon to his den, and when she lies in his arms beholds him transformed to a prince. But the prettiest tale of all is "The Maiden in Bird's Plumage" (No. 13).

One of the most noteworthy things in this ballad is the solemnity with which the enchantment is described. The form imposed on the maiden is not merely a disguise whence the human attributes peep out—she is forced to take on herself the real nature of the beast. She really becomes a hind, fleeing from the huntsman, unconscious of his desire to rescue her. When seized at last, she transforms herself into a still wilder creature, the greedy hawk; and no means avail for capture till the knight cuts the bleeding flesh from his own bosom and offers it as a bait—for human blood, in fairy tales, is the magical means of freeing the human likeness from its bonds. No less striking is the hero himself, the true "squire of dames," who risks all, and wins his love through a noble self-sacrifice.

In connection with these stories of transformation, the unique ballad must be mentioned, describing young Svejdal's wooing of his entranced bride, a ballad remarkable alike for its treatment and previous history. Two old Norse lays tell of young Svipdag, who went to the Magic Mountain and released Menglad from her restless lethargy of longing. These lays are generally regarded as a supplement, or postscript, to the Elder Edda, but their atmosphere is hardly congenial to the world of the Gods. It belongs rather to that of the fairy tale; the heroine is the sleeping Briar Rose, who could only be awakened by the entrance of the fated swain, and he the Fairy Prince, condemned by his stepmother never to be at peace till he found the maiden, and armed for the enterprise by his dead mother. In the Norse lays the story is veiled in dark, riddling dialogue, and illumined by a gleam from the mythic realms of Asgard and Jotunheim. Turning to the medieval ballad of Svejdal, we realize the truth of the proverb that what is hidden under the snow comes up in the thaw. All the sombre wintry majesty has fallen away, and only the simple fairy tale remains. Only the slightest of threads connects it with the splendour of Valhalla, but it shows how soon the Middle Ages began to mould the tales of adventure which played so great a part in their world of thought.

We have here, moreover, a ballad of love, conceived in a very different sense from anything familiar to the lays, a story of the obscure emotions controlling the will and rousing the gnawing ache of desire, which invade the soul by the most singular paths. We meet with this in the opening scene, when the maiden whose love is unrequited lays a curse of like nature on the hero—namely, that he is never to know peace till he has freed the entranced lady far away in an alien land.

In the magic of the runes a power was perceived which reduced mankind to greater helplessness than that of the Nature beings. Rune magic was a very ancient heritage, and the medieval method of practice was identical with that common in heathen times. The runes were incised (risted) on a "staff," a little flat slip of wood or the like, and thrown at the person who was to be influenced. All the same, the Christian ballad minstrel had a slightly different conception of the runes from that which prevailed in previous ages—he regarded them as a compelling force which overpowered a man's free will, so that, if the spell could not be broken, flight was the only means of security. In the ballads they mostly appear in the shape of love charms, capable of awakening an impulse as unaccountable as impossible to resist. Some late ballads merely make use of them as a trivial device for bringing knight and lady together. But if we turn to those which are full of real poetic feeling, we find dread and horror over the invoking of the wild forces which so easily bring unhappiness and are so uncontrollable by men. One such minstrel breaks out in conclusion:

> *Ill was the risting of that rune,*
> *And ill was it shaped, I wis,*
> *That two such noble King's children*
> *Should come to a death like this!*

This dread of blind desire may seem singular in modern eyes, but was inevitable at a period when natural feeling still bore the brand of uncanniness; if a dangerous allurement was felt in the greenwood and Elfin Howe, how much more must it have been perceptible in the sorcery working in man's innermost soul?

The ballad of "Sir Stig and His Runes" (Vol. II, No. 14) shows this belief in their irresistible power, yet maintains that, by dint of wisdom and strength of will, it can be evaded. When Stig casts the rune-staff, it misses the lady Kirsteen, and falls on the King's sister, who is seized with such longing for the knight as he cannot escape, even though he should go to the end of the world. But when the Princess steals up to his chamber and his bed, he lies "still as any bairn," and resists all her caresses. Next morning he tells the tale to the King, who, much amazed at his courteous behaviour, gives him the Princess, and the ballad ends with a magnificent bridal feast at the knight's homestead.

Sorcery does not always form the leading theme of the ballads, but sometimes appears incidentally. Thus it is only alluded to in one detail of "The Griefs of Hillelille" (No. 15). There was a belief that a sort of irresistible battle madness sometimes came over certain persons, a species of *Bersærks-Gang* (to use the ancient expression); they were, that is to say, possessed by a devilish entity, but when they were "called by their name" their human nature returned, and the madness was arrested. When Sir Hildebrand carries off Hillelille and is pursued by her kinsmen, he implores her not to name his name during the combat, but when her youngest brother is imperilled she disobeys him, his supernatural power is broken, and he is slain by his enemies.

Strangest of all ballads of magic is "The Avenging Sword" (No. 16). Its theme is identical with that of "Sir Stig and His Runes"—the idea of an occult power in Nature, which can be aroused, but neither understood nor controlled till its madness has resulted in woe to the world of men. All the berserk fury of old times seems concentrated in the clang of the sword. And yet this is the one and only ballad of magic which presents us with a detail of essentially Christian origin. The minstrel must have been influenced by a sight not infrequently witnessed during the Middle Ages. Amongst the great flocks of penitent pilgrims, some might be met with who had iron bands welded round neck, arm, or body—specially heinous sinners, parricides or fratricides, condemned to rove from one saint's shrine to another until the bonds should fall away. The unlimited bloodshed of this story is just such a crime in the minstrel's eyes. He therefore depicts his hero as condemning himself to the penance of iron bonds, and forgiveness as being granted, not at the shrine of a saint—the ballads are little concerned with ecclesiastical interests—but at that of his father's murderer. Thus the champion, who has "roamed the world round," returns at last, a true penitent, to the grave of his bitterest foe.

This ballad, with its religious conclusion, stands alone, but its underlying thought, that of an underworld of power striving to break man's free will, common to a multitude of ballads of magic, might well serve to deepen the spiritual life of the Middle Ages. This spiritual deepening was, apart from other issues, of great benefit to the minstrel's art. These ballads of magic sprang up in the rift between old and new as the fairest flowers of our Danish folk poetry.

### WARRIOR BALLADS

The name of warrior ballads was used towards the close of the medieval period to designate all ballads dating from the Age of Chivalry, and was used in that sense till modern times. It cannot, however, have originally borne that meaning, since many of the ballads in question have nothing to do with warfare; it must have applied to those dealing with the mighty, sometimes half supernatural, figures of the ancient past.

These ballads are dominated by two widely differing moods. One series, composed in a gay, sometimes a jesting, tone, is closely allied to foreign, mostly German, verse, while the second series, far graver in treatment, harks back to the heroic lays of antiquity. The favourite loan from the latter source was a love story. Sivord steals Brynhild from the Mountain of Glass, and gives her to his comrade, only to fall by her hand when she discovers the deception. Here we have the actors in the greatest Saga of our race, Sigurd Fafnirsbane and Brynhild, recurring in a beautiful medieval ballad with a haunting melody. The combat of Hjalmar and Angantyr for the daughter of the King of Uppsala was taken from Icelandic saga by a Norwegian ballad minstrel, and transformed once again when it reached Denmark. An echo from a third lay is to be found in "Aage and Else" (No. 3). Here their love has a setting of medieval Christianity, but the dialogue between dead lover and living maid recalls the lay relating how Helge Hundingsbane, recalled to earth by their mutual longing, revisits his love Sigrun, and complains that her tears drip on his heart like drops of blood.

But of all old tales of love and the fall of princes, only one stamped a really deep impression on the medieval ballad world —the love story of Havbor and Signe (No. 1).

This particular story was a special favourite with the Danes from time immemorial. Its origin goes back to the period of folk migration previous to that of Rolf Kraki and the other famous Skjoldung Kings. In the medieval ballad period, its scene was pointed out at Sigarsted in Sælland, near the old royal seat of Ringsted, with the howe where the King hanged his daughter's lover, the foundations of his palace and Signe's bower, and the battlefield where his entire army was defeated by Hagbard's avenging kinsfolk, who laid the haughty palace waste, never to be rebuilt. The faithful, defiant love of Hagbard and Signe was celebrated in an ancient lay, fragments of which were incorporated by Saxo Grammaticus in the seventh book of his History, with a more detailed description of the royal family and its ruin. The ballad poet drew on this source, though omitting much ancient history of combat, treachery, and revenge. In fact, he took over none of it except the allusion to the quarrelling Kings, and a remarkable reminiscence of the Shield Maidens (v. 20). He retained, however, every detail of the love story, and added a few new and beautiful ones on his own account.

The story of Havbor's disguise, for instance, follows the main lines of the lay, but the scene where he accounts for his masculine appearance has a fine original touch in his reply, more bold than prudent, to the suspicious serving-maid. The lay places most emphasis on the nocturnal interview between the lovers when Signe promises to follow her lover to the death she regards as inevitable, and Havbor's discourse when his mantle is hoisted on the gallows and her bower goes up in flame—a burst of rejoicing over the keeping of the vow, and the coming reunion of the lovers in the land of the dead, despite all who desired to part them. The ballad handles these scenes with a novelty and power which increases as they lead up in swift succession to the climax of the drama. Instead of dwelling on the dialogue, the action proceeds to the serving-maid's treachery, Havbor's desperate combat, and her suggestion of binding him with Signe's hair—which gives occasion for a fine trait of true medieval chivalry in his refusal to break the bond. At this moment, when he is doomed, we have the dialogue when she vows to die with him. The action gains pace without dwelling on words, since the events speak for themselves. Havbor's rejoicing at the gallows-tree is concentrated in his cry:

> Take down, take down my cloak of red,
> That well its task has done!
> For had I now ten thousand lives
> I would not ask for one.

The ballad ends on a note of atonement; the King, seeing the bale-fire, tries to save the lives of the lovers, and bursts out in a lamentation which would, no doubt, express the sentiments both of the minstrel and his audience. The two victims, moreover, are granted a posthumous revenge on the faithless serving-maid who betrayed her mistress. This, comparatively speaking, is a milder ending than the ferocious revenge in the lay on the entire race of Sigar. The public, unlike the ancient skalds, was no longer preoccupied with the devious windings of fate and the deaths and dying words of heroes.

In this ballad we discern the traits which usually characterized medieval loans from the Old Norse lays. A number of great and tragic love stories were adapted, to form some of our finest ballads, but the wars and doughty deeds of the heroes were left aside, and all that connected them with a long-vanished civilization.

Danish minstrelsy was enriched by another group of warrior ballads, dealing with those favourite medieval heroes, Didrik of Bern and Holger Danske. Their tone is gay and bold, their endings invariably happy. Their subject matter deals exclusively with warfare against trolls or human enemies, love being merely a secondary consideration.

King Didrik was by origin an historical personage, Theoderik, King of the East Goths, who subjugated Italy; his royal seat of Verona is the Bern of the ballads. His legend was early remodelled in the ancient German lays. Not long after the christianizing of Germany, the story was carried on in a cycle of warrior ballads, composed and recited by wandering minstrels or "fiddlers" (Spillemœnd). For the diversion of their mixed audiences in castle or market-place, they soon invented a multitude of new heroes and new adventures, treated in a more jovial, not to say coarser, vein. These minstrels visited Denmark, where they were known as "Saxon singers" during the reigns of Knud Lavard (d. 1131) and Svend Grade (d. 1157). It seems an obvious conclusion that these warrior ballads were taken over as giving examples of true knighthood. Many of them, however, seem to have reached Denmark by a more devious way. A great Saga of Didrik was compiled in Bergen during the thirteenth century from the tales told by the German merchants, and much of it got to Denmark through newly composed Norwegian ballads.

The leading theme of the Didrik legend—the long years of exile and warfare endured by the legendary hero before his conquest of Italy—was not assimilated by the Danish minstrels. Interest was confined to individual champions and their adventures—the wild young squire Vidrik Verlandson, the sagacious Raadengaard, and so forth. In the most popular ballads King Didrik himself does nothing whatever, but his doughtiest champions provide the whole of the entertainment.

With "twice seven and seventy champions" (No. 4) we see Didrik sallying forth against King Isung, and pitching camp at Birtingsborg. Isung stands watching on the castle tower, and beside him Sivord Snarensvend, doughtiest of warriors, who points out the shields hanging outside each tent —for the minstrel cannot deny himself the pleasure of going through the entire list of Didrik's much-loved champions, and recalling the remarkable feats of one and all. Amongst them we find Helled Haagen (Hero Högne) none other than the grim warrior of the Volsung Saga, who slew Sigurd, and has the fierce vulture as a bearing. Next comes the merry Fiddler Folkvar, who bears viol and bow by way of crest, a figure created by the wandering fiddle-men for their own pleasure. By way of honouring their Danish neighbours the Saxon singers also brought in a certain Detlev Danske; the elephant on his shield not only betokened his strength, but exemplified the predilection of the crusading period for Oriental decoration.

The whole ballad mirrors contemporary warfare from the chivalrous point of view. (We may recall the expedition of Valdemar the Victorious [1215], when his army confronted that of the Emperor Otto, and the victory of two Danish champions—Svend Starke and Ganling—in the tournament, won glory for the whole Danish nation.) The ballad shows us the challenge to single combat in the area between the two armies, the casting of lots to decide who shall accept it, the secret misgivings of the youth who wins the distinction and dares not evade it, the borrowing of weapons, exchange of pledges, negotiations for a marriage, and so forth, followed by the joust itself and the binding of the vanquished man to a tree-trunk. The leading figure in it all is Sivord Snarensvend, that antique hero who, under the name of Sigurd Fafnirsbane, was the ideal of the Norse and Germanic races, the perfection of valour and self-control. This place he retains, but the Saxon singers were chiefly preoccupied with his prowess as a fighter. The climax of the ballad shows him tearing up the oak-tree to which he was bound in sport, and coming home with it to the town. For all that, he is not merely the man of thew and sinew, this "blind fellow" who scarcely looks before he strikes, since, with knightly magnanimity, he passes off the vanquished youth as victor in the combat. If these warriors show less soul than body, they have at least plenty of fun in them, as appears above all in the war dance added by Danish adapters by way of conclusion to the Birtingsborg expedition.

Holger Danske was the other chief figure of the medieval warrior ballad. His origin was to be found in French heroic poetry, but as a Danish folk hero he differed essentially from his foreign prototype.

The earliest ballad of Holger describes his combat with Burmand the Troll for the King of Hungary's daughter, who releases the Dane from prison so that he may fight for her sake and that of her betrothed lover King Karvel, and rewards him with a kiss after his victory. This is par excellence the ballad of true chivalry fighting the oppressor and delivering the helpless, with no admixture of desire for personal advantage. The migration of this theme from France to the North coincided with an expansion of chivalrous principles in their simplest and loftiest forms.

The French poems of Holger include many other scenes. Ogier le Danois is a participant in that immense national achievement, the warfare of Charlemagne against the infidel in Spain, and his more fabulous expeditions to Italy. Ogier appears as an independent vassal who long defies his sovereign, and, in later poems, as the Crusader of romance, conquering and converting far-away' regions in the East. These features are all peculiar to the ideas of the Frankish nobility. That one picture alone, of the pure act of knightly protection, found its way into Danish minstrelsy, and was depicted with a gusto which elevates it over any mere survival from the heroic age. When chieftain and peasant sang the burden ("So Holger Danske conquered Burmand"), they regarded the feat as glorifying the whole Danish people, and Holger as the man who had increased Denmark's renown among foreign nations.

The next step taken by native singers was to represent the hero as fighting, not only for the honour, but the independence of his country. Thus originated the ballad "Holger Danske and Stout Didrik" (No. 5). Its beginning was borrowed from the earlier ballad which shows the King of Verona asking if any yet remain who can resist him. Then the subject is given a new turn; Didrik no longer appears as the pattern of chivalry, but as an embodiment of the German Emperor's power and presumption. Holger Danske confronts him as typifying the sturdy independence of the Danish people. For which reason he "dwells in North Jutland," and has himself "crowned with the red, red gold." His name occurs nowhere else on the list of Danish sovereigns, and the minstrel handles the old saga figures pretty freely. He places the Giants Sverting (the Swarthy) and Bermer-Ris amongst Didrik's followers, to show his irresistible power, and on the other hand turns over the most popular heroes to Holger, even when they rightfully belong to Didrik. Despite this free handling, however, he is able to breathe life into his pictures, of enemy presumption, of the faithful fellowship between the King and his men, and the bloody violence of the battle. He sang in epic form the first patriotic song of Denmark. With that, Holger's place as national hero was firmly established. Popular faith has assigned to him a hiding-place in hill or cavern whence he is to issue in time of need to save his people.

Meanwhile, the more comprehensive Ogier poetry of France became known through Kristjern Pedersen's "Chronicles of Holger Danske," 1534. Ingemann's "Holger Danske" was an attempt to amalgamate the French material with the picture of Holger as national hero.

The fabulous figure of Svend Felding sprang up as a species of imitation. As against the well-born and ever-chivalrous hero, this Jutland fighter is placed as a kind of spokesman for the powers, so long ignored, of the people in general, but in championship of women and Denmark's honour he is the true heir of Holger Danske.

The warrior ballads as a whole belong to the most ancient class of folk poetry, and exercised no little influence on other classes. The tone of the Didrik cycle finds an after-echo in "Lovel and John," and the tragic note of our native heroic verse recurs still more frequently.

### SATIRE AND LYRIC

The style and method developed by the ballads of chivalry was turned later on to other subjects. Alongside of those ballads, sometimes more or less facetious in treatment, there grew up the purely satirical ballad of daring caricature. As the former were connected with the dance, so the latter found their true home in the tavern. The chief theme was the feast or assembly, with its boisterous, sometimes unseemly incidents, the relationship of husband and wife, or the wedding of young couples. As chief characters they have the Gaffer and Gammer, or the fiddler who goes a-roving with fiddle at his chin. Occasionally they touch on the lusting of monk or priest after women, and the "bishop's daughter" is the stock figure for a lady not overburdened with modesty. Another caricatures the ideal of the times, the courtly maiden, slim as a lily-wand, who is pictured as the "strong woman," recalling the comic accounts of giantesses in native folk poetry. We find an example in "The Bride of Ribe" (No. 51), who does violence to priest and deacon, and so scares even the cattle that they stampede off home. There are many of these satirical ballads, but few have any poetical significance. For all that, they are full of amusing scenes, and the special diction of chivalry produces a comic effect when used in this grosser connection.

This coarse and lowly reflection of ballad minstrelsy had its more refined offshoots. One took the form of love poems, in which the treatment is more seemly, and the expression of feeling the principal object. One example is to be found in the little poem (No. 49), noteworthy because lover and lady were real persons, belonging to the nobility of South Sælland about 1330. The small bird singing his complaint to the linden tree was Sir Jens Due of Tessebölle, who was betrothed to Anne Nielsdatter, while the falcon which drives him away was the wealthy Falk of Vallö whom the lady subsequently married.

Moreover, the folk ballad developed among the more cultured gentry into the romance, a long-winded narrative in one hundred or even two hundred verses, all sung to the same tune and with the same burden. Sometimes the scene was set in faraway places like Spain or Myklegaard (Constantinople), or still more frequently in Norway. The plot usually includes a number of far-fetched and startling incidents, the favourite being that of lovers parted on account of the maiden's forced marriage to a wealthier suitor. With their constant insistence on virtuous conduct and courteous bearing, they form a strong contrast to the earlier ballad, with its violent and lawless characters.

A time came when the ballad ceased to accompany the dance, and this was due chiefly to the changes which came over the dance itself. The fifteenth century saw the building of many splendid country-houses, and the coming in of the Polish dance (polka), accompanied by viol and flute which made singing an impossibility. The ballad withdrew from the din and lived on in retirement among the everyday doings of the people. At this period, however, about 1550, the fashion came in of committing the ballads to writing. The gentry of the period, especially the ladies, possessed "poetry books" or albums, in which their friends and acquaintances wrote verses, and signed their names by way of friendly remembrance. Sometimes the verses were of a moralizing description, sometimes long-winded laments over the gossip and evil-speaking which separated lovers, and sometimes the old narrative ballads. The first collections of ballads, properly so called, were compiled in process of time from the varied contents of these poetry albums. The great folio manuscript in the home for noble ladies at Odense (Karen Brahe's Library) was written about 1550 in the house of an East Jutland gentleman, and contains some two hundred ballads. It was soon succeeded by a number of others, such as "Queen Sophy's Ballad Book," presented to one of her court ladies by the consort of Frederick II, by Anders Vedel's collection, and others. One or more of these comprehensive anthologies was usually to be found in the ladies' apartments of a great house, and one of them would sing from it to enliven the spinning and sewing during the long winter evenings.[8] This practice had not always the happiest influence on the text, the object being to draw out the poem to the utmost possible extent. "Axel and Valborg," with its two hundred verses, was widely circulated after 1600. Midway in the seventeenth century the ancient ballads found a formidable rival in the imported pastoral poetry in the rococo style, and when autocracy came in, they began to die out with the passing of many old noble homesteads into the hands of new owners.

Native poetry began to be confined to the market towns, which had never been very closely associated with the ancient ballad singing. The country folk, on the other hand, remained stubbornly attached to the songs of their forefathers. If the ballads have been handed down to modern times, we owe it, after the noble ladies, to the peasant and country-woman. Even in the early Middle Ages, this latter class had adopted the ballads of chivalry, for the yeoman often sat at the feast with his own overlord, and the squire from the castle sometimes set up house as a farmer. Amongst them the ballads got a new lease of life, without the lengthening and overrefining process they underwent in the great houses; they were, on the contrary, often curtailed and sometimes coarsened. In course of time they were added to from outside sources. The richest importation was that of the most popular folk ballads of Germany, a few of which were freely adapted, though most literally translated. There was also a number of new poems (murder stories, moral verses, laments over unhappy love, and the oppression of the peasants), composed by printers and other half-educated persons, and sold as broadsheets in the market or by the way-

[8] Sometimes we find directions given:

> Finis *means the end.*
> *Take the volume in hand,*
> *Sing loud and clear,*
> *So that all may hear.*

side. Despite all this competition, however, the old ballads held their own far into the nineteenth century, most remarkably so in the heath country of Jutland. This state of affairs was only altered by increased facilities for schooling, travel, and newspaper reading. From the beginning of the century till now (especially during the national revival of the 1840s) a vast number of ballads have been reduced to writing, and our knowledge of their tunes, so far as it goes, is almost entirely due to the singing of the country folk during this period.

The Danish ballads were edited earlier and much more fully than those of any other country. The historian Anders Sörensen Vedel published A *Hundred Chosen Danish Ballads* (chiefly of the warrior and historical classes) in 1591. *Tragica, or Love Ballads* followed by way of supplement in 1657, long after Vedel's death. "The Hundred-Ballad-Book" was frequently reprinted, and in 1695 the grammarian Peter Syv augmented it to *Two Hundred Chosen Ballads*. To the revival of interest in popular poetry was due the publication (1811-1813) of *Danish Ballads of the Middle Ages*, in five volumes by Abrahamson, Nyerup, and Rahbek. But the great pioneer work of the century was that of Svend Grundtvig, *The Ancient Folk Ballads of Denmark*, designed to present all the ballads, each in every version still surviving on the lips of the people, and each with its own historical introduction. Our own two volumes represent a selection from Grundtvig's work.

The number of Danish ballads which have been preserved is about five hundred, together with some fifty which were composed or translated during the sixteenth and seventeenth centuries. We have in addition at least a hundred purely satirical ballads, which for the greater part date from the Middle Ages.

No ballad is known to us in the precise form of its original composition. Before even the best of our versions were committed to writing, a long period, sometimes a couple of centuries, had elapsed since the actual birth of the ballad. In many examples later modifications were confined to the remodelling of separate phrases, and the addition or omission of single verses. There are, however, numerous cases of much more drastic alteration. Where a ballad as originally conceived contented itself with a definite scheme of treatment and certain characteristic expressions, later minstrels by accident or design would add a number of new stanzas, and narrow or expand the whole course of the narrative.

The texts given in the present edition have consequently been selected according to various different methods. (1) Where only one copy exists, or where one copy presents a consistently clear and beautiful version of the story, that text has been chosen. (2) When a number of copies exist, it is often possible to trace the original form of the ballad and follow its later developments. In such cases, this edition usually takes the earliest version ("Ebbe Skammelson," "Havbor and Signe"). Occasionally a later version has been preferred as more poetical ("The Maiden in Bird's Plumage"). (3) When a ballad has been handed down in a couple of different versions, a text has occasionally been put together according to personal judgment as to the merits or defects of each.

As a whole, the texts in this selection follow actual oral tradition more closely than those of any previous collection intended for general reading.

# WARRIOR BALLADS AND
# BALLADS OF MAGIC

# HAVBOR AND SIGNELIL

1   *Havbor the King and Sivord the King*
   *Have fallen out in strife,*
   *All for the stately Signelil*
   *That was so fair a wife.*
   *Ne'er wilt thou win such a fair one.*

2   *Havbor the King hath dreamt a dream,*
   *And woeful did he wake,*
   *He went to seek his mother dear*
   *And of the dream he spake.*

3   *"Methought that I was up in Heaven,*
   *And 'twas so fair a town;*
   *I held in mine arms proud Signelil,*
   *And we fell to earth adown."*

4   *"Didst dream the maid was in thine arm,*
   *And thou didst fall from sky*
   *It bodes that thou her love shalt win,*
   *And for her sake shalt die."*

5   *"When I dream of winning yon maiden*
   *Such happiness have I,*
   *That less than nothing I count it*
   *If I for her sake must die!"*

6    Now Havbor let his locks wax long
     And did on woman's gear,
     And so he rode to Denmark
     As though he a maiden were.

7    Oh his cloak he changed in the castle-garth
     All for the scarlet fair,
     And forth to the ladies' bower he went
     To seek proud Signe there.

8    "Here sittest thou, stately Signelil,
     With matrons and maids arow!
     Havbor hath sent me hither
     To learn to broider and sew."

9    "Now all the woman's craft I know
     Shall be for thee displayed,
     Shalt eat with me from the selfsame dish,
     And sleep with my serving-maid."

10   "Oh I have lain with King's children,
     And slept in their arms by night,
     And must I sleep with thy serving-maid
     I shall die of the sore despite."

11   "Now lithe and listen, fair maid, to thee
     Shall no such ill betide,
     Thou shalt eat with me from the selfsame dish,
     And slumber by my side."

12   He's ta'en a knife so small and fine,
     And cut as best he could,
     He's shaped them out, both hart and hind,
     That run in good greenwood.

13    Still sat all the dainty dames
       And sewed their seams aright,
       All save Havbor the Prince, and he
       His needle still did bite.

14    Up and spake the serving-maid,
       So evil a tongue had she:
       "Oh, never saw I so poor a seam
       Sewn by a fair ladye!

15    "Ever her needle is in her mouth,
       She sets no stitches fine,
       And still she drinketh the goblet out
       So fast as they pour the wine.

16    "Ne'er have I seen a lady's hands
       Stiffer than steel, I trow,
       Nor ever beheld so bold an eye
       Under a lady's brow."

17    "Now hold thy peace, thou evil maid,
       Let all thy prating be!
       Let me turn mine eyes where'er I may
       I'll turn them not on thee." ·

18    Now all were bound to slumber
       Whenas the even was spent,
       And Havbor with proud Signelil
       To the selfsame chamber went.

19    Her hand she laid on Havbor's breast
       That shone with gold so red:
       "Why hast thou a bosom so like a man's,
       And not the breasts of a maid?"

20    "Oh 'tis use and wont in my father's realm
      That maids to the Thing must fare,
      And therefore have I no woman's breasts
      Because of the mail we bear.

21    "Now tell to me, proud Signelil,
      Whilst we be all alone,
      Is there ever a wight in all the world
      Hast laid thy love upon?"

22    "Nay, there's never a wight in all the world
      That lies my heart within,
      Save only Havbor the King's fair son,
      And him I ne'er can win."

23    "And is it Havbor in very truth
      That to thy heart is dear,
      Then turn thee hither, mine own fair love,
      He lieth all so near!"

24    "And art thou Havbor the King's fair son,
      Why hast thou shamèd me?
      Why didst not ride to my father's hold
      With hawk on hand so free?"

25    "Oh, how should I ride to your father's hold
      With hawk on hand so free?
      Hath he not vowed, as well I know,
      To hang me on gallows-tree?"

26    "Now hush thee, Havbor, hush thee,
      And take thou heed, I pray!
      My serving-maid lies waking
      And listens to all we say."

27  "And doth she lie and listen,
    Thine evil serving-maid?
    'Neath my bolster blue lie hidden
    Both byrnie and trusty blade.

28  "Beneath my bolster lie hidden
    My byrnie and blade so true,
    And were a hundred warriors here
    The meeting they well might rue!"

29  Now she stood nearby to hear and spy,
    That evil serving-maid,
    And she stole away his byrnie brown,
    And stole his trusty blade.

30  Both trusty blade and byrnie brown
    She secretly stole away,
    And she hied in haste to the chamber
    All where King Sivord lay.

31  "Now sleep ye, wake ye, my noble Lord?
    Nay, your slumber is all too deep,
    For now lies Havbor the King's fair son
    By Signelil's side asleep."

32  "Now hold thy peace, thou evil maid,
    For an thou art a liar,
    Tomorrow or e'er the sun goes down
    Thou shalt be burnt with fire!"

33  "Now harken and hear, King Sivord,
    Well may ye trust my word,
    Behold, here is Havbor's byrnie brown,
    All with his trusty sword!"

34  Forth he sprang, King Sivord,
    And cried through bower and hall:
    "Now up, now up, my merry men,
    And don your byrnies all!

35  "Now don your mail, my merry men,
    And clasp it well enough,
    For here is Havbor the King's fair son,
    A warrior tall and tough!"

36  Oh they have knocked at the chamber-door
    With glaive and eke with spear:
    "Come forth now, Havbor, Havbor,
    Come forth and meet us here!"

37  Up sprang Havbor the King's fair son
    Or ever they spake the word,
    And gone I ween was his byrnie brown,
    All with his trusty sword.

38  "Oh gone, gone is my byrnie,
    And gone my blade so true,
    Now by my troth, proud Signelil,
    This meeting we shall rue!"

39  All hail to Havbor the King's fair son,
    Who fought like a warrior stout!
    Ne'er could his foes come nigh him
    Whilst the boards of the bed held out.

40  And some he slew with naked hands,
    And some underfoot did tread,
    Full thirty of King Sivord's men
    By Signil's bower lay dead.

41  They've taken him, Havbor the King's fair son,
    Fetters on him they draw,
    He burst them all asunder
    As though they had been of straw.

42  Now shame be on the serving-maid
    That gave them counsel there:
    "Never shall ye bind Havbor
    Save with proud Signil's hair!"

43  They took a hair of Signil's head
    To bind him foot and hand,
    His haughty heart would have broken
    Before he burst that band.

44  "Now lithe and listen, Signelil,
    Wouldst show thy love to me,
    Then burn thy bower and all therein
    When they hang me to a tree!"

45  "Oh, is there a man of my father's men
    That in thy death hath part,
    Be sure I will avenge his deed
    All on his own sweetheart!"

46  Up spake Havbor the King's fair son,
    When first he saw the tree:
    "Hang up my cloak of scarlet red,
    A sign for all to see!

47  "Hang up my cloak of scarlet
    That is both fair and fine,
    The ladies all will weep and wail
    When first they see the sign."

48 It was stately Signelil
   To roof and reed set fire,
   Both she and all her maidens
   Burned in the selfsame pyre.

49 Long stood doughty Havbor
   To look his last on land,
   Until he saw proud Signil's bower
   That all in flame did stand.

50 "Take down, take down my cloak of red,
   That well its task hath done,
   For had I now ten thousand lives,
   I would not ask for one!"

51 Up and spake King Sivord
   That looked and needs must speak:
   "Oh, what is the bale that burns so red
   All with the driving reek?"

52 Up spake the little foot-page,
   And fast his tears did fall:
   " 'Tis the deed of stately Signelil
   That shows her love to all."

53 "Save her, save her, Signelil,
   Ride ye in haste and run,
   Hie ye in haste to the gallows
   And save King Havbor's son."

54 When they came to the bower
   Signelil's soul was sped,
   When they came to the gallows
   Havbor was hanged and dead.

55   "Now had I known but yesternight
     How deep in love were they,
     Not for all Denmark had I done
     What I have done this day!"

56   Now woe is me for the gallows-tree
     And the bower in ashes laid!
     They buried her in the earth alive,
     The cruel serving-maid.

2

## ALF OF ODDERSKERRY

1   Now Alf dwells up in Odderskerry
     With store of the red, red gold,
     And two fair sons and tall had he,
     Were known for warriors bold.
     But now drives the storm o'er the white sands to north-
                                ward.

2   Now Alf dwells up in Odderskerry
     With sons of great renown,
     And both would woo the King's daughter
     That rules o'er Opsal town.

3   It was the doughty Helmer Kamp
     Bade saddle his steed so free:
     "Now forth to Opsal will I fare
     The Princess proud to see."

4   It was doughty Angelfyr
     Bade saddle his steed of pride:
     "What though the earth be rent beneath,
     To Opsal will I ride!"

5   They donned their cloaks of scarlet
     Beside the castle door,
     And entered in the high-loft
     To stand the King before.

6   In came doughty Helmer Kamp
     And stood the board beside:
     "O King, give me thy daughter fair,
     For I will not be denied!"

7   In came doughty Angelfyr,
     With shining sword in hand:
     "Sir King, give me thy daughter fair,
     And get thee from thy land!"

8   Long stood the King of Opsal
     And thought, and thought again,
     What answer should be given
     Unto those champions twain.

9   It was the King of Opsal
     Made answer good or ill:
     "No man shall have my daughter
     Save with her own good-will."

10  "Now thanks, now thanks, dear father mine,
     That leav'st the word to me!
     'Tis Helmer Kamp I fain would wed,
     So true a man is he.

11  "For Angelfyr, that is half a troll,
     Shall wed no Christian bride,
     The troll is in his parents twain,
     And half his kin beside."

12 Up and spake young Angelfyr
That came of wizard kin:
"Forth to the garth and fight with me,
The maiden's hand to win!"

13 Up stood the King of Opsal
That straight did speak and say:
"Brave are the words and keen the swords,
Ye well may prove their play!"

14 Now Alf he stood in Odderskerry,
And looked o'er hill and glade,
And long gave ear, and still did hear
The clash of blade on blade.

15 It was Alf of Odderskerry
Sprang on his courser red,
And straight rode forth to the castle-garth
Or ever his sons fell dead.

16 "Now lithe and listen, young Helmer Kamp,
Thou dear-loved son of mine,
Say, why dost guide thy sword so ill
All with that hand of thine?"

17 "Oh, seven deadly wounds have I
That are so deep and sore,
Had I but one of them, I wis,
I could not live an hour."

18 It was Alf of Odderskerry
Tore up an oak amain,
And struck young Angelfyr to earth,
Ne'er to rise up again.

19   "Lie there, lie there, young Angelfyr,
    And shed thy life-blood all!
    So sore the smart that pierced my heart
    When I saw Helmer fall."

NOTE: The material of this ballad is derived from very ancient sources common to all the Northern countries, and best known by the Hervarar Saga, which was itself founded on earlier epic poems. Its heroes, Hjalmar and Angantyr, become brothers in the ballad. As regards the father, Arngrim has apparently been changed into Örvar-Odd, "Alf i Odderskjer" being a species of anagram on "Oddr í Elfarsker." *Danmarks Fornviser*, by Ernst von der Recke (Möller and Landschultz, Copenhagen), Vol. I, p. 29.

# 3

# AAGE AND ELSE

1   Three maidens sit in a bower,
    Two broider with gold,
    The third she weeps her own true-love
    Under darksome mould,
    For her troth to him was plighted.

2   It was the knight Sir Aage
    That rode by land and lea,
    He loved the lady Elselil,
    So fair was she.

3   He wooed the lady Elselil
    With gifts and gold,
    On Monday thereafter
    He lay in the mould.

4   Sore wept the lady Elselil
    With wellaway,
    That heard the knight Sir Aage,
    Low where he lay.

5   Up stood the knight Sir Aage,
    His coffin black he bore,
    With mickle toil and trouble
    He sought her door.

6   He knocked there with his coffin,
    No cloak had he:
    "Rise up, thou lady Elselil,
    Open to me!"

7   Up spake the lady Elselil,
    With tears spake she:
    "Canst thou name the name of Jesu
    I'll open to thee!"

8   "Rise up, thou lady Elselil,
    Open thy door!
    I can name the name of Jesu
    As ever I could of yore."

9   Up stood the lady Elselil
    In dule and dread.
    So opened she the bower door,
    Let in the dead.

10  She took her golden comb
    To smooth his hair,
    For every lock she ordered
    Down fell a tear.

11  "Now lithe and list, Sir Aage,
    Dearest love mine,
    How goes it under mirk and mould
    In grave of thine?"

12    "So goes it under darksome mould
      Where I am laid,
      As in the happy realm of Heaven,
      Therefore be glad."

13    "Lithe and list, Sir Aage,
      Dearest love mine,
      Fain would I lie 'neath mirk and mould
      In grave of thine."

14    "So goes it under darksome mould
      There where I rest,
      As in the blackest depths of Hell!
      Cross thou thy breast.

15    "For every tear thou lettest fall
      In mournful mood,
      Adown into my grave doth drip
      A drop of blood.

16    "Up above my head
      The green grass grows,
      Down about my feet
      The dark worm goes.

17    "But when a song thou singest
      All in delight,
      Then all my darksome grave is hung
      With roses red and white.

18    "Now in the darksome entry
      The black cocks crow,
      And all the doors are opening,
      Forth must I go.

19 "And now the white cock croweth
In the high hall,
To earth I now betake me
With dead men all.

20 "Now croweth on the high-loft
The cock so red,
And I must back to earth again
With all the dead."

21 Up stood the knight Sir Aage,
His coffin took once more,
Forth fared he to the kirkyard
With travail sore.

22 Up stood the lady Elselil,
In mournful mood,
To follow him, her own true-love,
Through the greenwood.

23 And when they came to the kirkyard
With toil and care,
Wan it grew and faded,
His goodly golden hair.

24 "Behold now up in Heaven
The stars so bright!
There mayst thou see full surely
How goes the night."

25 She saw the stars a-shining
In Heaven so blue,
Down in the earth the dead man sank
Or e'er she knew.

26  Home went the lady Elselil
    With care so cold,
    And when a moon was over
    Lay she in the mould.

NOTE: Had she seen the dead man sink into his grave, she would (according to the popular belief) have been compelled to follow him, but this Sir Aage prevents by his sudden request that she should look up to the stars.

# 4
## OH, SEVENTY-SEVEN

1  Oh, seventy-seven twice told were they
   When out from Hald they went,
   And when they came to Brattingsborg
   They pitched full many a tent.
   There sounds thunder the captains under when they ride
                                                    forth.

2  King Isung stands on watchtower high,
   And looks forth far and wide:
   "Oh, little care for their lives have they
   That hither list to ride!

3  "Now harken, Sivord Snarensvend,
   Hast wandered far afield,
   What warriors are these who bear
   Each one his golden shield?"

4  "There shineth on the foremost shield
   A lion all so bold,
   Didrik the King doth bear that sign
   With crown of the red, red gold.

5   "And shining on the second shield
     Hammer and tongs are seen,
     For Vidrik Verlandson, who slays
     And brings no prisoner in.

6   "And on the third shield shining see
     A worm in fetters bound,
     That beareth Master Hildebrand,
     Cunning in counsel found.

7   "And on the fourth shield see where shines
     A leafy linden-tree,
     That beareth the lad young Humlunger,
     Earl Hornbook's son is he.

8   "There shineth on the following shield
     A wolf that roams the wold,
     The sign of Ulf van Jœrn the young,
     Who is a warrior bold.

9   "And on the sixth shield, red and grim
     A vulture shineth still,
     The crest of Helled Haagen,
     Who ne'er can slay his fill.

10   "And see, the seventh shining shield
     Viol and bow doth keep,
     And that bears Folkvar Fiddle-man,
     Would liefer drink than sleep.

11   "And on the eighth an elephant
     Is pictured with a swain,
     The bearing of Detlev Danske
     That swings his sword amain.

12   "All on the ninth shield shining, see,
     A swarthy eagle shows,
     The crest of young Sir Raadengaard,
     Full many a rune who knows.

13   "And on the tenth shield see where shine
     Two arrows wan and white,
     The bearer, Hvitting Hermandson,
     Is foremost still in fight.

14   "There shines on the eleventh shield
     Nought but a burning brand,
     That bears Sir Brand Vidfœrling
     Throughout all lordlings' land.

15   "And on the twelfth shield shining see
     A monkish cowl of grey,
     For Brother Alsing aye is fain
     To follow to the fray."

16   "Now harken, Sivord Snarensvend,
     Thou warrior bold and free,
     Shalt fight with one of Didrik's men
     For all my land and me!"

17   Up stood Sivord Snarensvend,
     And to the tents he hied:
     "Now is there ever a warrior stout
     A joust with me will ride?"

18   Now on the board they cast the dice
     They cast them far and wide,
     And the lot fell on young Humlunger
     That fateful joust to ride.

19  It was he, young Humlunger,
    That did to Vidrik speed:
    "I'll give thee a pledge to hold if thou
    Wilt lend me Skemming thy steed!"

20  "Oh, Sivord sees not the point of his spear
    Because his sight is dim,
    And if my Skemming gets scathe today
    No pledge will pay for him."

21  "But I, I have a sister,
    The mirror of maidens all,
    And if thy Skemming gets scathe today
    I'll pay it her hand withal."

22  "Oh, nought of Skemming thou'lt see today
    But for surety true and tried:
    Seven castles in Birtingsland,
    And thy sister fair beside!"

23  "Seven castles in Birtingsland
    Shall to thy forfeit fall,
    And therewith the maid my sister,
    Most precious pledge of all."

24  Now he has backed that steed so bold,
    And merrily ridden his way,
    Goodsooth but Skemming thought it strange
    To feel the spurs that day!

25  The red gold shone upon his shield
    Like sun in summer-tide:
    "God help me now, a simple swain,
    The brunt to bear and bide!"

26  The first course that they ran together
    Would neither champion yield,
    And both their shields were shattered there,
    And hurled so far afield.

27  "Methinks thou art a bold young swain
    That well can run and ride,
    Go now and take thy shield again,
    And I the brunt will bide."

28  But when they ran the second course
    The younger knight must yield,
    For Humlunger was smitten sore
    And hurled so far afield.

29  "Now have I struck thee down to earth
    And won thy steed so free,
    But who thou art and whence thou art
    I pray thee tell to me!"

30  "Oh, Hornbook hight my father
    In Birtingsland is lord,
    And I am called young Humlunger
    Whenas I ride abroad."

31  "Full well I knew thy father,
    For comrades kind we were,
    Now take thy shield and mount again,
    Son of my sister dear!

32  "And take the thongs from off my shield,
    Bind me to oaken-tree,
    Then ride and tell the champions all
    The game was won by thee."

33   Forth to the tents fared Humlunger,
      Cast brand upon the board:
      "Now have I bound the greybeard carle
      That spoke the vaunting word!"

34   "Now hold thy peace, young Humlunger,
      That needs must prate thy fill!
      Didst thou bind Sivord Snarensvend
      'Twas with his own good-will."

35   It was Vidrik Verlandson
      Bade saddle his courser free:
      "Now will I fare to the forest
      This conquered carle to see!"

36   Now Sivord all in greenwood bower
      Saw where the knight did ride,
      Up by its roots he reft the oak,
      For he would not in bonds abide.

37   Up by the roots he reft the oak,
      For in bonds he would not bide:
      "Comes Vidrik here, methinks he'll tear
      My ribs from out my side!"

38   The Queen stood up in the high-loft
      And looked both up and down:
      "Lo, here comes Sivord Snarensvend
      A-bearing summer to town!"

39   The Queen looked forth with her ladies
      All from her lofty bower:
      "Sivord hath been in good greenwood,
      And gathered a gallant flower!"

Gay went the round by Brattingsborg
Where champions danced amain,
There danced with oak-tree in his belt
Sivord the purblind swain!

5

## HOLGER DANSKE AND STOUT DIDRIK

1 Stout Didrik dwells in Berneland
With brethren eight all told,
And each of them twelve sons hath got,
All doughty knights and bold.
But the battle is raging northward up in Jutland.

2 Stout Didrik dwells in Berneland
With fifteen sisters bright,
And each of them hath twelve fair sons
That hold their lives full light.

3 And when they rode out all by Bern
A goodly host to see,
I say ye sooth, each warrior
Was tall as a beechen-tree.

4 "Now we have fought o'er all the world
And vanquished far and wide,
And news we hear of Holger Dansk
In Denmark doth abide.

5 "We have heard tell of Holger Dansk
That doth in Denmark bide,
And crowned is he with the red, red gold,
And ne'er will bate his pride."

6    Now Sverting seized a pike of steel,
     And vaunted loud and high:
     "An hundred of King Holger's men,
     I count them not a fly!"


7    "Give heed, give heed, thou swarthy swain,
     Or ever thou rue the day!
     We have heard tell of Holger's men,
     And bold young blades are they."


8    Oh, then up spake tall Bermer-Ris,
     And a vaunting word spake he:
     "Now will we up to Denmark,
     And try if the King will flee!"


9    Now all with eighteen thousand steeds
     From Berneland they fare,
     And they've drawn up to Denmark
     To meet King Holger there.


10   Stout Didrik sent a messenger,
     And bade King Holger yield
     To pay him scot and lot for aye,
     Or fight him in the field.


11   Up stood Vidrik Verlandson
     And spake a word so stout:
     "Now come they in to Denmark thus,
     They shall not thus go out!"


12   Oh, thus they met, a mighty host,
     All on the swarthy heath,
     And that was a woeful trysting-place
     Where warriors fought till death.

13   They fought for a day, for twain they fought,
     And stiff in stour did stand,
     King Holger and his warriors bold
     Slew many from Berneland.

14   Oh, mild of mood grew Bermer-Ris,
     And softly spake he then:
     "Now how shall we conquer Holger Dansk
     With scarce one hundred men?"

15   It was doughty Bermer-Ris
     Looked upward to the sky:
     "Small help for us is here, I ween,
     'Tis time to turn and fly!"

16   Stout Didrik took to both his legs
     To fly o'er hill and dale,
     And Sverting went the selfsame way
     For all his boastful tale.

17   Up spake little Iron Wolf
     That held the hill beside:
     "Oh, they that are come to fight the Danes
     Have little praise or pride!"

18   Oh, stern the stream of red, red blood
     That ran o'er land and lea!
     The reek of it rose up to heaven
     Till the sun was red as blood to see.

NOTE: Vidrik (Wittich) Verlandson. This last name harks back to the
Old Norse hero Völundr; English, Wayland the Smith. Ulf van Jœrn is
the same as Wolfart van Garten, the Italian Garda.

Raadengaard is Rüdegêr, who, like Haagen and Folkvar, comes through
the Nibelungen Lied.

Humlunger may be connected with Amelung, the name of Didrik's
royal race.—Ernst von der Recke, op. cit., Vol. I, p. 70.

# 6

# GERMAND GLADENSVEND

1   It was our King and our fair young Queen
     Went sailing o'er the seas:
     But their ship was held on the water,
     And they got no favouring breeze,
     So he flew over the sea.

2   "If one down under the water
     Our ship doth hold and seize,
     I'll give both gold and silver
     To win a favouring breeze."

3   "Nay, nought I ween can help thee,
     Neither silver and gold,
     What lieth under thy girdle
     That would I have and hold."

4   "Nought lieth under my girdle
     Save only my household keys,
     Come I living to landward
     Others I'll have for these."

5   She took the keys of her household
     And cast them out over the strand,
     And there sprang up a breeze so blithesome,
     And gaily they sailed to land.

6   The Queen she walked o'er the snow-white sand,
     And felt so sore a smart,
     And knew full well her little babe
     Was quick beneath her heart.

7   Long 'twas not thereafter,
    Or e'er five months were run,
    The Queen lay down in the high-loft
    And bore so fair a son.

8   Born was he at even
    And christened the selfsame night,
    They called him Germand Gladensvend
    And fostered him while they might.

9   Now well he waxed and well he throve,
    And well his steed could ride,
    But when his mother looked on him
    Full sore she wailed and cried.

10  "Now show me this, sweet mother mine,
    What I shall ask of thee,
    Why dost thou shed such bitter tears
    Whene'er thou lookst on me?"

11  "Now harken, Germand Gladensvend,
    Well may I weep for thee!
    An unborn babe, thou wert given
    To the fierce Troll of the sea."

12  "Now lithe and listen, sweet mother mine,
    And cast thy cares away!
    The weird that God hath laid on me
    I'll dree as best I may."

13  All on a Thursday morning
    When harvest did begin,
    The door of the bower stood open wide,
    And a fearsome voice came in.

14  Oh, there entered the Troll in vulture's shape,
    And sat by that fair ladye:
    "Hast thou forgotten, sweetheart mine,
    The gift thou gavest me?"

15  She swore by God and man and all
    Whereby could oath be sworn,
    No son nor daughter in all the world
    Was e'er of her body born.

16  With fearsome cry away did fly
    That grisly Troll and grim:
    "But mine he is for aye, I wis,
    Where'er I light on him!"

17  When fifteen years were past and gone
    He loved, as did befall,
    The King's fair daughter of Engeland,
    Mirror of ladies all.

18  So sore he longed to seek her
    As never a tongue might tell:
    "Now give me thy leave, sweet mother mine,
    To don the feather-fell!"

19  Oh, fast he flew o'er the billows blue
    And over the low green ground,
    But he heard the call of the grisly Troll
    From out the midmost Sound.

20  "Now welcome, Germand Gladensvend,
    Think not my power to scorn!
    To me thy life was given
    All as a babe unborn."

21    "Now let me fly 'twixt sea and sky
To find my bright ladye!
Behold, when I turn homeward,
A tryst I'll hold with thee."

22    "My mark I'll set upon thee
Or e'er thou cross the main,
Whate'er thy plight 'mid squire and knight
I'll know thee once again."

23    Now his right eye the Troll struck out,
And of hearts' blood drank his fill,
Yet on flew the swain in dule and pain
So strong was his steadfast will.

24    He perched on the beam of the ladies' bower
So bloody and wan to see,
And all the merry maidens there
Did cease their mirth and glee.

25    Little those merry maidens
Of woe so dire could dream,
But up she stood, fair Silverlad,
And cast down shears and seam.

26    She took a comb of silver
To smooth his shining hair,
For every lock she ordered
Down fell a bitter tear.

27    For every lock she ordered
She wept right bitterly,
She cursed and banned his mother
Who gave him that weird to dree.

28  "Now hush thee, hush thee, Silverlad,
    Let no such words be thine,
    She had no power in that past hour,
    So weary a weird was mine."

29  Oh, high he flew in the feather-fell,
    And swifter than the wind,
    And it was the lady Silverlad
    That followed close behind.

30  All the fowls of the air as she met them
    She sundered in pieces three,
    But mightier than all her magic
    Was the grim Troll of the sea.

31  It was the lady Silverlad
    Went flying o'er the strand,
    And nought she found of her lover
    Save only his right hand.

# 7
## THE ELFIN SHAFT

1   Sir Oluf rode by East and West
    To bid his friends to his bridal-feast.
    Gay goes the dance by the greenwood tree.

2   By the howe he took his way,
    And there danced elf and fay.

3   By four and by five danced the blithesome band,
    The Elf-King's daughter stretched out her hand.

4   The Elf-King's daughter spake up so free:
    "And will Sir Oluf tread a measure with me?"

5   "I dare not, I may not the measure tread,
    Tomorrow morn must I be wed."

6   "Oh, tread now a measure, Sir Oluf, with me!
    Two buckskin boots will I give to thee,

7   "Boots that well beseem a knight,
    With gilded spurs a-shining bright.

8   "Oh, tread now a measure, Sir Oluf, with me!
    A silken kirtle I'll give to thee.

9   "A silken kirtle so fair and fine
    That my mother bleached in the wan moonshine."

10   "I may not, I dare not, the measure tread,
    Tomorrow morn shall I be wed."

11   "Oh, tread now a measure, Sir Oluf, with me!
    An orb of gold I'll give to thee."

12   "An orb of gold I fain would win,
    But I may not dance with the fairy kin."

13   "And if thou wilt not dance with me,
    Scathe and sickness shall follow thee!"

14   She struck him 'twixt his shoulders broad,
    It pierced to his heart-roots like keenest sword.

15   She lifted him up on his steed of pride:
    "Ride home, Sir Oluf, and seek thy bride!"

16   Slow did he ride to his castle door,
    And it was his mother that stood before.

17  "Lithe now and list, Sir Oluf my son,
    Why is thy cheek so white and wan?"

18  "Well may my cheek be wan and white,
    I have seen the elf-maids' dance this night."

19  "Lithe now and list, dear son of mine,
    What shall I say to true-love thine?"

20  "Shalt say I am in the mead
    A-proving hound and steed."

21  All in the morning when dawned the day
    The bride rode in with glad array.

22  They poured the mead, they poured the wine:
    "But where is Sir Oluf, bridegroom mine?"

23  "Sir Oluf is in the mead
    A-proving hound and steed."

24  "Loves he hound and steed so free
    Better than he loveth me?"

25  Through house and hall in search she sped,
    She found him laid upon his bed.

26  She lifted up the mantle's fold,
    There lay Sir Oluf, dead and cold.

27  She kissed him all in bridal bower,
    She pined and died the selfsame hour.

28 All so early ere dawn grew red
   Were three in Sir Oluf's hold lay dead.

29 Sir Oluf lay dead and his bride also,
   The third was his mother who died for woe.

## 8

## THE MIGHTY HARP

1 Sir William and his plighted maid
  (The string is all of gold)
  All in her bower at dice they played.
  So meltingly he harped before his maiden.

2 Whenas the dice dropped, one and all,
  So many a tear did the maid let fall.

3 "Now dost thou weep o'er the gold so red,
  Or weepest thou for that we shall wed?

4 "Dost weep that I lack both land and fee,
  And deem me no fitting mate for thee?"

5 "I weep not o'er the gold so red,
  And 'tis with my good-will we twain shall wed.

6 "I weep not for lack of land and fee,
  And I deem thee a fitting mate for me.

7 "For Blide Bridge I cry
  That I must pass thereby,

8 "For there they drowned, my sisters twain,
  As they rode o'er with bridal train."

9  "Now weep not for that bridge of dread,
   By all my swains shalt thou be sped.

10 "All my swains shall with thee ride,
   A hundred gallants on either side.

11 "And this will I do to honour thee,
   Twelve knights shall lead thy courser free."

12 He shod her steed with the gold so red,
   And forth they fared to the bridge of dread.

13 But when they rode o'er the bridge eftsoon
   Then stumbled her steed on the golden shoon.

14 From the golden shoe a nail was gone,
   And down fell the maid in the water wan.

15 The knights they grasped at her saddle bow,
   But they might not help the maiden so.

16 The maiden stretched forth her lily-white hand:
   "My noble lord, now help me to land!"

17 "Call God and the Holy Ghost to aid,
   For I cannot help thee, mine own true maid!"

18 Sir William cried to his page so bold:
   "Now bring to me my harp of gold!"

19 Sir William took his harp in hand,
   And went beside the stream to stand.

20 He played so soft and low,
   No bird moved on the bough.

21  He played so loud and clear
    'Twas heard both far and near.


22  From oaken-tree the bough was torn,
    And from the lowing cow the horn.


23  The bark sprang from the birk,
    And the vane from Our Lady's kirk.


24  So strong the spell, so sure the charm,
    He played the bride from the Kelpie's arm.


25  Down to the deeps did William play,
    Till the Kelpie rose to the light of day.


26  He rose up from beneath
    With the maiden in his teeth.


27  And not alone his bride,
    But both her sisters fair beside.


28  "Now William, take thy bride to thee,
    But let me rule o'er my stream so free!"


29  "Right gladly I take my bride to me,
    But ne'er shalt thou rule thy stream so free."


30  In the scarlet fair he lapped his bride,
    And set her up on his steed of pride.


31  Now forth they fared o'er hill and dale,
    And gaily they drank the blithe bridale.

# 9

# SAINT OLAF AND THE TROLLS

1   *It was Saint Olaf the King so bold*
    *That ruled o'er Norroway;*
    *He set his sail for Hornelummer,*
    *The Trolls to seek and slay.*
    *(Red as the ruddy gold the sun shines over Trondhjem.)*

2   *Saint Olaf built a bonnie ship,*
    *And forth from land did fare:*
    *"Now we will sail to Hornelummer,*
    *And try our fortune there."*

3   *Up and spake the steersman bold*
    *That on the lading stood:*
    *" 'Tis no good haven by Hornelummer,*
    *Because of the goblins' brood.*

4   *"For Are hight the ancient Troll*
    *Hath dwelt there many a year,*
    *Each ship so tall with crew and all*
    *He draweth to his lair.*

5   *"For eyes hath he like a burning bale,*
    *Full loudly doth he roar,*
    *His nails stand out like the horns of buck*
    *A good ell's length and more.*

6   *"A beard he hath like a stallion's mane*
    *Hangs downward to his knee,*
    *His tail runs out a hawser's length,*
    *His claws are ill to see!"*

7   Up and spake King Olaf
    That swiftly sprang aboard:
    "Now cast off rope and cable
    In the name of God our Lord!"

8   Oh, on they sail and swift they sail,
    With wind and tide they go,
    Until they come to Hornelummer
    To work the goblin's woe.

9   Now forth he fared, the Giant Troll,
    All on the cliffs so steep,
    And spied the Ox, that gallant ship,
    A-sailing in the deep.

10  "Say, who is he, the overbold,
    That to my realm dare steer?
    I promise thee, thou Redbeard loon,
    Thou shalt abye it dear!

11  "For never today or yesterday
    Did good ship come to land,
    But I could haul it into my hill
    With the touch of a single hand."

12  "Now harken, Are, thou ancient Troll,
    Let be thy longings all!
    Cast off the rope and slip the chain,
    And see what will befall."

13  Oh, he seized the Ox by stem and stern,
    For an angry Troll was he,
    And into the rock he sank adown
    That held him to the knee.

14 "Here stand I sunken in the stone,
Here may I peak and pine,
Fain would I try a wrestling-bout
To prove that power o' thine!"

15 "Now hold thy peace, thou goblin grim,
Be stone from top to toe!
Shalt bide there till the Day of Doom,
And work no Christian woe!"

16 Now forth she fared and loud she roared,
The Troll-Wife old and grim,
But Saint Olaf bade her flee afar
And do no wrong to him.

17 Her neck she reared, and forth she peered,
And loud she roared and cried,
But Saint Olaf all with a word of power
Hath bidden her still to bide.

18 Then up and spake the little trolls
That sat within the hill:
"No word we hear from our mother dear,
Perchance she fareth ill.

19 "Perchance 'tis he, that Redbeard loon,
That harried our race so long,
But little his boot when we are afoot
With iron stake and prong!"

20 Up and spake Saint Olaf the King,
And a merry jest spoke he:
"Be each and all like stone and wall,
And good shall your gathering be!"

21   Now such was the hap at Hornelummer,
     That ne'er was seen of yore,
     He closed with that wall the mountain all,
     And left it ne'er a door.

22   Up and spake the smallest troll,
     And loud did he wail, I wis:
     "We have raised ere now on our shoulders broad
     A higher hill than this!"

23   Now tail and head in haste they laid
     To draw the hill adown,
     And they were broken to pieces small,
     And crushed from heel to crown.

24   Now thanks to Saint Olaf our King and Lord
     That did this mighty deed!
     Now all men may fare to Hornelummer,
     And well doth their sailing speed.

### 10

## THE MERMAID'S SPAEING

1   The King did a Mermaid catch and keep,
     (The Mermaids all a-playing)
     And chained her in a dungeon deep,
     His will was no gainsaying.

2   The Queen she spake to her pages three:
     "Now pray the Mermaiden to speak with me!"

3   In came the Mermaid and stood by the board:
     "What wilt thou, oh Queen, that thou sentest me word?"

4    *The cushion of blue she smoothed and pressed:*
     *"Tarry now, Mermaid, and take thy rest!"*

5    *"Wilt thou by leasing take my life?*
     *Beneath lies hidden a whetted knife!"*

6    *"Knowest thou that, then knowest thou more,*
     *Tell what the future hath in store!"*

7    *"Three sons of thee shall soon be born,*
     *But thy young life is lost and lorn.*

8    *"Denmark the first shall have and hold,*
     *The second shall wear a crown of gold.*

9    *"The third shall be so great on earth*
     *That thou must die to give him birth."*

10   *She decked the Mermaid with pomp and pride,*
     *She led her to the strand with all her maids beside.*

11   *Out swam the Mermaid into the deep,*
     *But ever the Queen so sore did weep.*

12   *"Now weep not for words thou didst hear from me,*
     *The gates of Heaven stand open for thee!"*

## 11

## AGNES AND THE MERMAN

1   *Agnes she walked on the edge of the steep,*
    *And up came a Merman out of the deep.*
    *Ha, ha, ha,*
    *Up came a Merman out of the deep.*

2   "Harken, Agnes, fair and fine,
    Wilt thou be true-love of mine?"

3   "Yea, goodsooth, that will I be,
    Canst thou bear me down into the depths of the sea."

4   Her ears he closed, her mouth he bound,
    And bore her down through the sea to ground.

5   She dwelt with the Merman eight years and more,
    Seven fair sons to him she bore.

6   Agnes she sat by the cradle and sang,
    And she heard how the bells of England rang.

7   She to the Merman did speak and say:
    "May I go up in the kirk to pray?"

8   "Thou hast my leave to go withal,
    But see thou come back to thy children small!

9   "When through the kirkyard thou dost fare
    Then see thou let not down thy shining golden hair.

10  "And when thou enterest in the door
    Then sit by thy mother's side no more.

11  "When the priest names the Name of dread
    Then bow not down thy head."

12  Her ears he closed, her mouth he bound,
    And bore her again to English ground.

13  When through the kirkyard she did fare,
    Oh, then did she let down her shining golden hair.

14 And when she entered in at the door,
  She sat by her mother as of yore.

15 When the priest named the Name of dread,
  Then she bowed down her head.

16 "Hark now and hear what I ask of thee,
  Where hast thou been eight years away from me?"

17 "I dwelt with the Merman eight years and more,
  Seven fair sons to him I bore."

18 "Harken, dear daughter, and fear no blame,
  What did he give for thy maiden fame?"

19 "He gave me a ring of golden sheen,
  Never a better one has the Queen.

20 "Of golden shoon he gave me a pair,
  Never a better the Queen might wear.

21 "He gave me a harp of gold to play,
  That I might touch the strings to wile my cares away."

22 The Merman made him a path so straight
  Up from the strand to the kirkyard gate.

23 In at the door the Merman hied,
  And all the holy images they turned their heads aside.

24 Like purest gold was his shining hair,
  His eyes were full of sorrow and care.

25 "Heed now, Agnes, what I say to thee!
  All thy little children are longing after thee."

26   "Let them long as they will, let their longing be sore,
      I shall return to them never more."

27   "Oh, think on the grown ones, and think of the small!
      Of the baby in the cradle think most of all."

28   "I think not of the grown ones, nor yet of the small,
      Of the baby in the cradle I'll think least of all."

12

## THE MAIDEN HIND

1   The mother to her son did say:
      (In the greenwood)
      "The little hind thou shalt not slay,
      That bears the band of gold.

2   "Mayst slay the hart and shoot the doe,
      But the little hind must thou let go."

3   Sir Peter rode in greenwood bound,
      And the little hind played before his hound.

4   The little hind sported his feet before,
      And he thought on his mother's words no more.

5   He spanned his crossbow with hand and knee,
      And shot the hind beside a tree.

6   His gloves from off his hands he drew
      To flay the hind without ado.

7   Her neck he flayed, and there
      Was his sister's golden hair.

8   He found in her bosom cold
     His sister's rings of gold.

9   In her side with sore affright
     He found her hands so white.

10   His hunting-knife to the ground he threw:
     "Now has my mother's tale come true!"

11   Cold on the river falleth the rime,
     There is luck for the lad who can take it in time.

12   Far the crane flieth up in the sky.
     Lucky the lad who from trouble can fly!

## 13
## THE MAIDEN IN BIRD'S PLUMAGE

Oh, well I wot where the greenwood grows
That standeth beside the firth,
For in it there blow the fairest trees
That a man may see on earth.

Therein do the willow and linden grow,
The fairest a man may find,
And under them play the lordly beasts
That men call hart and hind.

Therein they sport, both hind and hart,
And all beasts of the fair forest,
And there plays she, the lily-white hind,
With gold beneath her breast.

1   It was Nilus Erlandson
    Rode forth the deer to take,
    And there he saw the lily-white hind
    That ran through bush and brake.
    So the knight hath won his lady.

2   He chased her, Nilus Erlandson,
    That longed for her so sore,
    But swift was she, and still did flee
    For three days' space and more.

3   Now snares he set in every path
    Where'er a beast might go,
    But all so wise was the lily-white hind
    That he could not take her so.

4   Sir Nilus all through the greenwood
    Rode on, and rode in vain;
    His hounds loosed he by two, by three,
    To run her down amain.

5   Now can she spy no way to fly,
    So hot the hounds pursue,
    Her shape she changed to a falcon fierce,
    And aloft in the air she flew.

6   Her shape she changed to a falcon fleet,
    And perched on a linden green,
    All under the boughs Sir Nilus stood,
    And sighed for toil and tene.

7   Sir Nilus hath ta'en his axe in hand
    To fell the linden-tree,
    When forth there sprang a forester
    That smote the shaft in three.

8   "And wilt thou fell my father's wood
    And all to do me wrong,
    I promise thee, Nilus Erlandson,
    That thou shalt rue it long!"

9   "Now let me fell this single tree,
    This tree alone of thine,
    For but I can take the falcon fell
    I die of dule and pine!"

10   "Now hark and heed, thou fair young knight,
    The counsel that I bring,
    Ne'er shalt thou take her till she taste
    The flesh of a tamèd thing!"

11   A gobbet he cut from his bleeding breast,
    Right bitter pain he knew,
    She flapped her wings and down she dropped,
    And on the bait she flew.

12   She flapped her wings and down she flew,
    And on the bait she fell,
    And she changed her shape to the fairest maid
    That ever a tongue might tell.

13   She stood in a sark of silk so red
    Where the linden-tree did blow,
    And all in the arms of Sir Nilus
    She told her weird of woe.

14   "Oh, I sat and broidered lily and rose
    My father's board beside,
    When in she came, my false stepdame,
    Whose wrath was ill to bide.

15   "She shaped me all to a lily-white hind
To run in wild greenwood
And my seven maidens to seven grey wolves,
And bade them drink my blood."

16   The damsel stood 'neath the linden-tree,
And loosened her golden hair,
And thither came they that erst were wolves,
But now were maidens fair.

17   "Now thanks to thee, Nilus Erlandson!
Hast saved me from hurt and harm,
Never shalt thou seek slumber
But on my lily-white arm.

18   "Now thanks to thee, Nilus Erlandson,
Hast set my sorrow to rest!
Never shalt thou seek slumber
But on my lily-white breast."

## 14
## YOUNG SVEJDAL

1   And now the swain young Svejdal
Was playing at the ball,
It flew into the maiden's breast,
And her cheeks grew white withal.
Choose thy words well!

2   The ball flew into the maiden's bower,
And after went the swain,
And a bitter smart she felt at heart
Ere he came forth again.

3   "Oh, never shouldst thou venture
     Thy ball to throw to me!
     There lieth a maid in a far-off land
     A-longing after thee.

4   "Now ne'er shalt thou seek slumber,
     And never rest shalt know
     Till thou hast loosed that lovely maid
     That long hath lain in woe."

5   It was he, young Svejdal,
     Wrapped him in cloak of vair,
     And to the hall betook him
     To seek his captains there.

6   "Now sit in peace, my captains,
     And pledge your healths in mead,
     Whiles I fare forth to the grave-mound
     To ask my mother's rede!"

7   It was the swain young Svejdal
     That loud did cry and call,
     Till the marble-stone was rent and riven
     And the mound was nigh to fall.

8   "Now who is this that waketh me
     And calls with cry so bold?
     May I not lie and sleep in peace
     All under darksome mould?"

9   " 'Tis I, 'tis I, young Svejdal,
     Only son of thine,
     And all I ask is counsel
     From thee, dear mother mine.

10    "My sister and my stepmother
      Have made me peak and pine,
      All for a lovely lady
      That ne'er I saw with eyne."

11    "A palfrey will I give thee
      Shall serve thy need, I ween,
      He can bear thee as well o'er the billows
      As over the lea so green.

12    "A shining sword I'll give thee,
      Was tempered in dragon's blood,
      'Twill glow like a burning bale-fire
      When thou ridest through darksome wood."

13    It was the swain young Svejdal
      That spurred his steed so free,
      Forth fared he through the mirkwood
      And over the wide sea.

14    It was he, young Svejdal,
      That rode 'twixt sea and land
      And there he saw a herdsman
      That drove his flock to the strand.

15    "Now lithe and list, good herdsman,
      And speak thou sooth to me,
      Who owneth all this goodly flock
      Thou drivest by the sea?"

16    "Oh, there lieth a maid in this countrie
      In sorest dule and pine,
      All for a swain hight Svejdal
      That ne'er she saw with eyne."

17   "And knowest thou where the maiden dwells
     Then hide it not from me!
     When I am King of all this land
     A knight I'll make of thee."

18   "Oh, yonder under the linden-tree
     My lady's hold is dight,
     The walls are decked with the marble grey,
     And the doors with the steel so bright.

19   "The walls are decked with the marble grey,
     And the doors with steel laid o'er.
     She hath not looked upon the sun
     These seven long years and more.

20   "There lieth a bear by my lady's bower,
     And a lion so fell to see,
     But art thou Svejdal in very sooth
     Thou shalt pass by them free."

21   Forth fared the swain young Svejdal,
     And to the door he went,
     All the locks that held it
     Were riven asunder and rent.

22   The bear and the lordly lion
     They followed him from the door,
     The linden with all its silvery leaves
     Bowed down to earth before.

23   The linden bowed adown to earth
     With every silvery leaf,
     And up stood she, the damsel proud,
     That long had lain in grief.

24     Up she waked, the damsel proud
      That heard the spurs a-ringing:
      "Now thanks to God in Heaven above
      Who help to me is bringing!"

25     In went the swain young Svejdal
      That was both young and fair,
      Up stood the stately maiden
      To hail his entrancè there.

26     "Now welcome, welcome, Svejdal,
      Thou noble lord of mine,
      Praise be to God in Heaven
      Hath loosed us from dule and pine!"

NOTE: This ballad brings down the story of Svipdag and Menglad from the peaks of Valhalla into the flowery meads of fairy tale. "There is a vast difference between the simplicity of the ballad and the stately measure and rhetorical pomp of the original:

> "Svipdag is my name; Sunbright was my father's name.
> The winds have driven me far along cold ways;
> No one can gainsay the word of Fate
> Though it be spoken to his own destruction.

"The difference is as great as that between the Ballad of The Marriage of Gawayne, and the same story as told in the *Canterbury Tales*; or the difference between Homer's way of describing the recovery of lifted cattle, and the Ballad of Jamie Telfer of the Fair Dodhead."—W. P. Ker, *Epic and Romance*, Chap. II, Sec. 3.

## 15

## THE GRIEFS OF HILLELILLE

1    In bower sat Hillelil,
     (My grief knows none save God alone)
     And sewed her seam so ill.
     No living wight is there to whom I tell my woe.

2   She sewed with silken thread
    Where she should broider the gold so red.

3   The red gold did she choose
    Where she the silk should use.

4   With word unto the Queen they go,
    How ill the maiden did broider and sew.

5   The Queen she donned her cloak of vair,
    And to the high-loft straight did fare.

6   "Now lithe and listen, Hillelil,
    Say wherefore dost sew thy seam so ill?

7   "Thus dost thou sit and sew thy seam
    As one that turns from a joyous dream."

8   "Be seated, gracious dame, by me,
    And all my woes will I tell to thee.

9   "My father ruled o'er tower and town,
    My mother wore the queenly crown.

10  "My father showed me honour and praise
    With twelve bold knights to ward my ways.

11  "But one among those gallants so free
    Did lure my love and all from me,

12  "And he was hight Sir Hildebrand,
    Son to the King of fair England.

13  "With gold we loaded two coursers grey,
    And on the third we rode away.

14   "We found at eventide
      A place wherein to bide.

15   "At dead of night they smote the door,
      My seven bold brethren stood before.

16   "Now Hildebrand kissed my cheeks so white:
      'Name not my name, Oh heart's delight!

17   " 'What though my blood run red,
      My name must ne'er be said.'

18   "Forth he leapt, Sir Hildebrand,
      All with his doughty sword in hand.

19   "In the first onset straight did fall
      My seven yellow-haired brethren all.

20   "And next he slew in wrath and ire
      Twelve kinsfolk and the King my sire.

21   "Hildebrand, Hildebrand, stay thy sword,
      Hold in the name of God our Lord!

22   "Oh, spare my youngest brother dear
      To tell our mother the tidings drear!

23   "But ere those words of woe were said,
      With seven sore wounds the knight fell dead.

24   "My brother seized my lily-white hand,
      And bound me fast with saddle-band.

25   "He seized me by my golden hair,
      To saddle-bow he bound me there.

26   "Ne'er was a stream so deep and wide
     But his courser swam it from side to side.

27   "Never o'er stone so small we sped
     But the blood of my foot would dye it red.

28   "But when we came to the castle door,
     My woeful mother she stood before.

29   "My brother wished me in my grave,
     My mother sold me for a slave.

30   "A bell was the price they paid for me
     To hang in the kirk of Our Ladye.

31   "When first the bell rang out at morn
     My mother's heart in twain was torn."

32   When she had told her sorrow and tene,
     Dead she lay in the arms of the Queen.

33   When her tale was told and her sorrow was said,
     At the Queen's side Hillelille lay dead.

NOTE: In early medieval times, the father whose daughter engaged in a love-affair without his consent was permitted by law to sell her as a thrall-woman. This custom died out during the twelfth century owing to the increasing influence of the Church, and when the ballads were composed, it survived only as a far-away memory.

## 16

## THE AVENGING SWORD

1   Sir Peter rode to the castle door,
    The King of Danes he stood before.
    *Forward, hurrah, ride forward!*

2   "Welcome, Sir Peter, comrade mine!
     Hast thou avenged him, father thine?"

3   "Oh, I have been so southerly
     Until the sun bowed down to me.

4   "And I have been so westerly
     Until the sun sank near to me.

5   "And I have been so northerly
     Until the frost was frore to see.

6   "And I have been so easterly
     Until the day was fair to see.

7   "But never could I find the wight
     To rede me my father's death aright."

8   "Now say what wilt thou give the wight
     Can rede thee thy father's death aright?"

9   "Of silver he shall have his fill,
     And of golden coin whate'er he will.

10   "Yea, more I'll give to him,
     A ship in sailing-trim."

11   He smiled, the King, his words to heed:
     "Here stand I that did the deed!

12   "By God in heaven, I tell thee true,
     None but I thy father slew!"

13   Sir Peter smote himself on the breast:
     "Heart, bide still, nor break thy rest!

14   "Heart, lie still, bide patiently,
     Sure and swift shall my vengeance be."

15   Sir Peter walked abroad
     To speak with his good sword.

16   "Harken, sword so good!
     Wilt drink thy fill of blood?

17   "Good brown brand, wilt fight for me?
     No brother have I on earth but thee."

18   "Oh, say, how can I fight for thee?
     My hilt is broken in pieces three."

19   To the Smith his way he wended
     That the hurt might be amended.

20   He gave him iron, he gave him steel
     Of proof and price, the hurt to heal.

21   "Good brown brand, wilt fight for me?
     No brother have I on earth but thee."

22   "Be only in thy blows so stern
     As I'll be swift in point to turn!

23   "Be only in thy blows so stout
     As I in hilt will bear thee out!"

24   Sir Peter sought the hall
     Where the knights were drinking all.

25   To prove his brand he was full fain,
     Seven champions there lay slain.

26   Up and down he swung his blade,
     Neither matron he spared nor maid.

27   Up through the rafters did he thrust,
     The King and his sons they bit the dust.

28   Up spake the babe in cradle lay:
     "A red revenge dost thou wreak today,

29   "A red revenge for father thine,
     God give me a day for avenging mine!"

30   "And have I avenged him, father mine,
     Shalt see no day for avenging thine!"

31   He seized the babe amain
     And smote it straight in twain.

32   "Cease, brown brand, thy thirst to slake,
     Bide thou still for Our Saviour's sake!"

33   Wearily whispered the sword and still:
     "Fain of thy blood I'd have my fill!

34   "Hadst thou not named my name, I vow
     I would have slain thee, here and now!"

35   He sought the Smith again,
     Bade forge an iron chain.

36   In chains he bound him, foot and hand,
     For now he fain would leave the land.

37   When o'er the grave of the King he passed
     The chains of iron were riven and brast.

# HISTORICAL BALLADS

# 17

# VALDEMAR AND TOVE
## (1157)   (A)

1 King Valdemar sailed by isle and eyre,
  *(Goodsooth)*
  He wedded young Soffi, a maid so fair.
  *King Valdemar made vows to both.*

2 "Harken, Tove mine, and hear,
  Dost thou hold my Soffi dear?"

3 "Less dear to me, I ween,
  Than my son I hold the Queen.

4 "I will give her a good grey steed,
  And the name of Queen shall she bear indeed."

5 "Harken, Soffi mine, and hear,
  Dost thou hold my Tove dear?"

6 "I love her all so well
  As a wild wolf in the dell.

7 "I will give her castles three,
  She may burn therein for me!"

8 The Queen spake up to her page so small:
  "Now bid Tovelille hither to hall!"

9   So fain was Tove to look on the Queen
     She clad herself all by the tapers' sheen—

10   She clad herself in a kirtle of blue,
     At every seam the red gold shone through.

11   She clad herself in a silken sark,
     Of eleven maidens the handiwork.

12   She wrapped her in cloak of scarlet red,
     And thus to seek the Queen she sped.

13   "Art fainer with the King to speak,
     Or the bath with me to seek?"

14   "Fainer far with the King I'd speak
     Than the bath with thee I'd seek."

15   Soffi the Queen was strong of arm,
     She thrust her in to work her harm.

16   So hot she heated the fire beneath
     That Tovelille could scarce draw breath.

17   "Help me, Christopher, son of mine!
     Soffi will slay me in dule and pine."

18   "Now how shall I bring help to thee?
     Twelve armed men have hold of me."

19   Up spake the King, his men among:
     "Why cometh not Tove to Evensong?"

20   Up spake Soffi, red with wrath:
     "Thy Tove is wearied with her bath!"

21   "Well will I requite thy pain,
     Shalt never sleep in my bed again!

22   "Better was she with one cow for dower
     Than thou art, Soffi, with town and tower.

23   "Better was Tove in her sark
     Than thou art with all thy goldsmiths' work.

24   "Yea, dearer is Tovelil, though she be dead,
     Than thou with all thy gold so red!"

25   The way was long, the way was drear,
     The King himself bore up the bier.

## 18
## VALDEMAR AND TOVE      (B)

1   Gay went the dance in King Valdemar's hall,
     (By my troth)
     There danced the Queen with her ladies all.
     King Valdemar needs must love them both.

2   There danced the Queen with ladies fair,
     There danced Tove with waving hair.

3   "Harken now, Tove, my play-fellow sweet,
     Gird up thy silk skirts around thy feet."

4   "Small praise from me the King would gain
     If I might not trail a silken train."

5   "Tove, my play-fellow, tell thou me
     How first the King got his will of thee."

6   "Askest thou, I will tell thee why,
    Because the King was stronger than I.


7   "I was but a maiden small
    Dwelling in my father's hall.


8   "So little and fair by the gate stood I,
    The King and all his merry men they came a-riding by.


9   "By one, by two, his knights he sent,
    But never for their commands I went.


10  "The King he came himself with all his merry men,
    And I, Tovelille, must follow then."


11  "Tove, my play-fellow, tell thou me
    What morning-gift did he give to thee?"


12  "He gave me a casket of golden sheen,
    Better was never in Denmark seen.


13  "Nine rings he gave me of red, red gold
    That Sweden's Queen did have and hold.


14  "He clad me in silk and scarlet gay,
    Thou and all thy maidens ne'er go in such array."


15  Up spake the Queen in anger wild:
    " 'Twas enough, I vow, for a peasant's child!


16  "By God the Lord, if I breathe and live,
    Less by half to thee shall he give!"


17  The Queen she wrapped her in cloak of vair,
    To speak with King Valdemar did she fare.

18 "Now answer what I ask of thee,
    Why lovest thou Tove more than me?"

19 "For this Tovelille to me is so dear,
    Because she hath two sons that serve my person near.

20 "When Flensborg Town I first rode by
    Christopher bore my banner so high.

21 "When first I rode to Holsterland
    Knud bore my banner in his right hand."

22 Winters twain were gone and past
    Ere the Queen got her will at last.

23 All on holy Christmas Day
    Tove went in kirk to pray.

24 Tovelille fared forth in the street
    Golden silk and samite floated round her feet.

25 Forth from her window the Queen did spy,
    She saw proud Tovelille passing by.

26 The Queen she spake to her ladies three:
    "Now bid proud Tovelille hither to me!"

27 Tove wrapped her in cloak of vair,
    To seek the Queen she did repair.

28 "Lithe now and listen, Tove, to me,
    I would fain seek the bath tonight with thee."

29 "Ne'er of the bath can I have my fill,
    I'll do thy bidding with right good-will!"

30    *The Queen she spake to her pages three:*
       *"Take heed that the bath is hot for me.*

31    *"Heat it hot, and heat it red!*
       *There shall Tovelille lie dead."*

32    *Tovelille she went in before,*
       *The Queen herself she locked the door.*

33    *"Here is no water, here is no lye,*
       *Let me out for the sake of God on high!"*

34    *Christopher went riding by,*
       *He heard his mother wail and cry.*

35    *He struck the door a blow so stout*
       *That bolt and nail came leaping out.*

36    *In rue and wrath he burst the door,*
       *His mother from the bath he bore.*

37    *He bore her into the garden green,*
       *But she was dead ere day was seen.*

NOTE: The use of the steam-bath, now known as Finnish or Russian, was customary in olden days all over Scandinavia. Water was thrown on the heated stove to generate the steam; lye was used for washing and for bleaching the hair.

## 19
## THE DEATH OF KNIGHT STIG
## (1154)

1    *Up spake the King to Stig the Knight:*
       *"Now thou shalt bear up my banner in fight!"*
              *Alas, good knight, ill must he fare!*

2   "So poor a man and mean am I,
    I may not bear up thy banner so high."

3   "And wert thou poor as tongue could tell,
    Shouldst bear up my banner passing well."

4   "And if from my hand shall your banner be flown
    Then let a new banner be shapen and sewn!

5   "With gold, red, and blue that banner shall fly,
    And many a man 'neath those colours shall die."

6   Forth did they fare to an alien land,
    And ne'er was the banner loosed from his hand.

7   Fast flew the arrows and thick as hay
    Against the red sleeves of Stig that day.

8   Sore struck the arrows as burning brand
    Against the good knight's lily-white hand.

9   Loud cried the King amid the strife:
    "Now cast down the banner and save thy life!"

10   "Ne'er shall my true-love be told in the town
    That Stig bore the King's banner and cast it adown."

11   "Ne'er shall my true-love learn in the land
    Stig let the King's banner be loosed from his hand!"

12   Loud cried the King in dule and pain:
    "Sir Stig lies under my banner slain!"

13   The King was victor in hard-fought fray,
     But Stig the Knight was dead and away.

14   The King held up his lily-white hand:
     "We of the Danes have won the land!

15   "Right gladly to Denmark would I ride
     If Stig the Knight were by my side."

16   The King from the field fared home so fleet,
     And his sister went forth her brother to greet.

17   "Welcome, dear brother, and welcome again;
     Say, how hast thou fared with thy well-born men?"

18   "The fight we won and the land withal,
     But thine own true-love on the field did fall."

19   The maiden she wrung her hands so sore
     Her rings of gold ran over the floor.

20   "Dear sister, now cease thy tears to shed,
     With Sir Karl the rich shalt thou soon be wed."

21   Up spake the maiden and answered free:
     "Ne'er shall Sir Karl bear rule over me!

22   "Ye may call him the rich, but whate'er his plight,
     No match will he be for Sir Stig the Knight!"

NOTE: The Danish Royal banner after the time of the Valdemars bore three blue lions on a golden ground. The use of the Dannebrog as the national banner became more usual under Valdemar Atterdag and during the following period.

# 20

# ESBERN SNARE

1   Iver and Esbern both were merry,
    (The forest grows green and fair)
    They sat a-drinking at the Ferry,
    The summer and the meadow suit so well together.

2   "Harken, comrade true and tried,
    Give me little Kirsteen to bride!"

3   "Now what with little Kirsteen canst do?
    She cannot tie up her own ribbons of blue.

4   "She can neither shape nor sew,
    All her work to the town must go."

5   To Ribe did Sir Esbern fare,
    And bought new cloth of scarlet rare,

6   Cloth and samite of goodly show,
    Bade little Kirsteen shape and sew.

7   She sat her down on sewing-stool,
    She broidered the sun a-shining full.

8   Knife she took and shears withal,
    Roses and lilies she fashioned them all.

9   She shaped on the shoulders broad
    Two knights that drew the sword,

10   And at the seams on either side
    A ship that sailed the flowing tide,

11  And where the sleeves with knots were bound
    Fifteen maidens a-dancing the round,

12  And on the breast displayed
    A knight that kissed a maid.

13  "Shapen and sewn are the garments all,
    Would God they were carried home to hall!"

14  Up and spake the foot-page small:
    "I'll carry the garments home to hall."

15  When Esbern saw the kirtle bright:
    "Christ bless the damsel's fingers white!

16  "Christ bless the damsel's fingers white
    For every seam she sewed aright!

17  "I'll give her as fee for her tailor's gear
    Ribe and all the lands anear.

18  "And this shall she have for tailor's fee,
    Myself, if she will wed with me!"

19  "Now thanks, fair knight, for thy courtesie!
    'Tis thyself the maiden will take in fee."

## 21
## THE BATTLE OF LENA
### (1208)

1   It was the doughty Sverker
    Before the King who cried:
    "Now lend me men, that I may fight
    Because my father died!"
    The knights bore out their shields, and then
                    must many weep.

2  "From Sælland and from Jutland both
   My men with thee shall go,
   The bravest warriors are they
   That well can bend the bow."

3  'Twas all on the Sunday morning
   When the holy Mass was o'er,
   That Sverker fared to Öresund
   And sailed with his host from shore.

4  Now Sverker stood in the good ship's bows
   And looked forth over the Sound:
   "May God now grant us victory,
   Or sink us down to the ground!"

5  Oh, baleful that day of battle,
   And dearly that fight was won,
   When the lordlings raged together,
   And the sire smote down the son!

6  Forth he rode, young Engelbret,
   Girt with his golden horn,
   He mowed down the men of the Western Goths
   As the farmer cuts down the corn.

7  Oh, sore the price the Danes must pay,
   And bitter their dule and pain,
   So many a man that day did fall
   Where the blood ran down like rain!

8  For when they sailed from Denmark
   They were a thousand men,
   And none of all turned homeward
   But three times five and ten.

9   *The ladies stood in high-loft*
      *Their lords' return to see,*
      *But every steed with gore was red,*
      *And empty each saddle-tree.*

NOTE: Three times five: A custom still prevailed in the Middle Ages of reckoning by fives instead of tens, viz. by the fingers of one hand, not of both.

22

# THE BRIDAL OF QUEEN DAGMAR
## (1205)

1   *It was the Queen of Bejerland*
      *That to her daughter cried:*
      *"Great honour shall they show to thee*
      *When thou art Denmark's bride."*
      *They sailed from noblest Bejerland.*

2   *"When thou dost sail to Denmark's realm*
      *The queenly crown to wear,*
      *Forbear the peasant's plough to tax,*
      *And he will love thee dear.*

3   *"When first thy lord a boon bestows*
      *Then crave this morning-meed,*
      *That Valdemar, dear brother mine,*
      *May be from prison freed."*

4   *Eftsoon with silk and samite*
      *To lie her feet before,*
      *They took the lady Dagmar*
      *And led her to the shore.*

5   *They hoisted up their silken sails*
      *All on the masts of gold,*
      *And so they sailed to Denmark*
      *Or e'er two months were told.*

6   There did they cast anchor
    All on the snow-white sand,
    They took the lady Dagmar
    And led her up to land.

7   They took the lady Dagmar
    And led her up to land,
    And it was the King of Denmark
    Stretched forth his lily-white hand.

8   Eftsoon with silk and samite
    To lie her feet before,
    They led the lady Dagmar
    Up to the castle door.

9   So early in the morning,
    So long ere dawn of day,
    It was the lady Dagmar
    Her morning-meed did pray.

10  "The first boon that I beg, O King,
    I beg withouten fear,
    Let Bishop Valdemar go free,
    My mother's brother dear.

11  "Behold, I beg with right good-will
    A second boon of thee,
    Now tax ye not the peasant's plough,
    And set all captives free!"

12  "Now hold thy peace, Queen Dagmar,
    And crave ye no such boon,
    If Bishop Valdemar go free
    A widow thou'lt be eftsoon!"

13    All on the board her golden crown
       She laid the King before;
       "No greater am I in Denmark
       Than ever I was of yore!"

14    "Now bring to me Sir Strange,
       And bring Sir Knud to me!
       For they shall ride to Attingborg,
       And set the prisoner free."

15    Now when they loosed him from the tower
       He could not stand nor go:
       "Here have I lain for eighteen years,
       Long years, I ween, and slow."

16    Oh, she has ta'en a golden comb
       To smooth his locks withal,
       With every tress she ordered
       She let a tear down fall.

17    "Now hush thee, good Queen Dagmar,
       And dry thy rosy cheek,
       For an I live a twelvemonth more,
       A red revenge I'll wreak!"

18    "Now hold thy peace, mine uncle dear,
       Nor speak of death and bane,
       Dost thou return to Attingborg
       Thou'lt ne'er be loosed again."

NOTE: Attingborg, in all probability, was another name for Söborg in Sælland, where Valdemar was imprisoned.

# 23

# THE DEATH OF QUEEN DAGMAR
## (1212)

1 Queen Dagmar lay in Ribe sick,
  To Ringsted she needs must fare,
  All the dames in Denmark's realm
  She bade them seek her there.
  In Ringsted rested she, Queen Dagmar.

2 "Go bring me four, go bring me five
  Of those that wisest be!
  Send ye to Rise for young Kirsteen,
  Sir Karol's sister she."

3 Modest and mannerly young Kirsteen
  Entered the bower door,
  So fain of her coming was Dagmar the Queen
  That she lifted her head once more.

4 "Now canst thou read and canst thou write
  To drive my pain away,
  Then shalt thou wear the scarlet weed
  And ride my courser grey."

5 "And can I read and can I write,
  All shall be done, I trow,
  For sharper than steel is thine anguish,
  And fain would I help thee now."

6 Oh, she's taken the Book of Saint Mary,
  And striven to read withal,
  But she saw not the light of the crown so bright,
  So fast her tears did fall.

7    Oh, they led out the Queen and they led her in,
     And still waxed her anguish sore:
     "Now send ye word to the King our Lord
     To speak with me once more!"

8    Up he stood, the little foot-page,
     That was full fain to speed,
     His saddle he took from the beam adown
     And mounted the milk-white steed.

9    The King he stood in bower aloft
     And looked out far and wide:
     "Lo yonder I see a little foot-page,
     That doth a-weeping ride.

10   "Hither there cometh a little foot-page,
     All mournful is his mien,
     Now grant Almighty God in Heaven
     That all be well with the Queen!"

11   In he came, that little foot-page,
     Before the board stood he:
     "Now wouldst thou speak with the Queen again
     Thou must speak right speedilie!"

12   He's clapped the dice-board hard and close
     Till all the dice have rung:
     "Almighty God in Heaven forbid
     That Dagmar should die so young!"

13   The King rode forth from Skanderborg
     With an hundred swains and one,
     But when he came to Ribe
     Then rode he all alone.

14   Oh, woe was there in the woman's bower,
And bitter hurt and harm,
For the Queen or ever the King rode up
Lay dead in Kirsteen's arm.

15   And when at door he entered there
He saw the bier beside:
"Now help me, God our Father in Heaven,
My bitter grief to bide!

16   "Now pray, ye dames and damsels all,
Ye shall not pray in vain!
So fain am I a word to speak
With Dagmar once again."

17   Up rose the Queen upon her bier,
With eyes as red as blood:
"Alas, my noble Lord, alas,
We meet in woeful mood!

18   "The first boon that I beg thee now
I beg for love of me;
Give peace to every outlawed man,
And set the captives free.

19   "The second boon I beg thee now,
I beg for love of thee;
Oh, take not Bengerd for thy mate,
So sour a shrew is she!

20   "The third boon that I beg thee now
Thou'lt gladly grant to me,
I ask that Knud our youngest son
May King in Denmark be.

21   "I need ne'er have burnt in bitter pains
      Both by night and day,
      Had I ne'er on Sabbath tied my sleeves,
      Nor donned my head-gear gay.


22   "My hour is run, I must away,
      I dare no longer bide,
      For me the bells of Heaven ring,
      And the angels wait beside."

NOTE: After Knud Lavard's time, the abbey church at Ringsted became
the Royal burial place; the second line therefore intimates that the
Queen's sickness was fatal.

Reading and writing are mentioned together as the two allied arts.
The Book of Saint Mary was probably a collection of legends of the
Blessed Virgin, and seems to have been looked on as a source of healing
powers.

Valdemar's son Knud, who became Duke of Bleking, never ascended
the throne of Denmark. The author of the ballad apparently regarded
him as a son of Dagmar's superseded by Bengerd's sons, whereas he was
passed over as being illegitimate—evidence that the ballad was composed
long after Dagmar's death.


## 24

# QUEEN BENGERD
## ( 1 2 1 4 )


1   All in the morning, long ere day,
    She for her bridal-gift did pray.
    Woe be on her then, Queen Bengerd!


2   "Now give me Samsey to have and to hold,
    And let every maid pay a crown of gold!"


3   To Bengerd spake the King eftsoon:
    "Thou must beg another boon.

4   "So poor is many a maid today
     Were she to die, she could not pay."

5   "Dear my Lord, now heed my prayer,
     Let no lady scarlet wear!"

6   "Oh, can she buy it with gold and fee,
     She may wear it full well for me."

7   "Dear my Lord, my prayer now heed,
     That no son of a churl may ride a good steed!"

8   "Nay, can he come by it in honestie,
     He may ride it full well for me."

9   "Dear my Lord, now give commands
     To close all the havens with iron bands!"

10   "Now where can I so much metal win
     As to close all the harbours of Denmark in?"

11   "Up to Ribe will we fare,
     We shall find good blacksmiths there.

12   "How dare the peasant hope for more
     Than leather latch and wattled door?

13   "What more gear should a peasant gain
     Than a single cow and oxen twain?

14   "For every son his wife doth bear,
     A piece of gold should be my share.

15   "A piece of gold for every son,
     For every daughter half a one!"

16   When first the King slept in the dawn so dim,
     Good Queen Dagmar appeared to him.

17   "When on foray thou art bound,
     Leave not Bengerd on Danish ground!

18   "Leave Bengerd behind a year, I say
     The babe in the cradle must rue the day."

19   "Now busk ye and boun ye, Bengerd the Queen!
     Shalt fare on foray with me, I ween."

20   The first shaft that from string did dart
     Broke its barb on Bengerd's heart.

21   Now Bengerd in mirk and mould abides,
     And the peasant hath oxen and kine besides.

22   Now Bengerd lies in mirk and mould,
     And every maid keeps her red, red gold!

## 25
## THE KING-SLAYING IN FINDERUP
## (1286)

1   So many dwell in Denmark
     Would all be masters there!
     They've ridden up to Ribe,
     And close disguise they wear,
     And therefore the land lies in peril.

2   They've clad them all in close disguise
As friars of orders grey,
And up the land they've ridden,
Their liege lord to betray.

3   They watched him out, they watched him in,
They watched through time and tide,
They watched him till the woeful hour
He should to Finderup ride.

4   Into the goodman's garth they rode,
And shining spears they bore.
Was never a man might know them
For the monkish cowls they wore.

5   Oh, in they turned where the taper burned
In barn that was his bower,
They wakened him that was their King,
All in an evil hour.

6   "Harken, Ranild Jonson,
Wilt thou defend my life,
I'll give thee half my kingdom,
And my sister dear to wife!"

7   It was Ranild Jonson
That hewed at beam and board.
Goodsooth, most like a traitor
Did he defend his Lord!

8   Oh, they've struck in at the shoulder,
And out at the heart they smite:
"There shall be dule in all Denmark
For the deed we have done this night!"

9   It was the little foot-page
    That could not bear the sight,
    The saddle he took from the good grey steed,
    And set it upon the white.

10  The saddle he took from the good grey steed
    And set it on the white,
    And he rode and reached to Skanderborg
    Before the fall of night.

11  The Queen she sits in high-loft bower,
    And looks forth far and wide:
    "Yonder I see a little foot-page,
    And swiftly doth he ride.

12  "All on his master's steed he rides,
    And woe is me for fear!
    Now watch, Almighty God in Heaven,
    Over my Lord so dear!"

13  "Now God have mercy on his soul,
    For slain our King doth lie,
    Yea, foully slain in Finderup,
    And the land is in jeopardie!

14  "Now ward ye well your castle,
    Now ward ye well your realm,
    Now ward ye well King Erik's son
    Shall stand at Denmark's helm!"

15  "Now thou art a trusty messenger,
    Ill though thy tidings be;
    Food while I live and fire in my Court,
    This shalt thou have of me."

# 26

# MARSK STIG MADE AN OUTLAW
## (1287)

1  Now Marstig woke at the mirk midnight,
   And to his love he cried:
   "Oh, I have dreamt a weary dream,
   God knows what will betide!"
     My noble lord, the young Sir Marstig.

2  "Methought to savage swine was changed
   Each trusty hunting-hound,
   And they wasted all that grew so green
   Within our garden-ground.

3  "And then methought my gallant ship
   Was changed to shallop small,
   And anchor she had none, I wis,
   And nought to steer withal.

4  "And then methought across a bridge
   I fared with horse and man,
   But my courser threw me from his back
   And went where the wild mares ran."

5  "Now lay thee down, my noble lord,
   Thy dreams bode good to thee,
   The tax shall bring thee gain and gold
   From men of low degree."

6  "Nay, the Court shall be held on the morrow
   South by the riverside,
   And God alone doth know the hand
   Whereby King Erik died!"

7  Now Marstig and his gallant band
   Did on their byrnies brown,
   And forth they fared to Skanderborg
   So fast by dale and down.

8  The Queen of Danes in high-loft stood,
   O'er dale and down she spied:
   "Lo, hither he comes, Sir Marstig,
   King by the riverside!"

9  "Now cease for shame, my gracious dame,
   Thine ill-timed jests to fling!
   'Tis Ove, the lordly Seneschal,
   Should bear the name of King.

10 "Now lithe and listen, my gracious dame,
   Nor seek my cause to harm,
   'Tis Ove the lordly Seneschal,
   Lay last within thine arm."

11 Up and spake King Erik's son,
   Clad all in the scarlet red!
   "Full ill, I wis, such boot as this
   For my father fallen and dead!"

12 Up and spake King Erik's son
   A word of royal renown:
   "Shalt get thee from the land, Marstig,
   An if I wear the crown!"

13 "And must I depart from Denmark
   To hide in wrath and dule,
   My food will I fetch in Denmark,
   Both spring and summer and Yule!

14  "And must I depart from Denmark
    To sail the sea so deep,
    So many a widow will I make
    That the noblest dames shall weep."

15  Marstig he builded a castle proud
    That shone o'er wall and tower,
    Was never a man in Denmark's realm
    Could win that hold of power.

16  Forth to his field went the farmer,
    All for to sow his corn:
    "Now help us, God in heaven above,
    Since Hjelm hath gotten a horn!"

NOTE: In medieval pronunciation Marsk (Marshal) Stig was amalgamated into a single word, with the accent on the first syllable.

A "wild stud," consisting of a stallion with a few mares, was often
turned loose into the woods, so that the beasts should fend for themselves,
and allowed to run wild till they were caught again and trained.

The expression "King of the riverside" is obscure. "South of the river"
in the ballads usually signifies South Jutland, but this cannot be regarded
as Marstig's territory.

## 27

## MARSTIG AND·HIS LADY

1  It is young Sir Marstig
   Must journey far and wide,
   It is young King Erik
   That hath betrayed his bride.
   The lady sits in Sælland, and weeps right woefully.

2  It was young Sir Marstig
   Did home from foray fare,
   She would not rise, his lady,
   Nor give him greeting there.

· 157 ·

3   It was young Sir Marstig
    That entered in apace,
    She would not rise, his lady,
    Nor look him in the face.


4   Long he stood, Sir Marstig,
    And thought right heavily:
    "What aileth her, my wife so dear,
    That hath no word for me?"


5   "When thou didst go, my husband,
    I was a good knight's dame,
    Now am I Queen in Denmark,
    The greater is my shame!


6   "Never again shalt thou slumber
    All on my lily-white arm,
    Till thou hast slain King Erik
    That wrought me hurt and harm."


7   It was young Sir Marstig
    That answered ne'er a word,
    But rode in haste to the Land's Thing
    To meet the King his Lord.


8   It was young Sir Marstig
    Stood forth in all men's sight,
    Chieftain and squire he greeted,
    And many a noble knight.


9   Up stood young King Erik
    And took him by the hand:
    "Now welcome home, Sir Marstig,
    To thy Lord and to thy land!"

10　Up and spake Sir Marstig,
　　All in wrathful mind:
　　"Little I deemed when I fared forth
　　What falsehood I left behind!

11　"Both Revel and Riga I won for thee,
　　And that with mickle strife,
　　Whilst thou, King Erik, didst bide at home
　　To ravish my fair young wife!"

12　"Harken now, Sir Marstig,
　　And be not wroth with me!
　　Seven castles in Sælland
　　All will I give to thee."

13　"Seven castles in Sælland
　　Will ne'er assuage my shame.
　　Know thou, King of Denmark,
　　Dearer I hold my dame.

14　"Harken, King of Denmark,
　　And heed the words I say!
　　No fealty shalt thou have of me
　　Until my dying day."

## 28

# THE LONG BALLAD OF MARSK STIG

1　Marstig woke all at the mirk midnight,
　　And to his love he cried:
　　"Oh, I have dreamt a weary dream
　　God knows what shall betide!"
　　　　My noble lord, the young Sir Marstig.

2   "Methought my great and gallant ship
    Was changed to shallop small,
    And ne'er an oar did I behold,
    And nought to steer withal.

3   "And then methought that o'er a bridge
    I fared with horse and man,
    But my courser threw me from his back,
    And went where the wild mares ran."

4   "Now lithe and list, thou noble lord,
    Thy dreams bode good to thee,
    The tax shall bring thee gain and gold
    From men of low degree."

5   In came Marstig's little page
    And stood the board beside:
    "Behold King Erik's messenger
    That to our garth doth ride!"

6   Up stood young Sir Marstig
    That now to bed was boun,
    And to the garth he hastened
    To speak with the page eftsoon.

7   "Now hark and heed, Sir Marstig,
    The words I say to thee,
    The King doth bid thee come to Court,
    And thou shalt ride with me."

8   "Now hark and hear, thou messenger,
    The words I say to thee,
    If aught thou know'st of the King's counsel
    Then hide it not from me!"

9   "Oh, all I know of the King's counsel
    May'st learn as soon as I,
    Thou shalt anon to foray fare,
    And bear his banner high."

10  It was young Sir Marstig
    That donned his cloak of vair,
    And to the high-loft hastened
    To seek his lady there.

11  So dark of mood was Marstig,
    So pale and wan of hue:
    "Goodsooth, I ween, fair Ingeborg,
    Now shall my dreams come true!

12  "For when I dreamed my trusty steed
    Went where the wild mares ran,
    What should it bode but sore defeat,
    With loss of horse and man?"

13  "Now hold thy peace, my noble lord,
    Say no such words to me!
    The merciful Christ in heaven above
    Shall ward thy ways and thee."

14  It was young Sir Marstig
    To castle garth that sped;
    And there stood young King Erik
    Wrapped all in the scarlet red.

15  "Now lithe and listen, Sir Marstig,
    To foray shalt thou fare,
    And this shalt have for honour,
    My banner proud to bear."

16   "And must I fare to foray,
    And risk for thee my life,
    Then ward ye well young Ingeborg,
    That is so fair a wife."

17   Up spake young King Erik,
    And smiled 'neath cloak of vair:
    "No better should she be warded
    If she my sister were.

18   "So well will I watch and ward her,
    And guard thy beauteous bride,
    That harm shall no more befall her,
    Than if thou wert by her side."

19   It was young Sir Marstig
    That forth to foray rode,
    But still sat beauteous Ingeborg,
    And mournful was her mood.

20   It was young King Erik
    Bade saddle his steed so free:
    "Now landward will we ride, I wis,
    To visit that fair ladye!"

21   "Now greetings to thee, fair Ingeborg,
    Let be thy care so cold,
    And broider for me a kirtle
    Laid o'er with the burning gold!"

22   "And should I shape thee a kirtle
    With the red, red gold sewn o'er,
    Less kind should I be to Sir Marstig
    Than ever I was before."

23   "Now harken, beauteous Ingeborg,
    Wilt yield to me thy love,
    Thee will I hold in honour
    All other dames above."

24   "This chain of gold, this golden ring,
    On bridal day I bore,
    And n'er will I be false to faith,
    Nor break the vows I swore!

25   "Ye vowed to him, Sir Marstig,
    When he to fight should fare,
    No better should I be warded
    If I your sister were."

26   They kindled up the waxen lights
    That stood on the board arow,
    And with grief and shame that noble dame
    To Erik's bed must go.

27   It was beauteous Ingeborg
    That liked her lot full ill,
    Early and late he sought her love,
    And forced her to his will.

28   It was young Sir Marstig
    Fared home again from fight;
    But heavy and sore the tidings
    That waited the noble knight.

29   It was young Sir Marstig
    That hastened home apace;
    She would not rise, his fair young wife,
    Nor look him in the face.

30    Long stood young Sir Marstig
       And thought right heavily:
       "What ails her, beauteous Ingeborg,
       That hath no word for me?"

31    "When thou didst fare to foray
       I was a knightly dame,
       Now am I Queen in Denmark,
       The greater is my shame!

32    "When thou didst fare to foray
       Thine own true wife was I,
       Now am I Queen of Denmark,
       And shall rue it till I die.

33    "Never again will I slumber
       All on thy bosom white,
       Till thou hast slain King Erik
       That did me this despite.

34    "Never again will I slumber
       All on thy lily-white arm,
       Till thou hast slain King Erik
       That wrought me hurt and harm."

35    Sir Marstig has donned his armour of proof
       And ridden away to the Thing,
       With his merry men well weaponed in steel,
       All for to seek the King.

36    It was young Sir Marstig
       In open Thing stood forth,
       He greeted the redesmen of the realm,
       And the nobles of the North.

37   Sir Marstig stood in open Thing,
And thus did speak and say:
"For that my wife hath suffered wrong
Do I stand here this day.

38   "Oh, far did I fare in foray
To risk for the realm my life;
Thou sat'st at home, King Erik,
To ravish my fair young wife!"

39   Up spake young King Erik,
And smiled 'neath cloak of vair:
"Oh, her consent and will thereto
As good as mine they were!"

40   Up spake young Sir Marstig
In mood that needs must mourn:
"Right well we wot the ancient saw
That scathe treads hard on scorn.

41   "Now thou hast forced my fair young wife,
A mock of me to make,
But wot ye well, King Erik,
I'll slay thee for her sake!"

42   It was young Sir Marstig
That turned in open Thing:
"Bear witness, redesmen of the realm,
That I defy the King!"

43   "Now hold thy peace, Sir Marstig,
And calm thy wrathful mood,
I'll give to thee both tower and hold
And many a good greenwood."

44   "No good greenwood can calm my mood,
      No hold can hide my shame!
      I would the wrong had ne'er been wrought
      Against my noble dame."

45   "O Marstig, ne'er so fast canst ride
      But I can ride faster still,
      But wouldst thou be mine enemy
      Then follow thy wanton will!"

46   "Oh, let my riding be ne'er so slow,
      And ne'er so meek my mind,
      Yet have we seen a greyhound small
      Run down both hart and hind.

47   "Only do thou remember
      What cause I have to plead;
      Oft have we seen a hillock small
      Bring down a mighty steed."

48   Now a sister dear had his lady.
      And Rane hight her son,
      Was page to young King Erik,
      And small was the praise he won.

49   Now Rane was called to counsel
      All by that woeful wife,
      How to betray King Erik,
      And take away his life.

50   It was the page, young Rane,
      Before the King that stood,
      Tidings to tell of hind and hart
      That play in good greenwood.

51  "Where hart and hind in greenwood play
Right well in sooth I know,
And if thou wilt, my gracious lord,
We will a-hunting go."

52  It was young King Erik
Bade buckle his saddle-band:
"Now will we ride to the Council
And see how fares the land.

53  "Ride ye before, my trusty friends,
Prepare my dwelling due,
And I will ride with Rane,
And try if his tale be true."

54  So on before to Viborg town
They rode o'er holt and hill;
And little he thought or dreamed, God wot,
That Rane wished him ill.

55  And now alone to chase the deer
Both King and page are gone,
And on they rode till twilight fell,
And fast the night came on.

56  In mournful mood King Erik
Unto his page did say:
"So help me God in heaven above,
Now have I lost the way!"

57  The way they sought by waste and wild,
By holt and greenwood shaw,
Until in lowly hut and mean
A burning light they saw.

58    Now in went young King Erik,
    *Right mournful was his mind,*
    And there did see as fair a maid
    *As ever a man might find.*

59    *In lusty arm he seized her straight,*
    *And spake up plain and free:*
    "Now lend an ear, thou lovely lass,
    Tonight shalt lie with me!"

60    Oh, loud she laughed and long she laughed,
    *That lady fair and fine:*
    "Now tell me first, King Erik,
    That latest deed of thine!"

61    "And knowest thou that, my lady fair,
    Then more canst thou tell to me!
    *Fain would I learn ere fall of night*
    *How long my life shall be.*"

62    Then up and spake the beauteous maid,
    *And loud her laughter rang:*
    "Now ask that of the little hook
    Whereon thy sword doth hang!"

63    He strove to clasp that merry maid
    *His eager arms between,*
    But she went like a mist or e'er he wist,
    *And ne'er again was seen.*

64    Oh, the lights shone fair when the maid stood there,
    *And warmly burned the fire,*
    Now all was mirk in wailing wind
    *That blew o'er moss and mire.*

65   It was the page young Rane
      That up and spake eftsoon:
      "Now fare we from the forest
      While shineth yet the moon!

66   "I know where lieth a hamlet small
      All by the greenwood side,
      And if thou please my gracious lord,
      Thither we well may ride."

67   To Finderup they took their way
      All by the moonbeams wan,
      No fire nor sheen of light was seen,
      So late the night wore on.

68   At last a lowly barn they spied,
      And known to none were they,
      And little deemed King Erik
      That he must die ere day.

69   Up stood young King Erik,
      And to his page spake he:
      "Shut fast the door, young Rane,
      If I may trust in thee!

70   "An I may trust thee, Rane,
      Then shut thou fast the door,
      Remember bold Sir Marstig,
      And think of his chiding sore!"

71   "Oh, hot of mood is my kinsman,
      Wild are his words and vain,
      I rede thee forget them, gracious lord,
      Nor think on the knight again.

72   "The whaup will watch the lee-long moor,
      And ne'er her wings will rest,
      So she the little spot may ward
      Where she hath made her nest."

73   No man was there with sword and spear
      To watch beside the door,
      Goodsooth I say that traitor page
      Two straws he laid before.

74   Now scarcely had they set them down
      Upon the straw to lie,
      When word came from fair Ingeborg
      Unto the farm hard by.

75   So loud upon the door they smote
      With glaive and eke with spear:
      "Now rise up, young King Erik,
      Come forth and meet us here!"

76   Up and spake young Rane,
      A traitor foul was he:
      "And if ye deem the King is here,
      Some man hath cozened thee!"

77   All o'er the King the straw he cast,
      And cast o'er him the hay,
      And thus the traitor Rane
      Did show them where he lay.

78   Right lustily he laid about
      And struck at beam and board,
      Goodsooth, most like a traitor
      Did he defend his lord!

79  "Now who will ride to Viborg
  And follow the fallen King,
  Or who will ride to Skanderborg
  News to the Queen to bring?"

80  Was none would ride to Viborg,
  Nor follow the fallen King,
  And a page they sent to Skanderborg,
  News to the Queen to bring.

81  In he went, the little page,
  And stood beside the board,
  A lad of lither tongue was he
  That well could speak his word.

82  "Thou sitst in peace, thou Queen of Danes,
  Clad all in the scarlet red,
  But slain is young King Erik,
  And lieth in Finderup dead."

83  "Now this will I give thee for guerdon,
  Though woeful at heart am I,
  Both meat and drink in the royal court
  Until the day I die."

84  "Oh, they struck in at the left shoulder,
  And to the heart adown—
  Now ward ye well the bairn so small
  Shall wear the woeful crown!

85  "Oh, they struck in at the right shoulder,
  And down to the heart did smite—
  Now ward ye well the little lad-bairn
  Must wear the crown aright!"

86  Now when Sir Marstig slew the King
    Little he rued the deed!
    Forth he fared to Skanderborg
    All on his swiftest steed.

87  It was she, the Queen of Danes,
    That from the window spied:
    "Oh, yonder I see our self-made King
    That to our hold doth ride!"

88  "Nay, never a self-made King am I
    For all thy words, I ween!
    That name befits Sir Seneschal
    Lay last thine arms between.

89  "Oh, little to thee King Erik's death,
    And less thy dule and pine,
    So long as liveth the Seneschal,
    And thou dost hold him thine!"

90  Up spake young Prince Christopher,
    Clad all in the scarlet red:
    "Oh, little amends, God wot, ye make
    For my father fallen and dead!"

91  Up stood young Prince Christopher,
    And spake a royal word:
    "Shalt get thee gone from out the realm
    If I am King and lord!"

92  "And must I depart from Denmark,
    To sail the sea so deep,
    So many a widow will I make
    That the noblest dames shall weep.

93　　"And must I depart from Denmark,
　　　From wife and bairn, O King,
　　　My food will I fetch in Denmark,
　　　Both winter and summer and spring!"

94　　It was young Sir Marstig
　　　That home to hold did fare,
　　　And it was beauteous Ingeborg
　　　Went forth to greet him there.

95　　Up spake young Sir Marstig
　　　And took her in his arm:
　　　"Now have I slain King Erik
　　　That wrought thee hurt and harm!

96　　"Now wilt thou be a light-o'-love
　　　And bear a hated name,
　　　Or wilt thou follow an outlawed man,
　　　And live a landless dame?"

97　　"Fain would I follow an outlawed man
　　　And dwell an honest dame,
　　　Rather than be a light-o'-love,
　　　And bear a hated name."

98　　Now when Marstig from Denmark turned
　　　For Hjelm he set his sail,
　　　And many an eye must weep for that,
　　　And many a cheek grow pale.

99　　Marstig he builded a hold at Hjelm,
　　　A hold with tower and wall,
　　　Not to be won by engine of war,
　　　Nor yet by cannon-ball.

100    *Forth to his field went the farmer*
     *All for to sow his corn:*
     *"Oh, help us, God in heaven above,*
     *Now Hjelm hath gotten a horn!"*

101    *Marstig he builded a hold at Hjelm,*
     *A hold with wall and tower.*
     *The King in vain laid siege thereto*
     *With all his royal power.*

NOTE: An embroidered kirtle was the usual gift of a betrothed maiden to her lover, so that the King's request to Ingeborg was equivalent to a request that she should be his mistress.

Möllerup in the parish of Feldballe near Æbeltoft was, according to tradition, Marsk Stig's dwelling-place.

Cannons are first mentioned during the reign of Valdemar Atterdag, and were probably well known at the time of the ballad's composition, though certainly not when Hjelm was besieged by Erik Menved. The more ancient "engines" or catapults were still generally used at that period.

## 29
## NIELS EBBESON
### (1340)

1    *The Count to Denmark took his way,*
     *And would not be gainsaid,*
     *What though the spaeman told him true*
     *That there should he lie dead.*

2    *Was none could cross his wilful mind*
     *His fate to put to test,*
     *Yeoman and boor, and knight and squire,*
     *Must have him for their guest.*

3    *The Count has called Niels Ebbeson*
     *To come and meet with him,*
     *And peace should reign whilst the hour endured,*
     *With truce for life and limb.*

4 The Count he met Niels Ebbeson
   Northward beside the sea:
   "Now be thou welcome, Niels Ebbeson,
   Right welcome unto me!

5 "Blithe is thy cheer, Niels Ebbeson,
   Retainer dear of mine!
   Now what is the mind of the Northern Jutes,
   And what of kinsfolk thine?"

6 "Yea, kinsfolk enow are mine, I trow,
   And my wife hath kin also,
   And all of them shall do thy will
   If they thy will may know."

7 "Niels Ebbeson, thou art a valiant man,
   And a man of wit beside,
   And canst thou not ride straightforward
   The long way round thou'lt ride.

8 "Now lithe and listen, Niels Ebbeson,
   Wilt thou mine errand speed,
   Then say how many swains hast thou
   Will stand thee by at need?" ·

9 "Some five and forty swains have I,
   Such as they well may be,
   And are they many or are they few
   Right dear they are to me."

10 "And hast thou five and forty carles,
    Well art thou served, I ween—
    But last night were thou in Sir Bugge's hold
    With a hundred mail-clad men!"

11 Niels Ebbeson he stamped his foot,
   And straight made answer high:
   "Is any man here, or knight or knave,
   That dares maintain that lie?

12 "Is any man here, or knight or knave,
   Who dares that lie maintain,
   Never a foot will I retreat
   Till I answer him back again!"

13 "Now lithe and list, Niels Ebbeson,
   Of this we'll make an end,
   Go, ask of him, Sir Bugge,
   If he will be my friend.

14 "Sir Bugge and Povl Glob the young
   To do my will did swear,
   And Sir Anders Frost is one with them,
   And foremost in counsel there.

15 "Yea, more have sworn to do my will
   That now would work me woe,
   So hear and heed Sir Bugge's rede,
   And see how the thing will go!"

16 "Oh, nought know I of Sir Bugge's mind,
   What he may say or do,
   But Anders has kept his troth with thee
   As all men will tell thee true.

17 "Anders hath kept his faith with thee,
   As all men will tell thee true,
   But would he take leave of thy service
   Such leave is a free man's due.

18   "For this is the Danish custom,
    And hath been since days of yore,
    If a swain would change his service
    He should have leave therefor."

19   Up and spake Lord Gert the Count
    That liked his words right ill:
    "Nay, never a vassal may leave his Lord
    Save with his Lord's good will."

20   "Oh, none is bound with a holy vow
    Save a monk to his cowl of grey!
    Let chieftains come and chieftains go,
    Men serve them as best they may."

21   "Overbold is his speech, Niels Ebbeson,
    That bandies words with me!
    Or thou shalt depart from Denmark,
    Or I'll hang thee to a tree!"

22   "And must I depart from Denmark,
    From wife's and bairns' embrace,
    Oh, thou shalt call it a luckless hour
    That e'er thou sawest my face!"

23   "Get hence, get hence, Niels Ebbeson,
    And let thy prating be,
    Or I will do what well I may
    And break my truce with thee!"

24   "Oh, ne'er hast thou seen me so sore afraid
    As to tremble for curse and ban,
    Look well to thyself, Count Gert, I say
    And defend thy head like a man!"

25   "Niels Ebbeson, thy words are hard,
     As oft ere this was shown,
     But I will hold truce with thee today
     E'en till the sun goes down."

26   Niels Ebbeson waved his lily-white hand,
     And turned his steed on the shore:
     "Farewell, Count Gert, with all thy men!
     Soon shall we meet once more!"

27   Niels Ebbeson he fled full fast,
     Nor spur was fain to spare,
     And the Count held back with all his men,
     Was none durst follow there.

28   It was he, Niels Ebbeson,
     That home to hold did win,
     And it was his own dear lady
     Went forth to lead him in.

29   "Now lithe thou and listen, wife, I pray,
     Some counsel give to me,
     For the Count will make me an outlawed man,
     Or hang me on gallows-tree!"

30   "What counsel can I give to thee
     That have but a woman's wit?
     The worst of rede were here the best,
     Could we but light on it.

31   "The worst of rede were here the best,
     All in this evil hour,
     The Count to slay whilst yet we may,
     Or burn him in his bower.

32  "Now take thy steeds to the smithy,
    (This is my counsel true),
    And turn their shoon the backward way
    When they are shod anew.

33  "Turn thou their shoon the backward way,
    So the foeman thy track shall miss,
    And take heed and tell to no man
    That a woman taught thee this!"

34  Up and spake Niels Ebbeson,
    Unto his men spake he:
    "Now which of you will follow,
    And which take leave of me?

35  "Let him that now will follow
    Reach forth his hand to me,
    And he that now will take his leave
    Speak up right speedilie!"

36  Up they stood, his Danish squires,
    And answered their Lord so free:
    "Now all of us will follow
    And risk our lives for thee!"

37  Now up they rode to Ladywood,
    And there their steeds did bind,
    And into Randers town they went,
    Count Gert to seek and find.

38  And when to Randers Bridge he came
    He spake to his squires anew:
    "Now let him take his leave and go
    Who will not stand me true!"

39  Up and spake the little lad Trust,
    The truest of them all:
    "Now give me leave, my master,
    And saddle and steed withal."

40  He gave him leave, his master,
    And saddle and steed withal,
    And or ever the day was over
    He served him best of all.

41  It was he, Niels Ebbeson,
    Through cloak that smote the door:
    "Rise up, rise up, Lord Gert the Count,
    For thou must sleep no more!

42  "Stand up, Lord Gert the Count,
    And lend to me thine ear!
    Duke Henrik's messenger am I,
    And he hath sent me here.

43  "Rise up, Lord Gert the Count,
    Nor longer lay thee down!
    Kolding is beleaguered
    And burnt is Ribe town."

44  "And dost thou tell me tidings true,
    Then good are they to hear!
    Free in my hold whilst yet we live
    Thou shalt have steed and gear."

45  Oh, they have opened wide the door
    More of that news to know,
    And it was he, Niels Ebbeson,
    To the Count's bedside did go.

46   "Now thou and I, Niels Ebbeson,
     Can league us far and wide,
     Word will we send to Duke Henrik,
     And Sir Klaus his friend beside."

47   Up and spake the swarthy swain:
     "Now waste no further word!
     Let be, let be thy tedious tale,
     And harken to the sword."

48   They've seized him, Gert the Count,
     All by his golden hair,
     Body from head they've sundered
     Over his bedside there.

49   Now when the Count was done to death
     All on their drums they beat,
     Forth farèd he, Niels Ebbeson,
     And hastened down the street.

50   It was he, Niels Ebbeson,
     That fain would flee away,
     But Sir Ove Haas he barred the road,
     And strove to say him nay.

51   "Now lithe and listen, Sir Ove Haas,
     And seek not to hinder me,
     For thou art wed to my kinswoman,
     As well is known to thee."

52   "Yea, he that has wed thy kinswoman
     Is kin to thee, I trow,
     But thou hast slain my Lord this day,
     And thou shalt not pass me now!"

53  Niels Ebbeson he drew his blade,
    He would not flee the strife,
    Sir Ove and many a German foe
    Must there lay down their life.

54  It was he, Niels Ebbeson,
    To Randers Bridge did ride,
    And the little page that took his leave
    Was standing there beside.

55  Over the bridge rode Niels Ebbeson,
    For his foes came like the wind,
    And it was the little foot-page
    Broke down the bridge behind.

56  Niels Ebbeson rode to Noringsris,
    And fast he spurred his steed,
    Sore, good sooth, was his anguish,
    And sorer still his need.

57  She sheltered him, an old good-wife,
    Of loaves that had but two,
    And she's given one to Niels Ebbeson,
    Because Count Gert he slew.

## 30
## REVISED CONCLUSION
## (NIELS EBBESON B)

34  "Now eat ye and drink, my goodly squires,
    And see that your hearts be gay,
    For when the night is overpast,
    Then will we seize the day.

35   "When day doth dawn and sun doth rise
      We shall have tidings new,
      And then shall I see of all my men
      How many will stand me true."

36   Up they stood, his merry men,
      And answered their Lord so free:
      "Now we will venture goods and life
      And all to ride with thee!"

37   Now up they rode to Ladywood,
      And there their steeds did bind,
      And in they went to Randers town,
      Count Gert to seek and find.

38   It was he, Niels Ebbeson,
      To Randers Bridge did fare:
      "Let him take leave that has no mind
      With me to do and dare!"

39   And every doughty warrior
      To serve him gave consent,
      All save the son of his sister
      Who took his leave and went.

40   It was the knight Niels Ebbeson
      Through cloak that smote the door:
      "Open to me, Lord Gert the Count,
      Nor seek to slumber more!

41   "Open to me, Lord Gert the Count,
      And lend to me thine ear.
      Duke Henrik's messenger am I,
      'Tis he hath sent me here."

42   "And art thou Duke Henrik's messenger,
Then tarry thou not too long!
Tomorrow we'll meet in the Greyfriars' Kirk,
'Twixt Mass and Evensong."

43   "Rise up, rise up, Lord Gert the Count,
Nor longer lay thee down!
Kolding is beleaguered,
And burnt is Ribe town."

44   Forth from the window looked the Count,
And the shining spears he spied:
"Oh, luckless the hour that I came in!
Niels Ebbeson holds outside."

45   They knocked on the door with glaive and spear,
Till loosed were lock and link:
"Art thou within, Lord Gert the Count,
A health to thee we'll drink!"

46   "Now sit thou down upon my bed
Counsel anew to call,
Word will we send to Duke Henrik,
And Sir Klaus his friend withal."

47   "Oh, neither keep nor hold have I
To guard so rich a prey,
Spare not, but draw the shining swords,
And let them have their way!"

48   The goose did cackle, the sheep did bleat,
And the cock on the high-loft crew,
'Twas by daylight and not in darkness
That Gert the Count they slew.

49   God rest thy soul, Niels Ebbeson,
     All for that slaying's sake!
     Full many a German in Denmark
     The selfsame way shall take.

## 31
## THE BALLAD OF THE EAGLE
### (1523)

1   All the small birds in good greenwood
     Do sore of the hawk complain,
     Both feathers and down he rives from them,
     And to drive them afield is fain.
     But the eagle nests in the mountains high.

2   Now together they met and council held
     On high in the oaken-tree,
     A King to find who could defend
     And set his subjects free.

3   Up and spake the coal-black crow,
     All wild and woebegone:
     "Now choose we the eagle for our King,
     And our cause may well be won!"

4   Then answered all the lesser fowls
     And found the council fit:
     "Now shall the eagle rule our realm
     So long as God permit."

5   The haughty hawk he up and spake:
     "Herein our hope is small,
     For an that ancient rule our realm
     He'll harry us one and all."

6    Now the eagle heard that wanton word,
     And wroth was he, I ween,
     The hawk so haughty he wounded sore
     All with his talons keen.

7    But every lesser bird rejoiced
     And sang as best he could,
     Great weal and warbling did prevail
     Within the good greenwood.

8    The hawks they met in a mighty host
     With wings that hid the sky:
     "Now will we raid the greenwood glade,
     And the eagle old defy!"

9    Then forth she flew, the gentle dove,
     And all in sore alarm:
     "The hawks, O King, are on the wing
     To do thee hurt and harm!"

10   Up and spake the eagle old,
     That wept right bitterly:
     "Now an the mice would eat the cat
     'Tis time for us to flee!"

11   With all his young that Eagle King
     Did forth from forest fare,
     And wildly fluttered the lesser fowl
     With none to counsel there.

12   Now the hawk rules free in oaken-tree
     And spreadeth his wings with pride,
     And wrong is done to every one
     In greenwood far and wide.

13  The crow must sit, for all her claws,
    To starve on a withered tree,
    And the owl lies hid where the alders grow,
    So fearful and faint is she.

14  Fain would the whaup 'mid the growing corn
    Her lofty crest conceal,
    But the hawk swoops down despite her care,
    And maketh a savoury meal.

15  Now all is hushed in greenwood glade,
    The trees as stone are still,
    No warbling strain will be heard again
    Till the hour that God shall will.

16  Now woe is me for the forest free
    And the silence of mirth and song,
    And woe for every bird on bough
    That findeth the time so long!

17  Now the hound lies sleeping 'neath the board,
    The fox doth eat the geese,
    The hound shall wake his prey to take
    In the hour that God shall please.

18  The cat lies sick the gate beside,
    And that to all men's scorn,
    The mouse doth nest in pouch and kist
    Of women all forlorn.

19  God pity the eagle old and grey
    That flies o'er the weary waste!
    No rock he finds nor sheltered bower
    Where he may build his nest.

# BALLADS OF CHIVALRY

# 32

# NILUS AND HILLELILLE

1  *It was bold Sir Nilus*
   *Rode up by land and lea,*
   *He wooed the lady Hillelil*
   *That was so fair to see.*
   *Oh, there they played a game, and the game was all of*
   *wrath.*

2  *They drank their blithesome bridale*
   *Five days and more, I ween,*
   *And when they saw the seventh*
   *He led her home at e'en.*

3  *Now they made ready her chariot*
   *And saddled their steeds anew,*
   *But when they rode o'er the moorland*
   *Right fiercely the storm-wind blew.*

4  *"Oh, cold the rain is falling,*
   *And wildly blows the wind,*
   *Now rede thou me, proud Hillelil,*
   *Where we may shelter find.*

5  *"For if we fare to Hedingsholm*
   *It is so long a path,*
   *And if we fare to Frederlund*
   *I fear thine uncle's wrath."*

6   "Now ride we, I rede, to Frederlund,
    And bide till the dawning fair,
    And I will be thy surety
    If we find my kinsman there!"

7   It was bold Sir Nilus
    That through the garth did ride,
    And there he stood, Sir Peter,
    Wrapped in his cloak of pride.

8   "Hail now, all hail, Sir Peter,
    Thou kinsman dear to me!
    Now let Sir Nilus and his men
    Tarry this night with thee."

9   "God's pity on thee, proud Hillelil,
    Small good is thine, I wis,
    I would have found thee for husband
    A richer man than this!"

10  "And hadst thou found me a husband
    With riches too great to tell,
    Long would have been thy seeking
    For a man I loved half so well!"

11  "Now will I bid thy bridegroom
    To tarry and make good cheer;
    But well knows bold Sir Nilus
    He slew my brother dear."

12  They led the bride to the ladies' bower
    And the bridegroom to the hall,
    But Sir Peter has gone his armour to don,
    And so have his henchmen all.

13 He cast his sword upon the board
  Betwixt the mead and wine:
  "Hast thou forgotten, Sir Nilus,
  Who slew him, brother mine?"

14 "I that right well remember
  Will never the deed deny,
  But I will be thy sworn brother
  Until the day I die."

15 "Nay, thou shalt fare hence in peace, I trow,
  Thou and thy henchmen bold,
  Save only the sons of thy sister
  Shall tarry here in my hold."

16 Up they stood, those champions,
  Laid hand on sword and drew:
  " 'Tis we will order our going
  Wilt thou give leave thereto!"

17 Still stood bold Sir Nilus,
  And never a word he said
  Till he saw the sons of his sister
  Both at his feet fall dead.

18 "Oh, I have sworn by the holy Cross
  Whereon Our Lord did bleed,
  No sword to draw on the Sabbath day
  Save in the direst need."

19 It was bold Sir Nilus
  That drew his blade so bright,
  Heavy the blows he dealt there,
  And gallant was the fight.

20  Great pity it was of Sir Nilus,
    For never his blood was spilt
    Until the blade of his good sword
    Was broken at the hilt.

21  Both cushion of down and bolster blue
    He held his breast before,
    But they dealt Sir Nilus his death-wound
    There by the chamber door.

22  It was bold Sir Nilus
    That spake in dule and pain:
    "Now come with me, proud Hillelil,
    'Tis time to ride again."

23  It was bold Sir Nilus
    That set him on his steed,
    And forth they fared to Hedingsholm
    All in the sorest need.

24  It was bold Sir Nilus
    Into the garth did fare,
    And by the gate stood his sister
    Wrapped in her cloak of vair.

25  "Now wherefore, Nilus my brother,
    Dost thou so slowly ride,
    And where be they, my two young sons,
    Should serve thee by thy side?"

26  "To Frederlund I fared of late
    To please my lady's mind,
    And there I got my death-wound,
    And I left thy sons behind.

27 "Now lithe and listen, my sister,
  Make ready a bed for me,
  And be to my bride in a mother's stead,
  So fair a dame is she!"

28 "Oh, how should I love proud Hillelil
  When thou for her sake art slain?
  Why comes she here when my sons so dear
  Will ne'er turn home again?"

29 Oh, loud they wept in the high-loft,
  And bitter their dule and harm,
  When they saw the bold Sir Nilus
  Lie dead in his sister's arm!

30 Dead lay bold Sir Nilus
  With woe and wellaway,
  Proud Hillelil laid her beside him
  And died of her grief ere day.

## 33
## YOUNG ENGEL

1 It was the swain young Engel
  That was both free and fair,
  Up did he ride in the countryside
  And seized a maiden there.
  Will the day ne'er be dawning?

2 Now Malfred hight the maiden,
  Was honest as the day,
  And on the night of their luckless flight
  In greenwood wild they lay.

3    It was the swain young Engel
     At midnight did awake,
     And of his dream so dreary
     To her he up and spake.

4    "A wolf methought was on me,
     A wolf so grim and grey,
     That tore my heart with bloody teeth
     E'en when I waking lay."

5    "Small marvel if thus thou dreamest,
     Nor doth thy dream deceive,
     When thou by force hast taken me
     Lacking my kinsfolk's leave."

6    In he came, the little foot-page,
     And stood beside the board,
     Both swift of wit and sharp of tongue,
     He well could speak his word.

7    "Now harken thou, young Engel,
     And be for flight well boun,
     For Gode Lovmand and his host
     By four ways come to town!"

8    "Oh, not for four I tremble,
     Nor do I fear for five,
     I reck not of Gode Lovmand,
     Nor any man alive!"

9    "Nay, more than five the number,
     And a greater tale than ten!
     Here cometh Gode Lovmand
     With an hundred weaponed men."

10    It was the swain young Engel
      That kissed his fair ladye:
      "If aught thou knowst of counsel
      In God's name counsel me!"

11    "Now call thy squires together
      To saddle each his steed,
      And seek we the kirk of Our Lady
      So long as endures our need!"

12    And now round the kirk of Our Lady
      Was laid a leaguer close,
      And ever Gode Lovmand
      Was foremost among their foes.

13    Up spake the mother of Malfred
      Of mood so grim and cold:
      "An ye fire the kirk of Saint Mary
      Ye can build it again for gold.

14    "Now cast we our gold and silver
      Till it brims o'er a lordly cup;
      An ye level the kirk of Our Lady
      I trow ye can build it up!"

15    Oh, they fired the kirk of Saint Mary,
      And fast the flames leapt on,
      And 'twas the lady Malfred
      Must needs grow pale and wan.

16    Now heat like a fiery furnace
      Did in the kirkyard glow,
      But 'twas hotter within the walls, I ween,
      When the lead dripped down below.

17    Up spake the swain young Engel
      That was so bold of mood:
      "Now let us slay our coursers
      And cool us in their blood!"

18    Up spake the little horse-boy
      That loved the steeds so free:
      "Slay rather the lady Malfred,
      More worthy of death is she!"

19    It was the swain young Engel
      That took her in his arm:
      "Thou art not worthy death, dear love,
      And none shall do thee harm!"

20    Oh, they've set her on a shining shield
      To lift her with glaive and spear,
      They've hoisted her out of the kirk-window,
      A-weeping full many a tear.

21    With many a tear young Malfred
      Did through the kirkyard fare,
      Blackened were all her garments
      And burnt her golden hair.

22    Sore wept the lady Malfred
      Came in the meads so green:
      "Now burneth the kirk of Our Lady,
      And a gallant swain therein!"

23    'Twas so soon thereafter,
      Ere harvest time was done,
      The lady sought her bower,
      And bore so fair a son.

24   Born was he at even,
    And christened the selfsame night,
    They gave him the name of his father,
    And fostered him while they might.

25   She fostered him seven winters,
    And ever these words did say:
    "My brother slew thy father,
    And this must thou learn today."

26   She fostered him for a winter,
    And for nine winters yet:
    "My brother slew thy father,
    And never shalt thou forget!"

27   And now her son, young Engel,
    Unto his kinsfolk saith:
    "Fain would I seek my father's foes
    All to avenge his death."

28   It was Gode Lovmand
    Sat drinking at the board,
    And in he came, the little page,
    So ready with his word.

29   "Now harken, Gode Lovmand,
    Ye may to flight be boun,
    Here come young Engel and his men
    By four ways to the town!

30   "Young Engel and his merry men
    Upon the town advance,
    And wrathful is his mood, I ween,
    So high he shakes his lance."

31     "To Thing and meeting-place afar
      My way I oft have won,
      But the name of this young Engel
      Was spoken of by none!"

32     It was Gode Lovmand
      That clapped his cheek so white:
      "Now canst thou give me counsel,
      Then counsel thou me aright!"

33     "And if thou ask me counsel
      This will I give to thee,
      Seek we our stone-built tower
      So long as need there be.

34     "The doors are all of the lead so grey,
      And the walls of marble stone,
      And a wondrous lot will be ours, I wot,
      If ever that hold be won!"

35     And now that stone-built tower
      On four sides they beset,
      And 'twas the swain young Engel
      That would be foremost yet.

36     It was Gode Lovmand
      From loophole looked below:
      "Who be ye that come hither
      To make so proud a show?"

37     Up spake the swain young Engel,
      Decked all in scarlet gear:
      "Engel the name men call me,
      Son of thy sister dear."

38  Up spake Gode Lovmand
    All with a darkening brow:
    "Of that needs little boasting,
    For a bastard bairn wert thou!"

39  "And was I born of love, goodsooth
    The better is my breed!
    And I have gold and liegemen bold,
    And many a gallant steed.

40  "And was I but a bastard bairn
    The fault was thine, I trow,
    Yet am I lord of lands so broad,
    With towers and holds enow."

41  It was the swain young Engel
    Would sooner fight than fly,
    He fired the stone-built tower
    Till the flames leapt to the sky.

42  It was the swain young Engel
    That would not ride his way,
    Till he saw the stone-built tower
    Lie low in ashes grey.

43  It was the swain young Engel
    That clapped his lily-white hands,
    When he saw his father's slayer
    Lie dead 'mid burning brands.

44  It was the swain young Engel
    Did home to hold repair,
    And met by the gate his mother
    Wrapped in her cloak of vair.

45   "Now greetings, greetings, mother dear,
Let all thy sorrow be!
My father's death have I avenged,
And bring the news to thee."

46   It was the lady Malfred
Wrung hands in dule and pain:
"I had one daily sorrow,
And thou hast made it twain!"

47   It was the swain young Engel
That turned and rode away:
"Strange are the ways of women,
And that for sooth I say!"

48   Now lieth Gode Lovmand
All under darksome mould,
But Engel serves before the King
For goods and red, red gold.

## 34
## THE AVENGING DAUGHTERS

1   Sister to sister said:
(For him who loveth me)
"Wouldst thou not fain be wed?"
She dwelleth under greenwood tree.

2   "None will I wed while I draw breath
Till I avenge my father's death."

3   "Thou speak'st an idle word,
We have neither mail nor sword."

4　"Here are rich franklins dwelling in town,
　　Swords will they lend us and byrnies brown."

5　When they came to Rosy-bower
　　They met Sir Erlend that selfsame hour.

6　"Sure, ye twain are bridegrooms bold,
　　A-riding forth some tryst to hold!"

7　"Now nay, we are not bridegrooms bold,
　　But truly we ride a tryst to hold."

8　"I rede ye ride by wood and wold
　　To two fair orphans with store of gold."

9　"If they have store of pelf
　　Why dost not woo thyself?"

10　"I would flee them rather
　　For I have slain their father,

11　"And I have slain their brother,
　　And I have beguiled their mother."

12　"Yea, thou hast slain father and brother,
　　But thou liest concerning our mother!"

13　So womanlike their swords they drew,
　　So manlike did they hack and hew.

14　They hewed Sir Erlend to pieces small
　　As the leaves that under the linden fall.

15　Sorely the maidens wept for dread
　　When to shrive their souls they sped.

16  All the penance they got for Sir Erlend's slaughter
    Was Fridays three on bread and water.


## 35
### TORBEN'S DAUGHTER

We were so many children small,
(On the lea)
So early did our father fall!
The day it dawneth and the dew it driveth so free.


1   On the Sunday evening they scoured both spear
                                        and sword,
    On the Monday morning wrathful they rode abroad.


2   When they rode by the northern shaw
    Sir Torben a-ploughing his field they saw.


3   "There goest thou, Sir Torben, so fair and so fine!
    Now pay me blood-money for kinsman mine."


4   "I will give thee farm and stead,
    I'll give thee my daughter, so fair a maid."


5   "We come not hither for house nor land,
    We come for the blood of thy red right hand!"


6   They hewed Sir Torben to pieces small
    As the leaves that under the linden fall.


7   They've ridden up to Sir Torben's stead,
    And there stood his daughter, so fair a maid.

8   She stood there as slim as a willow-wand,
      With a goblet of gold in either hand.

9   In mirth and sport with wine-cup flowing
      She pledged the slayer, all unknowing.

10  "Now had I guessed thee so mild of mood
      Ne'er would I have spilt thy father's blood."

11  "And if my father thou hast slain
      Then must I dree full bitter pain."

12  "Have I done ill to thee thereby,
      Thou shalt fare hereafter as well as I."

13  He set her up on his steed so true,
      He wrapped her in his cloak of blue.

14  They rode away o'er the darksome heather,
      Nevermore did she see her father.

NOTE: This ballad has a special interest as showing how closely the life of a Danish knight in early medieval times was linked up with that of his Old Norse ancestors. The type of homestead, the journeys to Thing and other public meetings, the tradings and marriage treaties, all followed the pattern so familiar in the sagas of Iceland. As for the farm work, Sir Torben's death at his own plough-stilts can be paralleled again and again. The popular idea of a Viking is that of a pirate on the high seas; it is not generally realized that his home life was that of a man on the land, or that his keen eye for loot in foreign countries frequently extended to their agricultural methods. The idea of a windmill, for instance, was first brought to Denmark by a Viking.

It is a fruitful study in national temperament to observe, on the one hand, in what spirit the Danish minstrels dealt with their borrowings from the Old Norse sagas, which may on the whole be called thoroughly medievalized in comparison with the Faroëse treatment of similar themes; and how, on the other hand, the true ancestral spirit survived in the whole method of existence.—Translator.

# 36

# SIR JOHN THE OUTLAW

1  Little Kirsteen was so fair a maid,
  (*Thou must flee from thy country, Sir John!*)
  And many a wooer his courtesy paid.
  *To foreign land where many so proud a lord must dwell.*

2  Sir Peter of Engelsholm her favour did crave,
  And all his twelve brethren gallant and brave.

3  Sir John the rich she loved, and he
  Was fit her worthy mate to be.

4  Sir John prepared his bridal feast,
  The King of Danes must be his guest.

5  Sir Peter of Engelsholm fared to his hold,
  With all his twelve brethren gallant and bold.

6  To her foster-mother the maid did say:
  "Now when to the hall shall I take my way?"

7  "And when thou enterest into the hall,
  Then wear not thy golden adornments all.

8  "Eyes thou hast like a taper's sheen,
  Take heed lest their light too far be seen."

9  Straight did little Kirsteen prepare
  To deck herself in her garments rare.

10  She decked herself in a silken sark,
  That was of nine maidens the handiwork.

11    *She decked herself in a mantle of blue,*
       *At every seam the red gold shone through.*

12    *Ring after ring did Kirsteen don,*
       *On every finger they shimmered and shone.*

13    *With ribbons of silk and golden crown*
       *She decked her tresses that hung adown.*

14    *Two goblets she took of the silver sheen,*
       *And into the hall went little Kirsteen.*

15    *Sir Peter poured the red, red wine:*
       *"Now pledge me, thou maiden fair and fine!"*

16    *"Now nay, I will not drink with thee*
       *Until Sir John hath bidden me."*

17    *"A fair young bridegroom hast thou found,*
       *But fairer by far is my father's hound.*

18    *"Thou hast a bridegroom gallant and rich,*
       *My father hath bred a handsomer bitch!"*

19    *Little Kirsteen wrung her hands for woe,*
       *And fast o'er her cheeks did her salt tears flow.*

20    *Over the board bent her bridegroom strong:*
       *"Say, little Kirsteen, who doth thee wrong?"*

21    *"Sir Peter saith, fair may my bridegroom be,*
       *But his father's hound is better than he."*

22    *O'er the board he sprang when that word was said,*
       *Down on the floor ran the wine so red.*

23 His trusty sword he drew full fain,
  And hewed Sir Peter in pieces twain.

24 Sir John put up his sword by his side:
  "Now, little Kirsteen, wilt with me ride?"

25 Fleet was his courser and fine, I trow,
  He set up the maid on his saddlebow.

## 37
## LOVEL AND JOHN

Lo now I bid ye, my merry men all,
Put your armour on,[1]
Bind on your helms of the burning gold,
And follow Sir John!

1 Sir Peter home from the Thing did fare,
  (Put your armour on)
  Little Kirsteen came forth to greet him there,
  And ask after John.

2 "Welcome, dear father, home from the Thing!
  (Put your armour on)
  Tell me what tidings hast thou to bring?"
  What tidings of John?

3 "These are the tidings I have for thee,
  (Put your armour on)
  That young Sir Lovel thy bridegroom shall be."
  And not Sir John.

[1] Or: Be ye well boun—I være vel bon.

· 208 ·

4　"And must young Sir Lovel my bridegroom be,
　　(Put your armour on)
　　Sorrow and care shall he have with me!"
　　While liveth Sir John.

5　Sir Lovel to bridal feast doth speed,
　　(Put your armour on)
　　Sir John hath bidden them shoe his steed.
　　"I go also," says John.

6　Sir John he rode to the blithe bridale,
　　(Put your armour on)
　　High on his horse in his coat of mail.
　　"I come!" said John.

7　When dew fell fast and eve was sped
　　(Put your armour on)
　　The bride must go to the bridal bed.
　　"I go with her!" said John.

8　The bride they led to the bridal bower,
　　(Put your armour on)
　　Sir John himself bore the torch before.
　　"I'm first!" says John.

9　Sir John he locked the door aright,
　　(Put your armour on)
　　"Now bid Sir Lovel a gay goodnight!"
　　All from Sir John.

10　Straight to Sir Lovel the news they cried:
　　(Put your armour on)
　　"Sir John doth sleep with thy fair young bride!"
　　That did Sir John.

11    All in the morning when dawn was grey,
    (Put your armour on)
    To the King Sir Lovel did hasten away,
    "I go with thee," said John.

12    "My Liege, my Liege, now hark and hear!
    (Put your armour on)
    I've a tale of woe for thy gracious ear."
    "Of me!" said John.

13    "A fair young maid I thought to wed,
    (Put your armour on)
    But another knight took the bride to bed!"
    " 'Twas I," said John.

14    "Now since the maid to ye both is so dear,
    (Put your armour on)
    For her sweet sake ye shall break a spear."
    "I shall win!" says John.

15    When the first course they rode so free,
    (Put your armour on)
    Sir Lovel's charger fell on his knee.
    "Hold up!" said John.

16    But when they rode the course again,
    (Put your armour on)
    Sir Lovel's neck was broken in twain.
    "Lie there!" said John.

17    She clapped her hands, did the dainty dame:
    (Put your armour on)
    "Ne'er did I see so gladsome a game!"
    So he won, Sir John.
    Bind on your helms of the burning gold,
    And follow Sir John!

# 38

# THE MAIDEN'S MORNING-DREAM

1 *To the bower went Riseli,*
  *(But a Frankish mile away)*
  *To wake the damsels bright of blee.*
  *When the Wends are marching to the castle.*

2 With honour and praise did the damsels wake,
  But for Vesselil's shoulders a rod did she take.

3 "If thou dost lie and sleep so late
  Never a knight wilt thou win for mate!"

4 "Oh, I gain more good from my morning-dream
  Than other maids from their silken seam.

5 "Methought I was but a wild-duck light,
  To the land of the Wends I took my flight.

6 "So wide my wings were spanned
  They shaded lea and land.

7 "I sat me down on a linden-root,
  And the branches bowed to touch my foot."

8 "Now heed, dear niece, what I ask of thee,
  Shalt give thy morning-dream to me!

9 "Now give to me thy morning-dream,
  And I'll give thee all my summer's seam."

10 "Oh, keep to thyself thy summer's seam!
  Far dearer to me is my morning-dream."

11 Now scarcely had they done debate
   When the King of the Wends rode up to the gate.

12 The King of the Wends rode up to the door,
   Riseli went and stood before.

13 "Welcome, noble Lord of mine!
   Mead I'll pour for thee and wine."

14 "I reck nothing of mead nor wine,
   I fain would see Vesselil, niece of thine."

15 "But five years old is Vesselil,
   She bides with her foster-mother still."

16 "And if she were but three years old,
   These eyes the maiden must behold."

17 "My other maidens sew with a will,
   But ne'er of sleep can she have her fill."

18 Into the hall the King she led,
   And forth to seek her niece she sped.

19 Her hair she tore, her face she struck:
   "Woe worth thee, wretch, for thy good luck!

20 "Now do thou on thy garments bright,
   For thou shalt see the King ere night."

21 In at the door did Vesselil fare,
   And it seemed as the sun shone in with her.

22 "Oh, ne'er a damsel did I behold
   Was so well-grown for five years old!"

23    *He kissed her on her cheek so white,*
      *He called her love and heart's delight.*

24    *"My word I give thee, sweet Vesselil,*
      *Shalt sleep as long as thou hast a will!"*

25    *They clad her all in scarlet weed,*
      *They lifted her on the good grey steed,*

26    *On her flowing hair a crown of gold,*
      *And so Vesselil rode away from the hold.*

## 39

## THE GAME OF DICE

1    *"Now lithe and list, thou handsome squire,*
      *And play at dice with me!"*
      *"Nay, ne'er have I the red, red gold*
      *To wager here with thee."*
      *Because they played and threw the dice of gold.*

2    *"Now wager thou thy goodly hat*
      *Although it be of grey.*
      *And I will risk my snood of pearl,*
      *Shalt take it an thou may!"*

3    *When first the dice all golden*
      *Upon the board did run,*
      *The youth he lost his wager,*
      *And glad the damsel won.*

4  "Now lithe and list, thou handsome squire,
   And play at dice with me!"
   "Nay, ne'er have I the red, red gold
   To wager here with thee."

5  "Now wager thou thy kirtle,
   Though it be wadmal grey,
   And I will risk my golden crown,
   Shalt take it an thou may!"

6  When next the dice all golden
   Upon the board did run,
   The youth he lost his wager,
   And glad the maiden won.

7  "Now lithe and list, thou handsome squire,
   And play at dice with me!"
   "Nay, ne'er have I the red, red gold
   To wager here with thee."

8  "Thy hosen shalt thou wager,
   And shoon shalt wager both,
   And I will risk mine honour
   All with my plighted troth."

9  When next the dice all golden
   Upon the board were cast,
   The youth he won his wager,
   And sad the damsel lost.

10 "Now heed, thou little horse-boy,
   And get thee gone from me,
   My knife adorned with silver
   That will I give to thee."

11   "Thy knife adorned with silver
     I'll take whenas I may,
     But I will have the maiden
     I won with dice at play."

12   "Now hark, thou little horse-boy,
     And get thee gone from me,
     Seven silk-sewn kirtles
     All will I give to thee."

13   "Thy seven silk-sewn kirtles
     I'll take whenas I may,
     But I will have the maiden
     I won with dice at play."

14   "Now hear, thou little horse-boy,
     And get thee gone from me,
     A white steed and saddle
     I'll freely give to thee."

15   "White steed and saddle
     I'll take whene'er I may,
     But I will have the maiden
     I won with dice at play."

16   "Now hark, thou little horse-boy,
     And get thee gone from me,
     My hold and my castle
     Those will I give to thee."

17   "Thy hold and thy castle
     I'll take them when I may,
     But I will have the maiden
     I won with dice at play."

18  The damsel sought her bower
    And there her locks arrayed:
    "Now for the match that I must make
    God help me, luckless maid!"

19  All with his sword a-playing,
    The youth he up and spake:
    "Oh, better far than thy deserts
    The marriage thou shalt make!

20  "For I am ne'er a horse-boy
    Although it be thy word,
    My father is the noblest King
    That ever walked abroad!"

21  "And is thy sire the noblest King
    That ever walked abroad,
    Then shalt thou have mine honour
    All with my plighted word!"

## 40
## THE MAIDEN AT THE THING

1  Young was Inge the maid,
   (In the green grove)
   Yet she rode to the Thing unafraid,
   To ride to the maiden's bower.

2  Up and spake to his knights the King:
   "I spy a maiden that rides to the Thing!"

3  The little foot-page made answer then:
   "Be sure she comes hither to gaze on the men!

4   "But her kirtle is over strait and short
     Or her mantle o'er-full for the mode at Court."

5   For all that the maiden was modest and meek
     Full well she heard what the page did speak.

6   "And if I knew no trouble and tene
     I had been better at home, I ween.

7   "And did I not know mine errand well
     I had done better at home to dwell.

8   "But my kirtle is neither strait nor short,
     And my mantle is shaped for the mode at Court.

9   "Thou gracious King, I pray thee heed
     And hear the cause I come to plead.

10   "Only a little child was I
     When I saw my mother die.

11   "My father set me on his knee
     Gold and goods to share with me.

12   "But he died or ever two years were done,
     And I must rule my lands alone.

13   "In there came mine uncles three,
     All my goods they waste from me.

14   "The mown they mar, the sown they spoil,
     Both man and maid they lure from toil.

15   "Oxen and kine they drive abroad,
     They wile my serving-men from my board.

16    "And ere I'll live longer without relief
      I'll give thee my father's lands in fief."

17    "Thy gift I take, thy suit is sped,
      Which knight of mine art fain to wed?"

18    "And may I choose since my suit is sped,
      'Tis Sir Ove Stison I fain would wed."

19    "Stand up now, Sir Ove, and answer so free,
      Here is a maiden would marry thee!"

20    Up stood Sir Ove and answered so free:
      "Fair damsel, nought wilt thou win from me!

21    "Better can I tie a silken band
      Than play the farmer on lea and land.

22    "Better can I ride with hawk and hound
      Than drive the plough through the heavy ground."

23    "Oh, sit in my waggon all by me,
      So good a farmer I'll make of thee!

24    "Take plough in hand, lay the furrow featly,
      Take corn in hand and scatter it meetly,

25    "And let the harrow after go,
      Thou'lt make a goodly farmer so.

26    "Be no niggard with meat and drink at board,
      And the world will call thee a right good lord."

27    To laugh and be merry men were not loth
      When Sir Ove plighted the maid his troth.

28  All alone to the Thing she hied,
    But the King he led her home again with all
                                his men beside.

## 41
## TIT FOR TAT

1  So merry the knights sat drinking
   All at the board of the Queen,
   Gay went the word amongst them,
   With many a jest between.
   Under the linden-tree, there will I bide.

2  Oh, little they talked of the kirk,
   And less they talked of the cloister,
   But much they talked of the ladies
   That had fair maids to foster.

3  "I will wed a maiden
   That can both broider and sew,
   I will not wed a maiden
   Goes gadding to and fro.

4  "I will have a maiden
   That well can spread the board,
   I will not have a maiden
   Too ready with her word."

5  Still sat all the maidens
   And never a word replied,
   All but the smallest maiden
   That stood the board beside.

6   "An I so old were waxen
    That I might wedded be,
    So help me God in heaven
    I would not ask for thee!

7   "I must sit in the high-loft,
    And well may I broider and sew!
    Thou mayst bestride thy courser,
    A-gadding in town to go.

8   "I must sit in the high-loft,
    And well may I spread my board!
    Thou to the Thing canst betake thee,
    To waste fully many a word.

9   "I must sit in the high-loft,
    My household gear to guide,
    Whilst thou mayst talk and never think
    With lordlings by thy side."

10   Up stood young Sir Peter,
    So ready with his tongue:
    "Now have I found the selfsame maid
    That I have sought so long!"

11   Oh, merry that hour in ladies' bower,
    So rare a jest to see!
    The Queen she gave the maid away,
    Sir Peter's bride to be.

# 42

# THE WOUNDED MAIDEN

1   *They danced all on the wold,*
    *(Now tread ye high, my lordlings all!)*
    *There danced the knights so bold.*
    *The maidens must be honoured in the dance.*

2   *There danced the knights in scarlet sheen,*
    *There danced the fair maiden, little Kirsteen.*

3   *There danced the knights of pride*
    *With swords drawn by their side.*

4   *Out it slid, the shining brand,*
    *And wounded the maid in her lily-white hand.*

5   *It wounded her in her five fingers so small,*
    *Ne'er could she broider red gold withal.*

6   *In all her ten fingers it wounded her so*
    *That never again could she shape nor sew.*

7   *While the blood ran down from her wounds so sore,*
    *She went to stand the King before.*

8   *"Now tell me, Kirsteen, daughter mine,*
    *Why the blood runs down o'er thy scarlet fine?"*

9   *"Into the bower I sped*
    *To make ready my brother's bed.*

10   *"And on the wall, I ween.*
    *There hung his sword so keen.*

11   "And when I drew the shining brand
   It wounded me in my lily-white hand.

12   "All my ten fingers it wounded so sore
   That ne'er shall I broider with red gold more."

13   "Now who for thee shall the red gold lay,
   Or tie up thy sleeves with ribbons so gay?"

14   "My sister shall lay the gold so free,
   My mother tie up my sleeves for me."

15   Sir Peter stood behind the board,
   And harkened to Kirsteen's every word.

16   He kissed her on her cheek so white:
   "Wilt be my love and heart's delight?

17   "My sister shall lay the gold so free,
   My maidens tie up thy sleeves for thee.

18   "My maidens shall tie up thy ribbons so gay,
   And I'll lead thy courser the best that I may."

19   Up spake the King in scarlet red:
   "How canst thou love her, this maimèd maid?"

20   " 'Tis by my fault the mischance befell,
   And therefore I love the maiden well!"

21   He plighted her troth with his lily-white hand,
   And led her away to a far-off land.

## 43
## SIR PETER'S HARP

1   To little Kirsteen spake Sir Peter the knight:
"Wilt be my love and heart's delight?"
*(Ladies and maidens, why wake ye us from slumber?)*

2   "Right gladly thy true-love would I be
Could I know thou wouldst not cozen me."

3   "May we be cozened by Christ the Lord
If we cozen each other in deed or word!

4   "May we fall to Hell from the Bridge of Dread
If false to the other, living or dead!"

5   Together they lay so late at e'en
When Sir Peter went from little Kirsteen.

6   She searched and sought with mournful mind,
But never Sir Peter could she find.

7   Unto his bed went the maiden fair,
And found his harp a-hanging there.

8   "Wist I my love thou wouldst not scorn,
Thy harp with gold would I adorn.

9   "Five rings that on my fingers shine
I'd use to deck this harp of thine!"

10   On high-loft stair Sir Peter stayed,
And heard what she spake, the mournful maid.

11     And when he heard, to himself said he:
        "Great shame it were to cozen thee!

12     "As my leman I deemed thou shouldst lead thy life,
        But I will make thee my wedded wife."

13     All praise to Sir Peter, so true a knight,
        That led her with honour to bridal bright.

NOTE: Bridge of Dread (Old Norse Gjallarbro), leading to the realms of the departed, was conceived in the Middle Ages as the place of judgment, whence the wicked were cast into Hell, and the good passed into Heaven.

## 44
### EBBE SKAMMELSON

1     Skammel he dwells up North in Ty,
        And Skammel is rich and gay,
        Five sons hath he both fair and tall,
        But two went an evil way.
        And therefore treads Ebbe Skammelson so wild
                              a way alone.

2     Ebbe doth serve for fame and fee
        The royal court within,
        Whilst Peter his brother bides at home,
        And strives his bride to win.

3     "Dost sit so still, proud Adelus,
        And broider my brother's gear?
        Sir Ebbe serves in the royal court
        And scorns thee, nor holds thee dear!"

4   "Right well do I know him, Ebbe,
     And a steadfast mind hath he,
     And scorns he never a maiden proud,
     The less hath he scorn for me."

5   "Now plight me thy troth, proud Adelus,
     And let us twain be wed,
     For true are the tidings I bring thee,
     That Ebbe my brother is dead."

6   All on the selfsame evening
     They drank to the plighted pair,
     All on the Monday thereafter
     To bridal feast did fare.

7   It was Ebbe Skammelson
     At midnight did awake,
     And he called to the swain that nearest lay,
     And of his dream he spake.

8   "Methought that o'er my tower of stone
     The flames shone far and wide,
     And Peter my brother burned therein
     Beside my beauteous bride."

9   "Didst dream that o'er thy tower of stone
     The leaping lowe shone red,
     Then know that Peter thy brother
     Thy beauteous bride doth wed."

10  It was Ebbe Skammelson
     That girded on his sword,
     And leave he won ere an hour was run
     In haste to ride abroad.

11  *It was Ebbe Skammelson*
    *That paused not on his way,*
    *He came to his father's castle*
    *All on the bridal day.*

12  Forth they fared, his sisters twain,
    With golden cup in hand:
    "Now welcome, Ebbe, welcome
    Home to our father's land!"

13  "Now lithe and listen, my sisters twain,
    And let the truth be told!
    Say wherefore this goodly company
    Have gathered home to hold?"

14  Up spake his youngest sister,
    For needs must the words be said:
    "Behold, 'tis Peter thy brother
    Must to thy love be wed."

15  To the one he has given a brooch for her breast,
    To the other a ring for her hand:
    "Oh, I brought them both to mine own true-love
    All from a far-off land!"

16  The one has bidden him bide at home,
    The other to ride again:
    "For an thou tarry this night, be sure
    'Twill work us dule and pain!"

17  Now Ebbe turned his courser's head
    Forth from the hold to ride,
    But his mother seized on his bridle-rein
    And begged him at home to bide.

18 His mother to the highest place
Hath borne him cushion and chair,
His father has given him a goblet of gold
To pledge the bridal pair.

19 He pledged them in the red, red wine,
And in the mead so brown,
But when he gazed upon the bride
Full fast his tears ran down.

20 Now when the dew was falling,
And even was well-nigh sped,
Up she rose, the beauteous bride,
To seek the bridal bed.

21 They followed her, the bridal train,
Up to the chamber door,
And first went Ebbe Skammelson
To bear the torch before.

22 He led her to door of bridal bower
That bride so bright of blee:
"Hast thou forgot, proud Adelus,
The troth thou didst plight to me?"

23 "The troth I swore in times of yore
To thy brother is given away,
But I'll love thee e'en as a mother mild
Unto my dying day."

24 "I wooed thee not for a mother,
I wooed thee for my wife,
For this shall Peter Skammelson
Yield up to me his life!

25 "Now fly with me, proud Adelus,
 Far from this land we'll fare,
 For I will slay that traitor false,
 And doom for thee will dare."

26 "And wilt thou strike thy brother down,
 Ne'er will I be thine, I vow,
 And thou shalt sorrow thyself to death
 Like lone bird on the bough."

27 It was Ebbe Skammelson
 That drew his brand so brown,
 It was the bride, proud Adelus,
 That he to earth struck down.

28 Now he has hidden the blood-stained brand
 Beneath his cloak of pall,
 And sought out Peter Skammelson
 Sat drinking in the hall.

29 "Now harken, Peter Skammelson,
 A laggard art thou to wed!
 The bride is longing after thee
 Now in the bridal bed."

30 It was Peter Skammelson
 Spake up with mickle spite:
 "My leave thou hast with right good-will
 To sleep by the bride tonight!"

31 It was Ebbe Skammelson
 That drew his brand so brown,
 It was Peter his brother
 That he to earth struck down.

32    *Oh, sore has he wounded his father,*
      *And struck off his mother's hand,*
      *And so roams Ebbe Skammelson*
      *The wild ways of the land.*

NOTE: Weddings were always celebrated after ancestral tradition with a great feast, lasting several days, and attended by a multitude of relations and friends. The church service, which was general among the upper classes, played quite a subordinate part. The climax of the feast, and what gave lawful validity to the marriage, was the leading, first of the bride and then of the bridegroom, to the bridal bed. The procession went from the hall, or "stone-hall," where the festivities took place, along the gallery to the chamber in the "high-loft" which was to serve as bridal bower. Some knight, usually a near relative, preceded the bride with a torch, partly to light her, partly as a defence against evil spirits in this decisive moment of her life. This walk to the bridal bower afforded the best opportunity of speaking with the bride unperceived.

## 45
## SIR PETER'S LEMAN

1    *Sir Peter and Kirsteen sat over the board,*
      *(While summer doth blow)*
      *They spake so many a jesting word.*
      *But day is dawning all in the East.*

2    *"Now tell me, Sir Peter, and do not fail,*
      *When shall we drink thy blithe bridale?"*

3    *"Oh, so far hence is my bridal gay*
      *No lady thither can find the way."*

4    *"And were it two hundred miles or more,*
      *Yet would I ride to that castle door!"*

5    *"And wilt thou to the bridal come,*
      *Then leave my golden gifts at home."*

6　　"And may I not bear them and fear no blame?
　　　Thou didst not bestow them for my shame!"

7　　She wrapped herself in the scarlet fine,
　　　She went to the high-loft and poured the wine.

8　　Up spake the bride to her serving-maid:
　　　"What lady now poureth the wine so red?"

9　　The serving-maid up and spake so free:
　　　"Sir Peter's light-o'-love is she."

10　 "And is she his love, that gay ladye,
　　　Why rideth he hither to wed with me?"

11　 They feasted till far the night was sped,
　　　And the bride must go to the bridal bed.

12　 To bridal bed the bride must fare,
　　　And the bridal torch did young Kirsteen bear.

13　 The sheets of silk o'er the bed she drew:
　　　"There lies the swain I loved so true!"

14　 Young Kirsteen locked the door with speed
　　　And the fire she set to roof and reed.

15　 The fire she set and did not stay,
　　　And most o'er the place where Sir Peter lay.

16　 Sir Peter waked not in bridal bed
　　　Till the flames in his young bride's hair shone red.

17　 "Kirsteen, Kirsteen, spare thou me!
　　　In time to come I'll be good to thee."

18   Loud she laughed then, little Kirsteen:
     "Right well wilt thou keep thy word, I ween!"

19   Greater than all was his hurt and harm,
     That the bride must burn in the bridegroom's arm.

20   All must die in that woeful hour—
     Fifteen maidens that lay in the bower.

21   And in that hour so sore
     Died thirty knights and more.

## 46
# VALRAVEN AND THE DANISH KING

1   Valraven rode up by land and lea,
     He wooed young Gerborg so fair to see.
     So far as the green leaves fall.

2   Now word through the land went near and far
     That all the King's lieges must go to war.

3   Young Gerborg out of the gate did spy,
     And counted the King's men a-riding by.

4   Sir Iver Helt rode first, I ween,
     And next the King himself was seen.

5   Valraven the rich the next did fare,
     He took young Gerborg and kissed her there.

6   Down to the strand they bore
     Anchor and sail and oar.

7 The King's men steered their smacks from land,
  Little Gerborg swooned on the snow-white sand.

8 So moodily Raven went aboard,
  Three days he sat and spake never a word.

9 Up spake the King in the bows that stood:
  "Now wherefore is Raven so heavy of mood?

10 "Now blow for sport on thy horn of gold,
  Young Gerborg thou never shalt have and hold!"

11 Up spake the King an ireful word:
  "Now cast ye Valraven overboard!"

12 Long stood the King, and long watched he
  How Valraven sank down to the depths of the sea.

13 The King's men laid their smacks to land,
  The King trod first on the snow-white sand.

14 Young Gerborg stood by the gate to spy,
  And counted the King's men a-riding by.

15 By one, by two, the King's men passed,
  But she saw not Valraven first nor last.

16 "Welcome, ye King's men, home to the haven!
  But where is my true-love, the bold Valraven?"

17 "Valraven the rich in foray hath died,
  And thou, young Gerborg, shalt be my bride."

18 "And if Valraven in foray hath died,
  Ne'er will his true-love be thy bride!"

19     Of the red, red gold she took her store,
And entered the cloister for evermore.


## 47
## SIR VERNER'S ESCAPE

1     The ladies sat in Lindholm hold
While the knights were a-drinking so blithe and bold:
Ne'er could the ladies keep so rich a captive.

2     The knights sat a-drinking, so merry were they,
That heard Sir Verner in dungeon that lay.

3     Sir Verner he bore up a burden of power,
And that heard the ladies aloft in the bower.

4     Fair Ingeborg wakened and thus did she say:
"Which one of my maidens harpeth so gay?"

5     "Nay, none of thy maidens toucheth the strings,
Sir Verner it is that so merrily sings."

6     Fair Ingeborg spake to her pages three:
"Now bid ye Sir Verner come hither to me!"

7     In came Sir Verner and stood by the board:
"What wilt thou, lady Ingeborg, why sen'st thou me
word?"

8     "And wilt thou to my wish give ear,
A song of love I fain would hear!"

9     "Ne'er have I learnt of love a lay,
I'll sing thee another the best that I may."

10  Sir Verner he bore up a burden of power,
    Till they slumbered, the ladies that sat in the bower.

11  Ladies and lasses, they slept like the dead,
    Fair Ingeborg slept where the scarlet was spread.

12  He spied in the corners both one and all,
    Till the keys he found that hung on the wall.

13  Both small and great, he tried them o'er,
    Till he found the key of the castle door.

14  Such faith with the ladies kept the good knight
    That he hung up the keys in all men's sight.

15  And when to the open town he drew,
    He bore up a burden and sang anew.

16  So gaily he flourished his hat on high:
    "Goodnight to fair Ingeborg, that wish I!

17  "She bade me sing, I bless her therefore,
    Ne'er shall I be her captive more.

18  "I had proffered a bushel of gold in vain,
    And now not a penny shall Ingeborg gain!"

## 48
## KING ERIK AND THE
## SCORNFUL MAID

1   So rich and proud a damsel
    Dwells southward in our land,
    She will not dance with a poor young squire,
    Nor touch his horny hand.
    Damsel, great is thy favour! I thank thee right courteously.

2    She will not dance with a poor young squire,
      Nor touch his horny hand:
      She's tied up her sleeves with ribbons of silk
      And many a golden band.

3    It was young King Erik
      Bade saddle his steed so free:
      "We will fare to the Southland,
      And visit this proud ladye!"

4    It was young King Erik
      That forth to dance did stand,
      He's taken that dainty damsel
      All by her lily-white hand.

5    "Now nay, I will not dance with thee,
      Too hard are thy hands indeed!
      Thou hast been raising of fences,
      Or forking of hay in the mead."

6    "Oh, yestre'en I played at a bridal feast
      A-tilting with knights so tall,
      And hard is my hand with grasping the brand
      That won me the prize from all!"

7    "And wert thou yestre'en at a bridal feast,
      There tilted no knights so tall;
      Wert loading thy father's wain with muck,
      And deeper in dirt than all!

8    "Ill do thy garments become thee,
      Thy hosen are rent at the knee,
      Thy master hath given thee holiday,
      So thou must ride speedilie!"

9   "Are there no tailors, women or men,
    Here in this town of thine,
    Can cut me clothes of the scarlet cloth,
    And sew them with silk so fine?"

10  "Tailors there are, both women and men,
    Here in this town of mine,
    Can cut thee breeches of wadmal coarse,
    And sew them with hempen twine."

11  "Now lithe and listen, thou haughty maid,
    Wilt yield thy love to me?
    All the gold that in Denmark lies
    Thy portion it shall be."

12  "All the gold that in Denmark lies
    Is held in strong duresse.
    Get thee gone and patch thy shoon!
    Thy feet will ache the less."

13  Up spake the lady's serving-maid
    As boldly as she might:
    "And 'tis the young King Erik
    That thou dost scorn and spite!"

14  "And if 'tis young King Erik
    That I have scorned and shent,
    Methinks I have done an evil deed,
    And sore do I repent.

15  "All in the midst of my father's garth
    There standeth a linden green,
    And many a knight and lady bright
    Hold tryst beneath unseen."

16   "Yea, all in the midst of thy father's garth
There standeth a linden green,
And many a thief and rascal wight
Hold tryst beneath unseen!"

49

SONG OF THE FALCON

1   I know where stands a linden
With many a flower,
That sheltereth all from frost and snow
In wintry hour.
That causeth she alone I bear within my heart.

2   Therein the throstle and nightingale
Do sing their lay
And therein singeth the little bird
Sweeter than they.

3   But still I know the falcon grey
Buildeth beside,
The little birds to scare away
In all his pride.

4   And were it not for the falcon's rage
(Trust what I tell)
All in the linden I'd build my nest
Ever to dwell.

5   It is no linden-tree so green
Whereof ye hear,
It is the courteous maiden
I love so dear.

# BALLADS OF SATIRE

# 50

# THE LAST RESORT

1   The maiden and the lither lad
    They spake in jest so free:
    (For thee I long so sore)
    "How wilt thou find me meat and drink
    If I should wed with thee?"
    Alas, for the green leaves all are fallen.

2   "How wilt thou find me meat and drink
    That hast no store of pelf?"
    "Oh, I will get both line and net
    And catch thee fish myself."

3   "How wilt thou find me meat and drink
    If fish and all should fail?"
    "Then I will thresh the farmer's corn
    All with my trusty flail."

4   "How wilt thou find me meat and drink
    If farmer hath no corn?"
    "Then will I be a shepherd-boy
    And gaily wind my horn."

5   "How wilt thou find me meat and drink
    If sheep are none to see?"
    "Then will I take mine axe in hand
    And fell the tallest tree."

6    "How wilt thou find me meat and drink
     If axe refuse to bite?"
     "Oh, then I'll be a miller,
     And grind the flour so white."

7    "How wilt thou find me meat and drink
     If floods o'erwhelm the weir?"
     "Why then I'll be a captain bold
     And ride with sword and spear."

8    "How wilt thou find me meat and drink
     If thou art turned away?"
     "Then will I take a potter's wheel,
     To fashion pots of clay."

9    "How wilt thou find me meat and drink
     When frost the clay doth freeze?"
     "Oh, then a goldsmith will I be,
     The ladies fair to please."

10   "And when the ladies' gold is spent
     How wilt thou feed me full?"
     "Oh, then I'll be a hatter,
     And shape out hats of wool."

11   "If none will buy thy wares of thee
     How shall my food be found?"
     "Oh, by the hand I'll take thee then
     To run the land around."

12   "How wilt thou find me meat and drink
     If all the land lies bare?"
     "The devil may take thee then, good sooth,
     And I will not seek thee there!"

13 "How wilt thou find me meat and drink
   If the devil says No to me?"
   "Then will I take both shovel and spade,
   And deep I'll bury thee."

14 "How wilt thou find me meat and drink
   If still I will not lie?"
   "Then together we'll bide whate'er betide
   Until the day we die!"

## 51
## THE BRIDE OF RIBE

1 There dwelt a man in Ribe town
   So rich and full of pride,
   He gave his daughter a silken sark
   Was fifteen fathoms wide.
   She swept the dew from all the earth.

2 And fifteen tailors sewed the sark
   That were of great renown,
   And some dwelt up in Ribe
   If they dwelt not in Ribe town.

3 And fifteen maids of good repute
   That sark must wash and dry,
   And some got cramp in every limb,
   While some lay down to die.

4 And fifteen were the carpenters
   That hung it out to air,
   Some broke their arms and some their legs,
   And some lay sick a year.

5   And now the bride went forth to kirk
    All wrapped in cloak of skin,
    Full fifteen fathom must they unfurl
    Ere she could enter in.

6   And when she entered in the kirk
    Loud did she rage and roar,
    She struck adown the holy cross
    That stood therein of yore.

7   A penny was all the bridal-fee
    That she in pouch did find,
    She threw one deacon off his legs,
    And struck another blind.

8   Before the altar stood the priest,
    And by Saint Knud he cried:
    "No bridal can be hallowed here
    Till ye remove the bride!"

9   With nose in air that maiden fair
    From kirk returned again,
    And all the kine in field that fed
    Went galloping home again.

10  And when she sat at bridal feast
    She laughed both loud and high:
    "A penny we spent and to kirk we went,
    As nobody can deny!"

DANISH BALLADS
VOLUME II

——————

MISCELLANEOUS BALLADS

# RIBOLD AND GOLDBORG

1    "Now Goldborg, hear what I ask of thee,
     Wilt fly from thy father's hold with me?"
     When love was moving them.

2    "How should I fly from his hold with thee
     When so many keep ward over me?

3    "Wards me my father, and wards me my mother
     Wards me my sister, and wards me my brother.

4    "My true-love wards me morn and eve,
     Most of all for him I grieve."

5    "If all thy kin ward thee by wood and by wold,
     What thou hast promised, that shalt thou hold."

6    A steed had he both true and tried,
     He set her on the croup to ride.

7    As they went o'er the wold
     They met the Baron bold.

8    "Well met, thou gallant knight!
     Whence hast thou stolen the damsel bright?"

9    "My sister sick is she,
     That rides from cloister home with me."

10   "Untrue the tale thou hast to tell!
     Goldborg, Goldborg, I know thee right well."

11   "My scarlet cloak shall be thine, I wis,
     If thou tell my father no news of this."

12   "Mayst keep thy scarlet cloak, I wis,
     News to thy father I'll bear of this.

13   "Here sitst thou, Sir King, o'er the red, red wine,
     But Ribold's away with daughter thine!"

14   Loud cried the King through bower and hall:
     "Up, my men, with weapons all!"

15   Goldborg over her shoulder spied:
     "My father cometh, now what shall betide?"

16   "Let not thy lily hand disdain
     To hold my courser's bridle-rein.

17   "And though my blood run red,
     My name must not be said.

18   "Yea, though thou see me fall,
     My name thou must not call!"

19   Now first he struck down in mire and mould
     Her seven brethren with hair of gold,

20   And next o'erthrew in mould and mire
     Her six bold kinsmen and her sire.

21   "Ribold, Ribold, stay thy sword,
     Stay it, O God and Christ the Lord!

22   "Spare thou the youngest I love so well,
     That he may to our mother the tidings tell."

23   E'en as she spake the fatal word
     Wounded was he with many a sword.

24   His blade in sheath the knight bestowed:
     "Now 'tis time to take the road."

25   They rode by holt and heath,
     And he was still as death.

26   "Tell, thou who wert so gay at morn,
     Why thy mood is all forlorn?"

27   "God pity thee, all unknowing thou art!
     Thy brother's sword pierced near my heart."

28   And as they rode, ere close of day,
     They met his brother by the way.

29   "Welcome, brother dear to me!
     Whence hast thou lifted that fair ladye?"

30   "Hither, brother, draw thou near,
     To thee I give my lady dear."

31   "Never will I whilst I live
     My troth unto two brethren give!"

32   Ribold lay dead ere night was done,
     And Goldborg ere uprose the sun.

# SIR LUNO AND THE MERMAID

1    Sir Luno built him a ship so great
That ne'er on sea did sail its mate.
So they gained their red, red gold all up in Greenland.

2    A ship so great
That ne'er on sea did sail its mate.
On either side the red gold shone,
And Our Lady's name was written thereon.

3    The red gold shone,
Our Lady's name was written thereon.
On stem and stern did the red gold flame,
And thereon was written Our Saviour's name.

4    Did the red gold flame,
And thereon was written Our Saviour's name.
Of silk so fine the sails were spread,
And pied with stripes of blue and red.

5    The sails were spread,
And pied with stripes of blue and red.
The yards were all of silver white,
And with red gold the mast was dight.

6    Of silver white,
And with red gold the mast was dight.
Down to the strand they bore
Both anchor stout and oar.

7    They bore
      Both anchor stout and oar.
      Swiftly Sir Luno sailed the sea,
      And there met a Mermaid, and grim was she.

8    Sailed the sea,
      And there met a Mermaid, and grim was she.
      "Turn back now, Sir Luno, and get thee gone,
      Or thy ship will I straightway change to stone!

9    "Get thee gone,
      Or thy ship will I straightway change to stone!"
      "Ne'er shalt thou live to see the day
      When for a Mermaid I turned from my way.

10   "To see the day
      When for a Mermaid I turned from my way."
      With the first blue billow the Mermaid sent,
      Both mast and yard were asunder rent.

11   The Mermaid sent,
      Both mast and yard were asunder rent.
      With the second she sent against the boat
      The silken sail on the sea did float.

12   Against the boat,
      The silken sail on the sea did float.
      Up spake the steersman and said this word:
      "Is there no man who knoweth the runes aboard?"

13   Said this word:
      "Is there no man who knoweth the runes aboard?"
      Up spake Sir Luno, the well-born knight:
      " 'Tis I that can rist the runes aright."

14    The well-born knight:
      " 'Tis I that can rist the runes aright."
      On a linden-twig did he rist the spell,
      And there as a stone must the Mermaid dwell.

15    Rist the spell,
      And there as a stone must the Mermaid dwell.
      He risted the runes on a linden-bough,
      And bound the Mermaid with power enow.

16    On a linden-bough,
      And bound the Mermaid with power enow.
      "Sir Luno, Sir Luno, now loose thou me!
      Seven barrels of silver I'll give to thee.

17    "Loose thou me,
      Seven barrels of silver I'll give to thee,
      And another of gold will I bestow
      Wilt thou have mercy and let me go.

18    "Will I bestow,
      Wilt thou have mercy and let me go."
      "Sit thou a stone and starve for aye,
      I'll loose thee not till the Judgment Day!

19    "Starve for aye,
      I'll loose thee not till the Judgment Day.
      Tell all who come hither by sea or land
      Thou wert bound by Sir Luno's lily-white hand.

20    "By sea or land,
      Thou wert bound by Sir Luno's lily-white hand."
      He sailed back to Greenland, that knight so bold,
      And there sits the Mermaid, a stone so cold.

# WULFSTAN AND VENELIL

1  Wulfstan to Venelil spake up so free:
    (Mid wild bird and deer)
    "Wilt be my true-love and follow with me?
    See, the foal followeth the fallen o'er the heather.

2  "Lead thee to an isle will I
    Where thou shalt live and never die.

3  "The leek is all the grass that springs,
    The cuckoo is all the bird that sings.

4  "Fountains there be that run with wine,
    Trust ye my tale, true-love of mine!"

5  "Now how shall I ride away with thee
    When so many watchers keep ward over me?"

6  "Now gather thy gold in a casket gay
    While I saddle my steed to bear thee away!"

7  When they rode where the greenwoods grow
    The gold shone out o'er the saddlebow.

8  When they rode over land and lea
    They tarried to rest 'neath the greenwood tree.

9  'Neath greenwood tree did the maiden bide,
    Sir Wulfstan dug a grave beside.

10  "Now harken, Wulfstan, and tell me why
    Thou diggest a grave the grove nearby.

11  "O'er long it is for thy hound at need,
    O'er narrow to bury thy good grey steed."

12  "Now lift up thine eyes and look toward the town,
    And see where the red blood comes streaming down!

13  "Seven maids had I to wife,
    From seven maids I took their life.

14  "Thou shalt be the eighth, I ween,
    A sacrifice for all my sin."

15  Still she sat and thought eftsoon:
    Help shall be mine by the power of the Rune!

16  "Thou hast courted me this many a year,
    But ne'er have I ordered thy golden hair."

17  His head he laid in her lap so still,
    He slept a sleep all for his ill.

18  She took from his neck the golden band,
    And bound Sir Wulfstan's lily-white hand.

19  The hobbles she loosed from his steed so fleet
    And fast she bound Sir Wulfstan's feet.

20  "Now wake, Sir Wulfstan, and speak with me!
    Whilst thou sleepest I'll work no woe to thee.

21  "Seven maids hast thou had to wife,
    From seven maids thou took'st their life.

22  "The eighth shalt thou be to die, I ween,
    A sacrifice for all thy sin."

23    "Spare me, Venelil, spare thou me!
      Never will I prove false to thee."

24    "Let be thy pleadings sore!
      Shalt cozen maids no more."

25    She drew Sir Wulfstan's sword from sheath,
      Worthy was he to die therewith.

26    So womanlike the sword she drew,
      So manlike did she hack and hew.

27    "Lie now and see thy red blood run!
      A maid I'll live till my days are done."

# 4
## THE KNAVISH MERMAN

1    Gay went the dance in the kirkyard there,
      (On the lea)
      There danced knights with sword-blades bare.
      Methinks 'tis hard to ride away.

2    There danced maidens with hair unbound,
      It was the King's daughter sang the round.

3    Proud was the maiden, sweet was her song,
      That heard the Merman the billows among.

4    Up stood the Merman, thus spake he:
      "Perchance the King's daughter shall wed with me!"

5    Garments he shaped all golden and green,
      He called him Sir Alfast, son to the Queen.

6 He shaped him a steed so black and bold,
  He rode like a knight in a saddle of gold.

7 He bound his steed where the shade was mirk,
  Withershins went he round the kirk.

8 Into the kirk the Merman hied,
  And all the holy images they turned their heads aside.

9 Up spake the priest by the altar that stood:
  "Whence cometh hither this knight so good?"

10 The Princess smiled 'neath the scarlet fine:
  "Would to God that the knight were mine!"

11 "Harken, proud Princess, and love thou me,
  A crown of gold will I give to thee."

12 "Over three kingdoms my father was King,
  But ne'er did he give me so fair a thing!"

13 He wrapped her in his cloak of blue,
  Forth from the kirk they stole, they two.

14 They met upon the wold
  The steed with saddle of gold.

15 As they rode o'er the lea
  He became a troll so foul to see.

16 As they rode down to the water's brim
  He became a troll so fierce and grim.

17 "Sir Alfast, thou art christened man,
  What wilt thou with this water wan?"

18   "No knight am I nor christened man,
     My home is in this water wan!"

19   And when they reached the midmost sound
     Fifteen fathom they sank to ground.

20   Long heard the fishers with dread and dree
     How the King's daughter sobbed under the sea.

5

## SIR BOSMER IN ELFLAND

1   *Down by the stream dwelt the franklin free,*
     *(So sore is my longing)*
     *And his daughters twain were fair to see.*
     *For all my days are sorely filled with longing.*

2   *Five sons he had and daughters twain,*
     *And Sir Bosmer of all was the fairest swain.*

3   *The Elf-maid dwelt in the water clear,*
     *She loved Sir Bosmer for many a year.*

4   *Full fifteen winters were past and gone,*
     *But the love of Sir Bosmer she ne'er had won.*

5   *When the dew fell fast in the gloaming grey,*
     *She went to Sir Bosmer in loft where he lay.*

6   *Softly she knocked, and soft said she:*
     *"Rise up, Sir Bosmer, and open to me!"*

7   *"No tryst have I set tonight, I ween,*
     *None enters my door so late at e'en."*

8 Fair and white were her fingers small,
  Locks and bolts she loosened all.

9 She sat her down by Sir Bosmer's bed,
  She played with the locks of his golden head.

10 "Now pledge me thy troth to meet me alone
  Where the stream is spanned by the bridge of stone!"

11 At the mirk midnight did Sir Bosmer wake,
  And freely of his dream he spake.

12 "Methought a maiden came to me,
  White as molten wax was she.

13 "Methought I saw a maiden fair
  In silken sark with flowing hair.

14 "And my troth I pledged to meet her alone
  Where the stream is spanned by the bridge of stone."

15 "Now heed not thy dream, but slumber still,
  'Twas an Elf-maid sought thee to have her will."

16 "Let my dream go like wind and breath,
  But I will be true to my plighted faith!"

17 Sir Bosmer bade his pages speed,
  And saddle for him his good grey steed.

18 When from the garth he rode away,
  Sore wept his mother with welladay.

19 And when they came to the bridge of stone,
  Then stumbled the steed on his golden shoon.

20   On a golden nail tripped the courser brave,
     And the knight fell down in the weltering wave.

21   And when he won to fair Elfland,
     The Elf-maid met him on the strand.

22   "Welcome to this home of mine!
     Mead I'll pour for thee and wine.

23   "Tell me in the tongue of earth
     What land bred and gave thee birth?"

24   "Denmark bore me, blood and bone,
     There were my garments shapen and sewn.

25   "There my true-love dwells, and I
     Fain with her would live and die."

26   Unto her serving-maid she said:
     "Now fill a horn with wine so red!

27   "Now fill with wine an auroch's horn,
     And cast therein two grains of corn."

28   The serving-maid came in at the door,
     Wan as the moon shone the horn she bore.

29   And when he drank with the fairy-kind
     Then all the world went out of mind.

30   "Now tell me in the tongue of earth
     What land bred and gave thee birth?"

31   "Elfland bore me, blood and bone,
     Here all my garments were shapen and sewn.

32    "Thou art mine own true-love, and I
     Fain with thee would live and die!"

33    No more need the Elf-maid wail and weep,
     Sir Bosmer by her side doth sleep.

34    But sore wept all his kin
     When home he might not win,

35    And sorest the maid he might not wed,
     Who wept and sorrowed till she lay dead.

## 6

## KING OLUF AND HIS BROTHER

1    The King and his brother both were fain
    In Norway's land to rule and reign.
    So fair it is in Trondhjem to tarry!

2    Both were fain
    In Norway's land to rule and reign.
    "Who best can sail a ship, I say
    He shall be King in Norroway!"

3    "I say
    He shall be King in Norroway!"
    "No wager this of mine,
    The Serpent swift is thine.

4    "Of mine
    The Serpent swift is thine."
    "The Serpent swift for thee,
    The sluggish Ox for me!

5　"For thee,
　　The sluggish Ox for me!"
　　To kirk King Oluf straight did fare,
　　Like the red, red gold was his shining hair.

6　Straight did fare,
　　Like the red, red gold was his shining hair.
　　Word to the King eftsoon they bore:
　　"Thy brother is setting sail from shore."

7　They bore:
　　"Thy brother is setting sail from shore."
　　"Let him sail if sail he may,
　　But the Holy Mass will we hear today.

8　"Sail he may,
　　But the Holy Mass will we hear today,
　　The Mass doth Our Saviour's words repeat;
　　Then will we wash and go to meat.

9　"Words repeat,
　　Then will we wash and go to meat;
　　When we have eaten, then will we
　　Hoist our sail and fare to sea.

10　"Then will we
　　Hoist our sail and fare to sea."
　　Down to the strand they bore
　　Their anchor and their oar.

11　They bore
　　Their anchor and their oar.
　　Then fared King Oluf to the strand
　　Where the good ship Ox lay off the land.

12     To the strand
Where the good ship Ox lay off the land.
He clapped the Ox on the gilded horn:
"Now go as thou wouldst to growing corn!"

13     The gilded horn:
"Now go as thou wouldst to growing corn!"
The steersman bold did up and say:
"Now where shall we shape our course this day?"

14     Did up and say:
"Now where shall we shape our course this day?"
"O'er height and hill our ship shall haste,
Steer thy course as best thou mayst!

15     "Our ship shall haste,
Steer thy course as best thou mayst!"
When they sailed o'er the mountains blue,
Out came the trolls by three and by two.

16     The mountains blue,
Out came the trolls by three and by two.
"Ho, Redbeard, with thy ship so tall,
Why sailest thou o'er our house and hall?

17     "Ship so tall,
Why sailest thou o'er our house and hall?"
"Be turned to stone and stand thou still!
Thou knowest no good, thou shalt do no ill.

18     "Stand thou still!
Thou knowest no good, thou shalt do no ill."
He spanned his crossbow by his knee,
And the arrow fell aft of the mainmast tree.

19   *By his knee,*
     *And the arrow fell aft of the mainmast tree.*
     *He shot from the bows, and it fell far abaft,*
     *For the ship sailed swifter than the shaft.*

20   *Far abaft,*
     *For the ship sailed swifter than the shaft.*
     *The race he won by two nights and a day,*
     *So he kept the Kingdom of Norroway!*

NOTE: This ballad mirrors perfectly the popular conception of King Olaf as a saint. The essential point is his power over manifested Nature, and his piety as the source of it. In the picture of him as he goes to Mass, with his shining golden hair, we see the union of saint and folk-hero. The burden hints at the blessed repose of his body in his shrine at Trondhjem, still the defender of his people, and the helper of all who call upon him.

The theme originated in a Norwegian legend, associated with a mountain cliff resembling the prow of a vessel. It also recalls some historical memories, though Harald (Haardraade) disputed Norway, not with his brother Olaf, but with Olaf's son Magnus. Actually the "Serpent" was Olaf Tryggvason's vessel, though the "Ox" (Bison or Aurochs) was that of Saint Olaf. As the latter was the hero, so Harald was the villain, in Northern eyes; hence the necessity for placing them in opposition the one to the other.

The ballad was always sung with the repetition of one-and-a-half lines of the preceding verse (cf. Vol. II, No. 2). In all probability, one singer took the repetition and another the narrative.

# 7

## THE MOTHER UNDER THE MOULD

1   *Sir Björn rode up by land and lea,*
     *He wedded a maid so fair to see.*
     *He wedded the maiden Sölverlad.*
     *(Soft words ensnare so many a soul.)*

2   He wedded the lady Sölverlad,
    Sorrowful was she and seldom glad.
    They dwelt together eight years and more.

3   They dwelt together eight years and more,
    Seven fair babes to him she bore.
    Death walked abroad through all the land.

4   Death walked abroad through all the land,
    Then died that lady, the lily-wand.
    Sir Björn went faring far and wide,

5   Sir Björn went faring far and wide,
    And wooed another to be his bride.
    Home to his garth did the train repair.

6   Home to his garth did the train repair,
    And his bairnies went forth to greet them there.
    They kissed her cloak of the scarlet fine.

7   They kissed her cloak of the scarlet fine:
    "Now be thou welcome, sweet mother mine!"
    And with her foot she thrust them away.

8   And with her foot she thrust them away:
    "Are these the first faces that meet me today?"
    Sir Björn he gave her purple and pall,

9   Sir Björn he gave her purple and pall,
    To love and cherish his children small.
    Sir Björn gave her the gold so red,

10  Sir Björn gave her the gold so red,
    But she let the bairnies starve for bread.
    She took from them the bolsters of blue,

11    She took from them the bolsters of blue,
And straw for their bed was all their due.
Oh, sorely the bairnies wailed and wept,

12    Oh, sorely the bairnies wailed and wept,
Till they wakened their mother where she slept.
Late it was on Sabbath e'en,

13    Late it was on Sabbath e'en
When souls should rest from toil and tene.
To Heaven's hall she took her way,

14    To Heaven's hall she took her way,
Leave from Jesu Christ to pray;
"To Middle Earth would I go full fain,

15    "To Middle Earth would I go full fain,
And speak with my bairnies once again!"
"Yea, thou mayst go and do no wrong,

16    "Yea, thou mayst go and do no wrong,
But see thou tarry not over-long."
From her grave she rose once more,

17    From her grave she rose once more,
Her coffin on her back she bore.
To the house in haste she hied,

18    To the house in haste she hied,
Her eldest daughter stood there beside.
"And do I see thee, daughter mine?

19    "And do I see thee, daughter mine?
How fares it with brothers and sisters thine?"
"Goodsooth, thou art not mother mine,

20    "Goodsooth, thou art not mother mine,
     Wan is thy cheek as the white moonshine!"
     Into the chamber she took her way,

21    Into the chamber she took her way
     To see the bed where her bairnies lay.
     Into the bed she looked, and saw,

22    Into the bed she looked, and saw
     That her bairnies lay in the barren straw.
     Down she sat all on her chair,

23    Down she sat all on her chair,
     She combed and plaited their golden hair.
     The smallest on her lap she set,

24    The smallest on her lap she set,
     And wept till her eyes with blood were wet.
     She went her way by stair and loft,

25    She went her way by stair and loft,
     Till she found Sir Björn a-sleeping so soft.
     All with her coffin she smote the door,

26    All with her coffin she smote the door:
     "Rise up and speak with thy wife once more!"
     "No tryst have I set tonight, I ween,

27    "No tryst have I set tonight, I ween;
     None enter my chamber so late at e'en."
     "Now wake proud Blidelil,

28    "Now wake proud Blidelil,
      That treateth my bairns so ill!
      I brought thee a dower of gold so red,

29    "I brought thee a dower of gold so red,
      And thou lettest my bairnies starve for bread.
      I brought to thy homestead bolsters of blue,

30    "I brought to thy homestead bolsters of blue,
      And straw for their bed is all their due,
      And if I come to thee once again,

31    "And if I come to thee once again,
      Then shall Blidelil die in dule and pain,
      When thou hearest the watch-hounds howl so high,

32    "When thou hearest the watch-hounds howl so high,
      Thou shalt know the dead are drawing nigh.
      Now doth the black cock crow,

33    "Now doth the black cock crow,
      And to my grave I go."
      Scarce to her grave had she gone anew,

34    Scarce to her grave had she gone anew
      When her bairns were laid 'mid the bolsters blue.
      Blidelil plaited their locks so bright,

35    Blidelil plaited their locks so bright,
      She pleased and played with them from morn till night.
      Whene'er she heard the watch-hounds bay,

36    Whene'er she heard the watch-hounds bay
      With the red, red gold did the bairnies play.

# 8

# SIR OLUF AND HIS GILDED HORN

1   Oluf and Peter sat at the board,
    (All under the linden)
    And spake so many a merry word
    Under the linden-tree watcheth the maiden dearest to me.

2   "Harken, Sir Oluf, comrade mine!
    Thou shouldst wed a damsel fair and fine!"

3   "Now why should I wed maiden born
    While yet I have my magic horn?

4   "While yet my golden horn endures
    So many a maid its music lures.

5   "Never a maid beneath the moon
    But I can befool her by might of rune."

6   With hand Sir Peter struck the board:
    "Nay now, Sir Oluf, speak no such word!

7   "A love have I so true and kind,
    No rune can move her constant mind."

8   "Now will I wager my charger grey
    She shall come to my door 'twixt night and day.

9   "Yea, I will venture my neck so white,
    That thy love I'll befool this selfsame night!"

10  In the gloaming grey when the ways were blind
    Sir Oluf hath gone his horn to wind.

11  So well did he wind his horn of power
That maid Mettelil heard it afar in her bower.

12  Long she stood in wonderment:
"Shall I go thither ere night be spent?"

13  Long she stood a-musing there:
"No maid of mine shall with me fare."

14  Maid Mettelil called her hound so good,
And alone they went through the wild greenwood.

15  Softly she knocked and soft said she:
"Rise up, Sir Oluf, and open to me!"

16  "No tryst have I set tonight, I ween,
And none enters my door so late at e'en."

17  "Rise up, Sir Oluf, and open thy door,
Thy words have wounded my heart so sore."

18  "What though thy heart be sad and sore,
To thee I open not my door."

19  "Now open, Sir Oluf, and heed my call!
Cold on my mantle the rain doth fall."

20  "And if on thy mantle falleth the rain,
Then what was without turn withinwards again!"

21  "Now wilt thou grant not what I pray,
Then send thy squires to ward my way!"

22  "The moon shines clear o'er tree and toft,
And no lover will follow thee home to loft."

23     Proud Mettelil and her hound so good
       Went home alone through the wild greenwood.

24     Home in haste to garth they hied,
       And there stood Sir Peter the gate beside.

25     "Welcome home, my lady bright!
       Whither hast wandered all by night?"

26     "I have wandered by the stream,
       Fair shone the flowers in the wan moonbeam.

27     "Fair the roses red and white,
       Well-grown are they by Midsummer Night."

28     "Nay, this night's wandering, by my troth,
       Basely hath befooled us both!

29     "Lest fain thou follow what went before
       Thou shalt walk o' nights no more.

30     "Now, proud Mettelil, true-love mine,
       Go seek thy bed 'neath the linen fine!"

31     When first Sir Peter slumbered and slept
       Forth from his arms proud Mettelil crept.

32     From her sleeve of red she drew the knife:
       "I yet with honour may end my life!"

33     Then wakened Sir Peter, and up he stood,
       For the bed was drowned in his true-love's blood.

34     Against a stone he set his hilt,
       His heart's blood by the point was spilt.

35   Now shame on the knight with his gilded horn
     That hath brought so many a maid to scorn!

36   And shame on the horn of gold so red
     Hath cozened so many an honest maid!

## 9
### THE SERPENT BRIDE

1   There stood a courteous damsel
     Beside Sir Jennus' bed,
     Five silver cups she proferred him,
     And gifts of gold so red.
     The rose he fain would love.

2   "Five silver cups I proffer thee
     Whose beauty none may view,
     For when my brother dealt our goods
     Nothing of them he knew.

3   "Five foals so fleet I proffer thee
     That run in greenwood grove,
     Were I a knight, as thou art one,
     I'd give a maid my love.

4   "And twelve tall ships to thee I'll give
     That sail the salt sea-swell;
     A knight were I, as thou art one,
     I'd love a maid right well."

5   The lusty cock on high-loft crew,
     For night wore on so fast:
     "Now by my troth, Sir Jennus,
     The time to help is past!"

6    Oh, the cock crew high, for dawn was nigh,
     So swift the night did pass,
     And the maid was changed to a serpent small
     That crept amid the grass.

7    But Sir Jennus awaked, and up he stood,
     And to his page did say:
     "Now set ye straight my saddle of gold
     All on my courser grey!

8    "Now saddle for me my courser free
     All at this morning hour,
     For I will forth from castle-garth
     To ride in greenwood bower."

9    Forth fared the knight Sir Jennus
     Through greenwood dark and deep,
     And there he saw the serpent small
     That through the grass did creep.

10   The knight bent low o'er saddlebow,
     And kissed the serpent small,
     And a maid was she as bright of blee
     As e'er was seen in hall.

11   "Now thanks, now thanks, thou courteous knight,
     That thus hast set me free!
     Now never a boon canst ask eftsoon
     But I will give to thee."

12   "Now thanks to thee for thy bounty free,
     Thou maiden fair and fine!
     If thou to a knight thy troth canst plight,
     My love shall all be thine."

# 10

# THE BEAR OF DALBY

1   *There roamed a Bear by Dalby lea,*
    *Fierce and fell of mood was he,*
    *Both steed and ox he slew at will.*
    *But we are right merry in Denmark!*

2   *Both steed and ox he slew at will,*
    *The yeomen liked his deeds full ill.*

3   *They met in council every one:*
    *"Now shall the swine in greenwood run!"*

4   *Up spake the Bear beside his prey:*
    *"Why go the swine the greenwood way?"*

5   *Up rose the Bear so fierce of mood,*
    *And a christened man before him stood.*

6   *There they wrestled a little span,*
    *And the Bear o'erthrew the christened man.*

7   *A knight came spurring there amain,*
    *And he heard how the man's heart burst in twain.*

8   *"So fast thou needst not fare,*
    *To fight full well I dare!*

9   *"Hast nimble hands and spear so bright,*
    *But I have teeth so sharp and white!"*

10  *They fought for a day, they fought for two,*
    *On the third day they fought anew.*

11    "*Fight as thou mayst, I ne'er shall fly,*
      *Nothing wilt thou win thereby.*

12    "*A royal King was my sire so bold,*
      *My mother wore the crown of gold.*

13    "*Then by my stepdame banned,*
      *A Bear I roamed the land,*

14    "*Ne'er in man's likeness to appear*
      *Till I found a wight that knew not fear.*

15    "*From enchantment foul thou hast set me free,*
      *Thou shalt follow me home to mine own countrie,*
      *I'll give thee half the gold that's mine."*
      *But we are right merry in Denmark!*

NOTE: It was a very ancient belief that a bear fiercer and stronger than others was a man whose shape had been changed by enchantment.

The last line of the preceding verse should be repeated with the next, before the burden. Two singers would probably take part as in Nos. 2 and 7.

## 11

## THE WOOD-RAVEN

*Oh, the raven flies at fall of day*
*And loveth not the light,*
*And he must take the black fortune*
*That cannot take the white.*
*The raven flies at even.*

1     *It was the maid, fair Elver,*
      *That through the town did hie,*
      *And saw the wild wood-raven*
      *A-hovering in the sky.*

2   "Fly down, thou wild wood-raven,
    Fly down and speak with me!
    All my secret sorrow
    That will I tell to thee.

3   "To the son of a King my father
    Did plight my troth langsyne,
    But my cruel stepdame willed him
    In far-off land to pine,

4   "To pine in a far-off country
    All under her curse and ban,
    For she willed me to wed with her brother,
    Was liker a troll than a man."

5   "Now hark, thou maiden Elver,
    What gift wilt give to me,
    If I bear thee away to thy true-love
    So far o'er land and sea?"

6   "Oh, the silver white I'll give thee,
    And the red, red gold amain,
    Though wild of mood be the raven-brood,
    Wilt thou ease me of my pain!"

7   "A better boon than silver,
    A costlier gift than gold!
    The first-born son thou bearest,
    Him will I have and hold."

8   Oh, she set the claws of the raven
    Her lily-white hand upon,
    And she swore an oath by her Christian troth
    To give him her first-born son.

9    He took her athwart his back so swart,
     To lie his wings between,
     And fast he flew o'er the billows blue
     With mickle toil and tene.

10   All o'er the high-loft window
     A resting-place they win:
     "Be glad, thou maiden Elver,
     Thy true-love waits within!"

11   Forth came the bold Sir Nilus
     With silver cup in hand:
     "Now welcome, my true-love, welcome
     All to this far-off land!"

12   "Now fly thy ways, wild raven,
     Thy ways by sea and shore,
     And when a twelvemonth is over
     Come thou to us once more!"

13   He flew his ways, the raven wild,
     By moss and mount and moor,
     And he came again to their window
     When the twelvemonth well was o'er.

14   It was the wild wood-raven
     That perched upon the sill:
     "Think on thy vow, fair Elver,
     And let me have my will!"

15   "Now let him be dight in the linen white,
     The little babe I bore!
     He must go with the wild wood-raven,
     Nor see his mother more."

16   Oh, the raven has gored the bairnie's breast,
     And drunk his blood so red,
     And he changed his shape to as fair a knight
     As ever in land was bred!

NOTE: The raven, in medieval belief, was a wandering soul, yearning for deliverance. The "Valraven" was a fabulous creature, a blend of raven and wolf.

This latter word having no equivalent in English, I have used "wood-raven" for metrical reasons.—Translator.

## 12

# THE KNIGHT IN THE FEATHER-FELL

1   Once in our land there lived a maid
     (I will venture my life)
     Who vowed that she would ne'er be wed.
     I would venture my life for a lady.

2   Ne'er would she wed, was the maiden's cry,
     Till she found a husband who could fly.

3   That learnt Master Hildebrand,
     Son to the King of fair England.

4   Nine rings he took of gold so clear
     All to make ready his flying gear.

5   He wrapped him in the feather-fell,
     And flew to the land where the maid did dwell.

6   O'er the wild sea he took his flight
     Where never was day but alway night.

7   O'er a hill so high his way he won
     That over it never shined the sun.

8   He sat on a beam o'er the maiden's bower
    And sang so sweet in the evening hour.


9   Forth came the maiden fair and fine:
    "Would God, sweet bird, that thou wert mine!


10  "Never shouldst thou drink aught but wine,
    Never shouldst sleep but in bosom mine."


11  Forth went the maiden slim as a wand,
    And beckoned the bird with her lily-white hand.


12  She beckoned the bird till to her he came:
    "Would God, sweet bird, that thou wert tame!"


13  Down sat she where the green grass grew,
    And the bird into her bosom flew.


14  The bird into her bower she bore,
    And spread fair linen his feet before.


15  He took the wings from his shoulders both:
    "Fair lady, I have thy faith and troth!"


16  Off his feather-fell he cast:
    "Fair lady, the bird is tamed at last!"


## 13
## THE DRAGON


1   In bower fair Ingelil
    Her harp played soft and still.
    And they sported on the moorland.

2   Her harp she played so soft and sweet,
     And the Dragon came gliding to her feet.

3   "Ingelil, Ingelil, love thou me!
     Great store of gold I'll give to thee."

4   "May God me forsake when I call on Him,
     If e'er I love a Dragon grim!"

5   "If I no more of thy love may know,
     Then do thou kiss me and let me go."

6   She held to her lips a linen fold,
     And kissed the monster of goblin mould.

7   All with his talon the maid he tore,
     And red o'er her garment ran the gore.

8   Down crept the monster of goblin kind,
     Wringing her hands, she followed behind.

9   When they went down by the gallery stair,
     Her seven brethren met her there.

10   "Inge, our sister, we greet thee well,
     How hast thou fallen 'neath the Dragon's spell?"

11   "I needs must follow the goblin's brood
     When my luck was for ill, and not for good."

12   Into the mountain the monster crept,
     Followed the maiden who wailed and wept.

13   When they had entered the lair within,
     Lo, then did he cast the Dragon's skin.

14  The Dragon's shape he cast aside,
    He stood a Prince in all his pride.

15  "I thank thee for thy courage high!
    Ever with thee I'll live and die."

16  Now Inge no more her hands doth wring,
    For she lies o' nights with the son of a King.

17  Now she hath forgot her hurt and harm,
    For she sleeps o' nights in his lily-white arm.

## 14
## SIR STIG AND HIS RUNES

1   Sir Stig and Findal were brethren twain,
    Better will ne'er be seen again.
    Now give us leave, fair ladies!

2   Through women's tongues did Findal fall,
    Stig served the King in his castle hall.

3   Before the King stood that knight so fair,
    Damsels and dames curled his golden hair.

4   By the King's board he stood at e'en,
    And his mind ran ever on young Kirsteen.

5   "I have conned the runes these seven years past,
    And now will I try their worth at last!"

6   With his right hand the mead and wine he poured,
    Whiles his left unseen cast the runes abroad.

7 The runes should fall on Kirsteen the fair,
  But they flew 'neath Regise's cloak of vair.

8 Blacker than earth grew Stig the knight,
  And red as blood the lady bright.

9 He wrapped him all in cloak of vair,
  To his foster-mother he straight did fare.

10 "Now counsel, good counsel, of thee I pray,
  In peril sore stands my life this day!

11 "How may I living escape the King
  When the runes on his sister I chanced to fling?

12 "On little Kirsteen the runes should fall,
  But they flew 'neath Regise's cloak of pall."

13 "Through the realm of France shouldst thou take
             thy flight,
  Yet Regise would go to thy bed tonight.

14 "To the ends of the earth shouldst thou ride and run,
  She must find thee or ever the night be done!

15 "Go now to thy bed and bolt thou thy door,
  Do all as ever thou didst of yore.

16 "Though she stroke thy cheek with her fingers small,
  Lie like the dead and stir not at all.

17 "And what though she kiss thy cheek so red,
  Lie still and stir not as thou wert dead."

18     Late at even when soft fell the dew
       Regise wrapped her in mantle of blue.

19     Her mantle of blue the Princess did on,
       And to the knight's chamber in secret hath gone.

20     She went to his chamber and softly knocked she:
       "Rise up, thou good knight, and open to me!"

21     Slender to see were her fingers so small,
       But the nails from the lock she plucked one and all,

22     Fifteen were the nails, and the bar was fast,
       Yet into his chamber swiftly she passed.

23     Down by his bedside sat the maid,
       And with his golden locks she played.

24     She smoothed his cheek with her fingers white,
       But still as a dead man lay Stig the knight.

25     She kissed him on his mouth so red,
       But still did he lie as lie the dead.

26     She took him stealthily in her arm,
       But still he lay nor broke the charm.

27     All in the morning ere dawn was pale
       Unto the King they carried the tale.

28     Up spake the King to his pages three:
       "Now bid ye my sister come hither to me!"

29  In came the Princess and stood by the board:
    "What wilt thou, dear brother, that thou didst send
                                        me word?"

30  "Now sister, read me a riddle aright,
    Didst go to the chamber of Stig this night?"

31  "Yea, truly I entered therein, I wis,
    But little goodwill I won of his."

32  Up spake the King to his pages three:
    "Now bid Sir Stig come hither to me!"

33  In came Sir Stig and stood by the board:
    "What wilt thou, gracious King, that thou didst send
                                        me word?"

34  "Now speak, Sir Stig, and answer aright,
    Did my sister dear seek thy bower this night?"

35  " 'Tis God's truth that my chamber she entered in,
    But little goodwill from me did win."

36  Long stood the King with wondering mind:
    "What better match for her could I find?"

37  Great joyance was there in all the land
    When he gave to the knight his sister's hand.

38  Great mirth and joyance on every side
    When Stig won the Princess with honour and pride.

39  Good wine he prepared and mead of the best,
    And the King of the Danes was bidden as guest.

40    The King he bade with his liegemen bold,
       And the Queen of the Danes to his house and hold.


41    Up spake the Queen a-riding in state:
       "Behold now what honour on virtue doth wait!


42    "Yestre'en my Lord's courser this gallant did ride,
       Now wins he a Princess to wed for a bride.


43    "Yestre'en but a henchman was he to my Lord,
       Now he taketh a Princess to bed and to board!"


44    Up spake the Queen as she rode o'er the moor:
       "Now is this Stig's castle that standeth before?"


45    Up and spake the foot-page small:
       "The good knight's castle is known of all.


46    "Without, fair silver doth deck the hold,
       And within there beameth the burning gold."


47    And when they rode to the good knight's tower,
       There stood it all in a greenwood bower.


48    The lily was there and the linden green,
       The hind and hart played in between.


49    And when to the good knight's gate they hied
       Two snow-white bears were bound beside.


50    With silver the portals were overlain,
       And locked together with roses twain.

51    And when to the castle hall they came
      *It shone as bright as burning flame.*

52    Of amber rare was the loft aboon,
      *And the beams were gilded with many a rune.*

53    With marble stone the walls were dight,
      *And the pillars were all of the whalebone white.*[1]

54    And in the midst did a fountain rise,
      *All adorned with gold of price.*

55    Five goblets of silver stood thereon
      *With a napkin of silk for every one.*

56    With sweetest herbs the floor was spread,
      *Where dames and damsels a dance did tread.*

57    There danced Sir Stig as slim as a wand,
      *With a goblet of gold in either hand.*

58    He drank to his bride, that knight so good,
      *Till the flowers all blossomed in wild and wood,*

59    Till the flowers all blossomed in wold and hill:
      *"Now shall we live happy by God's good will!"*

60    Here endeth the Ballad of Stig the Knight,
      *God's grace and good fortune to every wight!*

[1] Ivory of narwhal horn.

# 15

# THE STOLEN BRIDE

1   Gay on the wold at eventide
    There danced the ladies all,
    With Wooing Dance and Dance of Luck,
    While the swains they played at ball.
    Tread, noble knights, with pride and honour!

2   The maidens trod the Lucky Dance
    So lightly o'er the lea,
    When the King of the Wends with all his ships
    Came sailing in from sea.

3   The King of the Wends with all his ships
    Came sailing to the strand,
    And fifteen of the fairest maids
    He carried off from land.

4   Two months they lay in harbour
    And never hoisted sail,
    For the waves ran high and the clouds hung low,
    And they found no favouring gale.

5   It was the gallant steersman,
    That up and spake his word:
    "Ne'er shall we find fair weather
    While we have these maids aboard!"

6   A-smiling all in secret,
    Up spake the King amain:
    "Goodsooth, then all the maidens
    Shall straight go home again!

7   "Now bear up a burden, ye maidens,
    All ye that most sweet can sing,
    And home in peace shall ye depart
    On the faith of the Wendish King!"

8   It was the maiden Kirsteen
    Looked over her shoulder small:
    "Now Karen, my little sister,
    Sing thou the first of all!"

9   Kirsteen and beauteous Karen,
    So sweet a song sang they
    That all were glad that walked on wold,
    And all in ship that lay.

10  Yea, glad were all the little fish
    That swam in sea and flood,
    And glad was every hart and hind
    That played in good greenwood.

11  And glad were all the men that rowed
    In boats upon the sea,
    And loud he laughed, the King of the Wends,
    For gladder than all was he.

12  "Now all ye courteous maidens
    Homeward in peace may ride,
    Save Kirsteen and proud Karen,
    That both must here abide."

13  Up spake little Kirsteen,
    And bitter the tears she shed:
    "Oh, a luckless hour it was for me
    When my mother dear lay dead!

14    "And when I learnt a lay to sing
     It was a luckless chance,
     But most luckless of all the evil hour
     When I stood up to dance."

15    It was the King of Wenderland
     That kissed her cheek so white:
     "Now weep not, little Kirsteen,
     Shalt be my heart's delight!

16    "For thou shalt wed the King of Wends,
     And live his consort fair,
     And Karen thy little sister
     Thy household keys shall bear."

17    That did the King of Wendland
     When home to port he came,
     He gave her a crown of red, red gold,
     And called her Queen by name.

18    And Karen her little sister,
     A maiden fair was she,
     Got a good knight for husband,
     And lands to hold in fee.

## 16

## SIR LAURENS STEALS A BRIDE

Forth by the light of day I dare not ride,
Sorrow I bear and pain all for a lady's pride,
My shield's known far and wide.

1   It was the knight Sir Laurens
    That loved a lady fair,
    But they closed her in a cloister
    All for his sorrow and care.

2   It was the knight Sir Laurens
    That to his brother said:
    "Now will I burn the cloister,
    And bear away my maid."

3   "And wilt thou burn the cloister
    To set thy lady free,
    Beware lest great King Byrial
    Should wreak revenge on thee!"

4   Unto his squires in anger
    Spake up that lusty lord:
    "We'll raze that cloister to the ground,
    And bear the maid abroad!"

5   Up they spake, those squires so bold,
    And to their lord they cried:
    "Now will we burn the cloister,
    And let what will betide!"

6   They rode to raze the cloister
    And all with sword and fire,
    And sweet as any nightingale
    The nuns sang in the quire.

7   Sweeter than any nightingale
    Did sing the maidens nine,
    And sweetest of all sang Bente,
    That maiden fair and fine.

8   They razed the wall of the cloister,
     They brake both bolt and door,
     And what though she stood by the altar,
     Fair Bente away they bore.

9   Up spake the lady Sesselil
     That by the altar stood:
     "Beware lest our lord, King Byrial,
     Should wreak revenge in blood!"

10   He took the lady Bente
     And set her on his steed,
     Down to the strand he led her
     As fast as they might speed.

11   Up spake the lady Bente
     That saw the pennon fly:
     "Would God that ship and all might sink,
     For a woeful maid am I!"

12   Up stood young Sir Laurens
     That spake a word so free:
     "The ship is well-found and her timbers are sound,
     To bear us o'er the sea!"

13   Now they have hoisted their sails of silk
     Up on the gilded mast,
     And swift they sailed to Norroway
     Or e'er two days were past.

14   Within his father's castle
     To bridal feast they went,
     Seven years and more they dwelt there
     In peace and sweet content.

15    Eight years were gone, the ninth came on,
      Swift as a tale they tell,
      And 'twas the knight Sir Laurens
      In deadly pains that fell.

16    It was the knight Sir Laurens
      That felt the pains of death:
      "Bid Bente come to my bedside
      While yet I draw my breath!"

17    It was the knight Sir Laurens
      Her rosy cheek did kiss:
      "No heir have we to lands and fee,
      And a woeful weird is this!"

18    Up spake the lady Bente,
      And fast her tears did flow:
      "The richer then are thy kinsfolk,
      The greater is my woe!"

19    "Now raise ye a gold cross o'er my grave,
      And a holy kirk beside,
      And hie thee back to thy brother
      Once more with him to bide."

20    She raised a kirk above his grave
      And set a cross of gold,
      Then fared the lady Bente
      Home to her brother's hold.

21    All in the garth of the castle
      She donned her cloak of vair,
      And to the hall she hastened
      To meet her brother there.

22   "All hail to thee, King Byrial,
     My brother dear art thou;
     What grace may be accorded
     Thine only sister now?"

23   "God wot thou wert, fair Bente,
     No sister dear of mine,
     When thou didst flee to a far countrie
     With that poor swain of thine!"

24   Up spake the lady Bente
     Most like a loving wife:
     "Ne'er would I seek thy favour
     Had God but spared his life!"

25   Up he stood, King Byrial,
     And a word so kind spake he:
     "All that I own of goods and grace
     I'll freely give to thee!"

NOTE: Of all the ballads dealing with the lover who carries off his lady from the cloister school, this is the earliest, or at all events the earliest historical example. In 1244 Laurens, the Lawman (President of the Thing) of East Gothland, carried off the Swedish Queen's sister Benedikte (Bente Sunesdatter) from the nunnery at Vreta, and took her to Norway. After his death six years later she was reconciled to her family.

The ballad, with its dry, matter-of-fact narrative, has more historical accuracy than poetical merit, which is chiefly apparent in the introductory verse. It only errs in making Bente the King's sister instead of the Queen's, and giving him the name of Byrial, a blend of King Erik's name with that of Birger Jarl, who was the real power in the land. The whole thing gives an interesting picture of the tumultuous life of the Middle Ages, especially during the time of the Folkungs.

# 17

# THE WEDDING OF RANE JONSON

1   Ranil bade saddle his steed so free:
     ('Twas told me oft of yore)
     "The mighty Margrave I'll go see,
     Though I am severed both from friends and kinsmen."

2   Now Ranil into the garth did fare,
     And there stood the Margrave all wrapped in vair.
     Now am I sundered both from friends and kinsmen.

3   "I greet thee, Sir Margrave, so fair and so fine,
     Now give me young Kirsteen, true-love of mine,
     So sorely am I sundered from friends and kinsmen."

4   Up spake her mother that loved her so dear:
     "Think not to seek thy true-love here
     Whilst thou art severed both from friends and kinsmen."

5   "And wilt thou not give me my heart's desire,
     All that thou hast will I burn with fire,
     Whilst I am sundered both from friends and kinsmen."

6   "And wilt thou burn all I have with fire,
     Then ride thou away with thy heart's desire,
     Though thou art severed both from friends and kinsmen!"

7   They lapped the damsel in scarlet weed,
     They set her up on his good grey steed,
     Though he was sundered both from friends and kinsmen.

8    Nought for their bridal bower they found
      But the wood and the wold and the new-mown ground,
      For he was sorely severed from friends and kinsmen.

9    "And hadst thou not King Erik slain
      In our own land we might have lain,
      But now we are sundered both from friends and kinsmen."

10    He struck her across the gaming-board:
      "When guests are by one must watch one's word,
      Now we are severed both from friends and kinsmen."

11    He struck her on the cheek so red:
      "I never wished King Erik dead,
      Though I am sundered both from friends and kinsmen.

12    "Forests have ears and fields have eyes,
      We must wander the world as the wild swan flies,
      For ever are we severed from friends and kinsmen!"

NOTE: The wild period of unrest after the assassination of Erik Klipping furnished many themes for ballads. By the side of the comprehensive cycle of which Marsk Stig was hero, others sprang up dealing with the adventurous lives or lamentable deaths of the other outlaws.

Most remarkable of these is the ballad of Ranil Jonson's marriage, as giving a picture of the hazardous daily life of an outlawed man. At a period which usually regarded the rover from the distrustful standpoint of the settled community, the minstrel hints at the poetry and excitement of the wandering life.

Between verses 8 and 9 there is a hiatus in the action, which passes from the wood and wild to the playing of dice in the presence of guests.

The ballad can hardly be contemporary with the life of its hero. The title of "Margrave" has never been known in Denmark; moreover, the two-lined stanza was less popular in the thirteenth than in the fourteenth century. One among the many legends of Ranil's escapes and captivities represents him as carrying off a girl from the crowd of youngsters playing in a village street, and some such incident may have inspired this ballad.

# 18

## MARSK STIG'S DAUGHTERS

1   Marsk Stig he had daughters twain,
And long they lived in sorrow and pain,
The elder took the younger by the hand,
All through the wide world to wander.

2   The elder took the younger by the hand,
And so they fared to King Malfred's land.
King Malfred home from the Thing did ride.

3   King Malfred home from the Thing did ride,
And there stood the sisters his gate beside.
"What manner of women may ye be?

4   "What manner of women may ye be
That stand here alone to meet with me?"
"Marstig's daughters, we come to plead.

5   "Marstig's daughters, we come to plead
For thy grace in sorest need."
"Get ye from my garth away!

6   "Get ye from my garth away!
Thy father did mine uncle slay."
The elder took the younger by the hand.

7   The elder took the younger by the hand,
And so they fared to King Sigfred's land.
King Sigfred home from the Thing did ride.

8   King Sigfred home from the Thing did ride,
And there stood the sisters his gate beside.
"What manner of women may ye be?

9    "What manner of women may ye be
That stand here alone to meet with me?"
"Marstig's daughters, we come to plead.

10   "Marstig's daughters, we come to plead
For thy grace in direst need."
"Get ye from my garth away!

11   "Get ye from my garth away!
Thy father did my brother slay."
The elder took the younger by the hand.

12   The elder took the younger by the hand,
And so they came to King David's land.
King David home from the Thing did ride.

13   King David home from the Thing did ride,
And there stood the sisters his gate beside.
"What manner of women may ye be?

14   "What manner of women may ye be
That stand here alone to meet with me?"
"Marstig's daughters, we come to plead.

15   "Marstig's daughters, we come to plead
For thy grace in direst need."
"Can ye brew and can ye bake?

16   "Can ye brew and can ye bake?
And what besides can ye mend or make?"
"We can neither bake nor brew.

17   "We can neither bake nor brew,
But other work we well can do.
Gold can we spin a web to weave.

18   "Gold can we spin a web to weave,
     All to delight and never to grieve."
     The elder did the web prepare.

19   The elder did the web prepare,
     The younger wove it smooth and fair.
     And first she wove for all to see.

20   And first she wove for all to see
     Our Saviour and our dear Ladye.
     And then she wove in purple and pall.

21   And then she wove in purple and pall
     The Danish Queen and her maidens all.
     And then the maiden wove.

22   And then the maiden wove
     All saints in Heaven above.
     And when the younger her work had done,

23   And when the younger her work had done
     The bitter tears from her eyes did run.
     "Had we a father dear,

24   "Had we a father dear
     Then should we make good cheer.
     Had we a mother kind,

25   "Had we a mother kind
     Great solace should we find."
     In sickness sore the elder lay.

26   In sickness sore the elder lay,
     The younger tended her night and day.
     Dead lay the elder, for all was vain.

27   *Dead lay the elder, for all was vain,*
     *The younger lived in sorrow and pain.*
     *But the King he gave her his youngest son,*
     *For all through the wide world had they wandered.*

NOTE: We have two versions of this ballad. One depicts the two daughters of the King of England, or the King of Cologne, who rove the world trying to earn their bread, and finally marry two princes. This, a fairy tale pure and simple, is undoubtedly the earlier. The later version, dealing with Marsk Stig's daughters, is tragic in tone, but the minstrel throws in the concluding line of the marriage with the King's son, probably with the feeling that the fairy-tale nature of the theme was bound to have a happy ending. What the ballad gives us is a vivid picture of the outlaw's miserable lot. The figures of the sisters seem to be borrowed from the Ballad of Erik Menved's Bridal, when the young Queen pleads for the "release of Marsk Stig's daughters from prison," and this semi-historical theme has been grafted on to the ballad, without any alteration of the fabulous names of the Kings visited by the sisters.

Both versions, however, picture the same social conditions—the hard work by which homeless women had to earn their livelihood, and the industry and thoroughness which went to the making of medieval works of art.

## 19
# NIELS STRANGESON'S STONE TOWER

1   *It was the King of Denmark*
     *Rode forth the town to view:*
     *"Now whose may be this castle*
     *That shines so fair and new?"*

2   *Up and spake the lither lad*
     *That rode beside his knee:*
     *"Now that is Nilus Strangeson's,*
     *Who best is known to thee."*

3   It was the King of Denmark
    Spake to his pages three:
    "Go, bid ye Nilus Strangeson
    To come and speak with me."

4   In came Nilus Strangeson
    And stood beside the board:
    "What wilt thou, King of Denmark,
    That thou didst send me word?"

5   "Harken now, Nilus Strangeson,
    And look thou tell me true,
    Wilt sell to me thy castle
    That shines so fair and new?"

6   "My father set me on his knee
    In tender age,
    And bade me bargain not away
    My heritage.

7   "My father set me on his knee,
    So young was I,
    And bade that none my heritage
    From me should buy."

8   Up spake the King of Denmark
    To those that stood beside:
    "Seize him, Nilus Strangeson,
    In dungeon deep to bide!"

9   It was Nilus Strangeson
    His sword that drew with speed:
    "Who sets me in dungeon this day, methinks,
    Shall do but a luckless deed!"

10   "Put up thy sword, Nilus Strangeson,
      And hear what I shall vow,
      My daughter I will give to thee,
      For worthy of her art thou!"

11   That gained Nilus Strangeson,
      For a valiant man was he,
      The King's fair daughter of Denmark,
      And half the land in fee!

NOTE: This story of Nilus Strangeson's "stone tower" has a genuine historical foundation. He was a powerful chieftain in Ty, belonging to a celebrated family, and nephew and namesake of Niels Ebbeson, who fell at Skanderborg. The tower seems to have been situated at Smerup in Tyholm, the ancestral heritage of his wife. In 1408 young King Erik and Queen Margaret visited North Jutland to reclaim certain Crown lands which had been alienated, and set up a claim to that of Sir Nilus. This claim, as frequently was the case under the wise Queen's management, was amicably settled. Sir Niels conveyed the disputed homestead to the Crown, together with twenty-four adjacent farms; in consideration of payment as previously "agreed on." Immediately afterwards the King and Queen visited him at Ty, and endowed him with the property as long as he and his wife should live.

The ballad was composed in his own neighbourhood, which by no means understood the details of the transaction, but judged by the upshot, that Niels remained secure in the controverted possession. The story followed the lines so familiar to the ballads—the picture of the bold fighter compelling the King at the sword's point to spare his life, and frequently to hand over his daughter into the bargain. We may see that the art of composing terse, vigorous ballads survived even as late as the beginning of the fifteenth century, but it is none the less obvious that this art, after the lapse of a couple of centuries, had become definitely dependent on literary models, and no longer sprang from a creative impulse in direct contact with life.

# 20

# YOUNG DANNEVED AND
# SWAIN TRUST

What shall I do in Denmark?
My corselet sore doth gall,
The Danish knights make mock of me
For I am young and small.
  Ne'er shall I speak good Danish!


1  Firm he sat in saddle,
His spurs were sharp and long,
At Lunde Kirk in Skaane
There heard he Evensong.


2  He heard them sing, he heard them read,
Till Evensong was o'er,
Then listed him, young Danneved,
To mount his steed once more.


3  Up and spake Sir Peter
That was his parish priest:
"Now by my troth, young Danneyed,
This night shalt be my guest!"


4  "For meat I will not tarry,
Nor will I wait for wine,
Until I come to Berneskov
To speak with mother mine."


5  "Nay, neither for eating nor drinking
Crave I thy companie,
But well do I wot thy foemen
Are lying in wait for thee!"

6   "Oh, first I trust in my biting blade,
     And therewith my steed so tall,
     And next do I trust my liegemen true,
     But myself the most of all."

7   "Well mayst thou trust in thy biting brand,
     And well in thy steed so tall,
     But trusteth thou in thy liegemen's troth
     They'll cozen thee first of all."

8   It was the knight young Danneved
     That laughed and rode his way,
     And there he met his foemen false,
     Thrice nine in number they.

9   There did he meet his foemen false,
     Thrice nine in number they,
     And all his squires took leave of him
     In haste to flee away.

10   Leave took all his liegemen,
     And from their lord withdrew,
     All but the little swain hight Trust,
     Who service did renew.

11   "Lo, I have worn thy garments,
     And eaten have I thy bread,
     And this day will I stand by thee
     Whiles thou art sore bested.

12   "Lo, I have worn thy garments,
     And ridden have I thy steed,
     And this day will I stand by thee
     To help thee in thy need."

13   Now back to back their stand they took
     There in the greenwood bower,
     And those twain I ween struck down fifteen
     Ere they had fought an hour.

14   They set their backs together
     There in the greenwood brake,
     And they won great praise and honour
     All for that slaying's sake.

15   It was the knight young Danneved
     That sheathed his sword at side:
     "Now come thou hither, thou little swain Trust,
     'Tis time for us to ride!"

16   It was the knight young Danneved
     To home and hold did fare,
     And there she stood, his mother,
     Wrapped in her cloak of vair.

17   "Now greet us well, my mother,
     And pour for us the wine!
     For I will give to little swain Trust
     The hand of sister mine."

NOTE: The introductory verse and burden must not be regarded as part
of this ballad. Both were borrowed from an earlier one describing a joust
between a young foreign knight and some Danish champions. The motive
for this borrowing was probably desire to make use of a well known
melody, and the fact that both ballads deal with a valiant young warrior.

21

## SIR HJELM

1   Sir Hjelm he rode in the Rose Wood's bound
    And with him went both hawk and hound.
    So free sits the swain in his saddle.

2   Over the lea he looked and saw
      Where his true-love's brethren rode by the shaw.

3   Sir Hjelm to his page spake up so free:
      "Hast thou good counsel, then counsel thou me!"

4   "I rede thee, Sir Hjelm, thou gallant knight,
      Set spurs to thy steed and take to flight."

5   "Ne'er to my true-love shall tale be told
      That I fled from her seven brethren bold."

6   Sir Hjelm spake up to his page so free:
      "Hast thou good counsel, then counsel thou me!"

7   "I rede thee, Sir Hjelm, thou gallant knight,
      Spur thy steed, fall on, and fight."

8   "Why ridest thou to us alone?
      Didst slay our uncle and ne'er atone.

9   "Hast ravished our sister, young Kirsteen,
      And asked no leave of us, I ween!"

10   "Red gold have I in a casket fine,
      That will I give thee for kinsman thine."

11   "No weregild seek we in all the land
      But thy left foot and thy red right hand!"

12   Straight Sir Hjelm his blade did bare,
      Body from head he sundered there.

13   Ebbe and Lang he hurled to ground,
      For now the sword its swing had found.

14  Asser the White and Wulf lay slain,
    Those four ne'er stood up again.

15  Terkel next he slew and Thor,
    Six lay on earth to rise no more.

16  The youngest brother up and spake:
    "Now spare my life for my sister's sake!"

17  "With right good will shouldst thou go free
    Did I deem thou wouldst be true to me."

18  "Sir Hjelm, Sir Hjelm, now spare thou me!
    Thy true sworn-brother I aye will be."

19  Sir Hjelm fared on in full content,
    Ole the false behind him went.

20  When the good knight turned to look on the swain
    Ole smote his head from his shoulders twain.

21  He set the head all on his spear,
    And went to seek his sister dear.

22  "Harken, sister fair and fine!
    Here hast thou the head of true-love thine."

23  "And have I the head of true-love mine,
    Come, I'll pour thee mead and wine."

24  Ere silver can from lip did part,
    She thrust a knife through his false heart.

25  "Lie thou there for hound and swine
    While I seek the body of true-love mine!

26   "Lie for crow and erne to tear,
      But my love shall have a burial rare.

27   "I'll do what I may for my knight so bold,
      His coffin shall be decked with gold.

28   "A kirk shall rise above his bier,
      All bedecked with amber clear.

29   "All the world that passes by
      Shall see where a squire of dames doth lie.

30   "Now will I seek the hall of stone,
      And weep my true-love all alone!"

## 22
## SVEND OF VOLLERSLOV

1   There dwelt a dame in Bredeby,
      And she had daughters twain,
      And many a mighty lordling
      Wooed once and once again.
      For she herself was proud of mood.

2   When Svend of Vollerslov wooed her
      In vain his pains were spent,
      But when Sir William wooed her
      To him she gave consent.

3   It was young Sir William
      To bridal feast did speed,
      It was Svend of Vollerslov
      That bade them shoe his steed.

4   They wept for young Sir William
    With woe and welladay,
    For he was slain on his bridal night
    In bride-bed where he lay.


5   Now it fell nine moons thereafter
    When woods grew green once more,
    The lady sought her bower,
    And a son so fair she bore.


6   Born was he at even,
    And christened the selfsame night,
    His father's name they gave him,
    And hid him as best they might.


7   They fostered him for a winter,
    And well for winters nine,
    And ne'er had eye beholden
    A babe so fair and fine.


8   Forth went the lads on the moorland
    To sport with staff and stone,
    So mightily cast young William
    He wounded them every one.


9   Then seized him by his golden hair
    A franklin's son so free:
    " 'Twere best avenge thy father's death
    And let thy comrades be!"


10  Up and spake young William,
    His cheek so white with pain:
    "My father's death shall be avenged
    'Ere I sport with ye again!"

11    It was young Sir William
      Wrapped him in cloak of vair,
      And entered in the high-loft
      To seek his mother there.

12    "Now lithe and list, my mother dear,
      To what I ask of thee,
      For if the sword my father slew
      Then hide it not from me!"

13    "Weapons thou canst not bear, I wis,
      That art but a half-grown boy,
      And long may Svend of Vollerslov
      His life in peace enjoy!"

14    It was young Sir William
      That penned a challenge high,
      And sent it by a secret hand
      The slayer to defy.

15    No squires had he but two and three
      To follow at his side,
      But he clad them all in byrnies brown,
      And to the Thing did ride.

16    And ten had Svend of Vollerslov
      That well could weapons bear,
      He clad them all in the silk so gay
      To meet Sir William there.

17    Up spake Svend of Vollerslov,
      Decked in the scarlet weed:
      "Now who hath summoned me hither
      In vain to tire my steed?"

18   From out his helm a-shining
      Did William answer fling:
      "Oh, well mayst thou weary thy courser's legs
      To meet me at the Thing!

19   "Now answer, Svend of Vollerslov,
      To what I ask this day,
      Tell me, hast thou forgotten
      Thou didst my father slay?"

20   All with his foot Svend Vollerslov
      Cast up the mud and mire:
      "No penny thou'lt get in payment
      Because I slew thy sire!"

21   It was young Sir William
      That wheeled his steed so fleet,
      And cast down Svend of Vollerslov
      Under his courser's feet.

22   It was young Sir William
      That home to hold did ride,
      And it was his lady mother
      That stood the gate beside.

23   And all with words of welcome
      The lady up and spake:
      "What didst thou at the Thing today
      For thy dear father's sake?"

24   "Now what was seen at the Thing, I ween,
      Hath caused full great annoy,
      For I saw Svend of Vollerslov
      Fall by the hand of a boy!"

25    *It was proud dame Mettelil*
      *That kissed his cheek so red:*
      *"Now thanks, my son, Sir William,*
      *That hast avenged the dead!"*

NOTE: This tale of a blood-feud harks back to remote antiquity, but is not derived from any legend in particular. The scene in the playing-field, when the lads avenge the little mishap by informing the hero of his father's murder, has its original source in the legends of Ireland, but reappears in a number of ballads, and occasionally in medieval Icelandic sagas. Various Norwegian and Faroëse ballads tell the same story as "Svend of Vollerslov," but the latter has features peculiar to the knightly customs of Denmark. The burden is noteworthy, as ascribing the lady's thirst for revenge to her proper pride.

## 23

# THE SLAYING OF THORD IVERSON

1    *Now Aage sat with proud Ellen,*
      *And she ordered his locks of gold:*
      *"Now whither wilt thou ride today,*
      *For my heart with care is cold?"*
      *All on the lea ye slumber.*

2    *"Now I will ride up the countryside*
      *To seek Thord Iverson,*
      *For his father slew my brother dear*
      *These eight long years agone."*

3    *"Now wilt thou seek Thord Iverson*
      *And that with sword and spear,*
      *I beg thee in the Name of God*
      *That he abye it dear.*

4   "Spare not his kine and oxen,
     Spare not his gold so red,
     And spare thou not his lily-white neck
     If thou canst reach his head!"

5   'Twas on a Saturday even
     They scoured both spear and sword,
     Early a Monday morning
     Wrathful they rode abroad.

6   It was the knight Sir Aage
     That rode in greenwood bower,
     And there he met Sir Iver's page
     All at the morning hour.

7   "Now hark and hear, thou little foot-page,
     The words I say to thee,
     If Sir Iver bides at his homestead
     Then hide it not from me!"

8   "My lord bides not at his homestead,
     He rode from us late yestre'en,
     Nor will his steps turn hither
     Till another Yule be seen."

9   "Nay now, if he bide at his homestead
     Then hide it not from me!
     Twelve marks behold of the good red gold
     That I will give to thee."

10  They spread on the mead their mantles,
     They counted the red, red gold,
     And there a knight so gallant
     For money was bought and sold.

11　"Down to the south in our castle-garth
　　　There standeth a tower of stone,
　　　And my master therein with young Kirsteen
　　　Doth lie o'nights alone."

12　Upon the door of the tower
　　　They knocked with glaive and spear:
　　　"Stand up, stand up, Thord Iverson,
　　　Stand up and meet us here!"

13　"Thord Iverson from the garth is gone,
　　　And nought but his guest am I,
　　　My spear is left in the high-loft,
　　　My steed in the field nearby."

14　"Now nay, thou art Thord Iverson,
　　　Thy words are leasings all,
　　　Thy spear stands in the chamber,
　　　Thy steed stands in the stall."

15　With glaive and spear a-shining
　　　Against the door they beat,
　　　And every nail in lock and bolt
　　　Fell inwards at his feet.

16　"Now thrust ye not through my bolsters of blue,
　　　Nor rend ye my sheets so fine,
　　　Nor wake from sleep mine own dear wife
　　　That lies in dule and pine.

17　"Now wake not from sleep mine own dear wife
　　　Hath lain in anguish sore,
　　　No longer ago than yesterday
　　　Two beauteous babes she bore."

18   Oh, they have ta'en Thord Iverson
     All by his golden hair,
     Body from head they sundered
     Over his bedside there.

19   Up and spake his wife so dear,
     Lay lapped in scarlet weed:
     "And if his sons do live and thrive
     They shall avenge this deed!"

20   Now the blades they clean of their swords so keen,
     And sheathe them at their side,
     And they sing "All hail to Christ the Lord"
     As from the garth they ride.

NOTE: In this grim ballad we have the blood-feud with no redeeming feature. It shows incidentally how the weregild could be assessed in terms of cattle, either "lifted" without permission, or bargained with as the most convenient form of portable property. Otherwise it was a case of a life for a life. The singing of the Alleluia by the victors is characteristic of that period when Christian hymns or psalms so frequently served as battle-songs. The burden, which has small connection with the subject, must have been picked up from another ballad.

The story seems to have had some historical foundation. A tradition of the early seventeenth century places the scene in West Jutland, south of Holstebro, where a hollow between Avhem and Lundgaard is supposed to have been the site of Thord Iverson's homestead. But nothing can be said as to the reliability of this tradition.

## 24

## THE LOVER'S DEATH

1   Sir Oluf lay smitten with sickness sore,
     (Up Northward)
     And fain would he see his love once more.
     But all the oars are drifting overboard.

2 The messenger stood the board beside,
  And his tale he told to Sir Oluf's bride.

3 "Sick lies thy true-love, and bids ye go
  To speak with him ere the cock shall crow."

4 Young Kirsteen donned her cloak of vair,
  To her foster-mother she straight did fare.

5 "Now tell me whether would shame be cried
  Should maid betrothed to her bridegroom ride?"

6 "Nay, honest it is and no shame, I wot,
  That she should go when he cannot."

7 Little Kirsteen fared to the stall,
  And sought amongst the coursers all.

8 She thrust aside the white and brown,
  The swiftest she laid saddle on.

9 Four leagues afar lay the greenwood bower,
  But thither she rode in the morning hour.

10 Into his garth did Kirsteen ride,
  And there stood his mother the gate beside.

11 "All hail, Dame Mettelil, fair and fine,
  Now say, how goes it with bridegroom mine?"

12 "In sickness sore doth thy bridegroom lie,
  Ever we tend him, his sisters and I."

13 In at his door went the maiden bright,
  Sir Oluf stretched forth his hands so white.

14 His hands he stretched to her and said:
  "Come, little Kirsteen, and sit by my bed!"

15 "Weary I am not nor oppressed,
  But good it is awhile to rest."

16 Sir Oluf called his page anear:
  "Mine iron-bound casket bring thou here!"

17 He set the casket on his knee,
  He dealt to her both gold and fee.

18 Gold rings he gave her many a one,
  Both hart and hind were graven thereon.

19 Rings he gave her beyond compare,
  Both rose and lily were graven there.

20 A brooch he gave her of golden sheen,
  And his mother was wroth when that gift was seen.

21 "Now give no more, now give not all!
  Sisters thou hast in house and hall."

22 "House and hold have daughters thine,
  But my love will dwell in no house of mine.

23 "Land and lea shall my sisters keep,
  But ne'er in my bed shall my true-love sleep."

24 Sir Oluf turned his head aside,
  And e'en as he spake he swooned and died.

25   *Home rode the maid with welladay,*
     *And forgot to bear her gold away.*

NOTE: The ballads make very clear the medieval respect for the claims of inheritance, which apparently extended to portable property. Sir Oluf outrages proper family feeling when he presents his betrothed with all his most precious treasures. Another strict convention of the period is shown in Kirsteen's consultation with her foster-mother. A girl was permitted to receive visits from her lover in her own home, but could not go to him without being accused of the greatest immodesty, and Kirsteen only dares break this rule when her lover is actually dying.

25

# DAME GUNDELIL'S HARPING

1   *Sir Franklin must to the Landsting go,*
     *And the King bade saddle his steed also.*
     *Proud was Dame Gundelil, Sir Franklin's spouse,*
     *And her they could not win.*

2   *Unto the garth the King did fare,*
     *And there stood proud Gundelil wrapped in vair.*

3   *"Welcome, Sir King, to homestead mine!*
     *Now will I spare neither mead nor wine."*

4   *"Little reck I of mead or wine,*
     *I pray thee, Dame Gundelil, be thou mine!*

5   *"Proud Gundelil, play on thy harp of gold,*
     *And all my love shalt thou have and hold.*

6   *"Proud Gundelil, play on thy harp for me!*
     *Saddle and steed will I give to thee."*

7   *"Harp I will not touch with hand*
     *Save when Sir Franklin doth command."*

8    "Proud Gundelil, strike the strings for me,
     Ribe and Ringsted I'll give to thee."

9    "I will not touch the strings, I wis,
     An thou give me no better gift than this."

10   "Proud Gundelil, play thy harp for me,
     Sælland and Skaane I'll give to thee."

11   When first proud Gundelil touched the string
     The King's grey courser did dance and spring.

12   There danced all the King's merry men
     By two and by three, and by twenty and ten.

13   When she played both high and low
     The King himself to dance must go.

14   So loud and clear the dame did play
     They danced out of the garth and far away.

15   He kissed her on the brow so white:
     "I thank thee, dame, for this hour's delight!"

16   She was courteous, fair and fine,
     She poured the King both mead and wine.

17   The King bade saddle his courser grey,
     In mood right merry he rode his way.

18   Home to the garth did Sir Franklin fare,
     There stood his dame wrapped all in vair.

19   "Welcome, dear husband, home today!
     The King but now hath ridden his way.

20   "Ribe and Ringsted both are thine,
     Sælland and Skaane both are mine."

21   "And have I Ribe and Ringsted now,
     The King thy honour hath spilt, I trow!"

22   "Now praised be God in heaven's hold,
     I won it all with my harp of gold!

23   "Thou'lt never gain more from kith and kin
     Than thy wife with her harp of gold did win."

### 26

## PROUD ELLENSBORG

1   Sir Peter went forth all in the garth
    With his good sword to play,
    And the long road to Jerusalem
    Was in his mind that day.
    And now I long so sore.

2   It was the knight Sir Peter
    Wrapped him in cloak of vair,
    And in the high-loft entered
    To seek his true-love there.

3   "Now say, how long wilt wait for me
    Thy maiden's bower within,
    While I fare afar o'er land and sea
    To wash away my sin?"

4   "A maiden will I wait for thee
    These seven long years and more:
    Wed will I not though King on throne
    Should give command therefor."

5   When seven long years were past and gone
     He came no more to land;
     Fair Ellensborg wrapped her in cloak of blue
     And sought the salt sea-strand.

6   "Now hark, thou goodly merchantman,
     What wares hast thou·to cry?"
     "Oh, linen I have both fine and fair,
     The best a dame could buy."

7   "Nay, linen is mine both fair and fine,
     And silks of coloured dye,
     But my sister's son doth sail the sea,
     And woeful for him am I."

8   "Now nay, full well the man I know
     For whom thou 'rt sorrowing,
     And his troth is plight to another maid
     In the land of the Eastern King!"

9   It was the lady Ellen
     Wrapped her in cloak of vair,
     And to the hall betook her
     To seek her brethren there.

10   "Now hail, my seven brethren bold,
     That are so dear to me!
     Now are ye boun for your sister's sake
     To sail across the sea?"

11   "Great peril it is for a carl, I wis,
     And worse for womenkind,
     The sea to sail through gust and gale,
     Full little gain to find."

12　It was the lady Ellensborg
　　That turned in wrath and pain:
　　"Long will it be ere day doth dawn
　　When I seek your rede again!"

13　It was the lady Ellensborg
　　Her serving-maids did call,
　　And took in hand her shears of gold
　　To clip their locks withal.

14　She clad them then in garments new
　　That were of knightly guise,
　　And sailed away to lands afar
　　Beyond the red sunrise.

15　Proud Ellensborg she took the helm,
　　Her maidens took the oar,
　　And or e'er two months were over
　　They came to the Eastern shore.

16　There did they cast anchor
　　All on the snow-white sand,
　　And it was the lady Ellensborg
　　That first set foot on land.

17　With sword at side proud Ellensborg
　　Did to the hold repair,
　　And greeting gave full courteously
　　To every lady fair.

18　Up spake the knight Sir Peter
　　That stood the board before:
　　"Christ's blessing on those beauteous eyne
　　I knew so well of yore!"

19  Up spake the knight Sir Peter
    With silver cup in hand:
    "Now welcome, thou son of my sister,
    Here to this strangers' land!"

20  "Now nay, no sister's son is this,
    With skin as white as milk,
    And locks that shine like gold spun fine
    Under the hood of silk!"

21  "Now lithe and listen, fair Mettelil,
    And tarry awhile for me,
    The whiles I walk with my sister's son
    Beneath the greenwood tree."

22  "Oh, pages hast thou and squires enow
    To follow the stranger's tread,
    But thou, goodsooth, like a gallant knight,
    Must follow thy bride to bed!"

23  "Pages have I and squires enow
    That my bride to bower may lead,
    But I will walk with my sister's son
    Over the blowing mead."

24  It was the knight Sir Peter
    That sailed away from land,
    It was the lady Ellensborg
    That steered him from the strand.

25  Right glad she loosed her locks of gold
    And cried her maids among:
    "Now doth Mettelil know the selfsame woe
    That I have felt so long!"

26   *Now where is the like of this lady?*
     *Her praise should all men sing,*
     *For she dared to loose her own true-love*
     *From the land of the Eastern King!*

27

### YOUNG SVEND DYRE

1   *Oh, gay are the King and his merry men all*
     *When to the Thing they go,*
     *But young Svend Dyre rides alone,*
     *And his heart is full of woe.*
     *That day the squire did of his lord take leave.*

2   *It was young Svend Dyre*
     *That to his mother cried:*
     *"Forth will I fare this day to greet*
     *Sir Magnus and his bride."*

3   *"And wilt thou fare this day to greet*
     *Sir Magnus and his bride,*
     *I rede thee by the Holy Rood*
     *That swiftly home thou ride!"*

4   *Oh, he girded aright his sword so bright,*
     *And spake up bold and free:*
     *"Now how can it be, my mother,*
     *That thou shouldst fear for me?"*

5   *It was the young Svend Dyre*
     *Rode forth the bride to meet,*
     *Silk and silvery samite*
     *Hung to his courser's feet.*

6    It was young Svend Dyre
     That rode along the strand,
     Of red, red gold was the bridle rein
     All glimmering in his hand.

7    Up spake the bride, a-smiling
     Beneath her mantle's fold:
     "Who may he be, this knight so young,
     That bears a brow so bold?"

8    Up spake the maiden by her side,
     And did reply with speed:
     "Oh, that is young Svend Dyre
     That rides so tall a steed."

9    "And is it young Svend Dyre
     That rides the steed so tall,
     May God in Heaven bear witness
     He loveth me best of all!"

10   Now scarcely had the bridal train
     Turned out their steeds to grass,
     Ere it was young Svend Dyre
     That to his seat would pass.

11   "Now bring to me a cushion soft,
     For I will choose my place,
     And sit beside our bonnie bride
     From sun to shade her face!"

12   Up stood the father of the bride,
     And spake in anger strong:
     "Thou shalt not sit by my daughter
     All with thy cozening tongue!"

13 "Oh, long have I dwelt in Paris town
　　Where many folk there be,
　　And my tongue is e'en as a dagger keen,
　　So well it wardeth me!"

14 "Goodsooth hast thou dwelt in Paris town
　　Where folk are fine and free,
　　And thine is the tongue of a rascal knave,
　　So ill it serveth thee!"

15 Late, so late at even,
　　When all men's beds were dight,
　　He up and asked, Svend Dyre,
　　Where he should lie that night.

16 "Oh, up on the roof of the high-loft,
　　Or down under beam and rafter,
　　There let him lie, Svend Dyre,
　　And no man follow after!"

17 Now when the bride to bower was boun
　　So late at evenfall,
　　Forth went young Svend Dyre
　　To arm his henchmen all.

18 "Now busk ye and boun in your byrnies brown,
　　And loosen your swords below,
　　And fare this hour to the bridal bower,
　　And see how the thing will go!"

19 And now they lit the tapers fair,
　　And lit the torches tall,
　　To lead the bride to bower
　　With knights and pages all.

20   When to the bower they led her
      With pomp beyond compare,
      Svend Dyre he quenched the bridal lights
      Or ever a man was ware.

21   Up spake the young bride's mother,
      And she was an angry dame:
      "Ill fare the wight that quenched the light,
      And on his head be shame!"

22   Up spake young Svend Dyre,
      So swift with tongue, I wis:
      " 'Twas I that blew your tapers out,
      And saved your breath for this!"

23   And now with speed he lapped the bride
      In scarlet cloak and hood,
      And lifted her when none espied
      Upon his courser good.

24   Now some in haste unlocked the bower,
      And some the torches lit.
      Svend Dyre bore the bride away
      Ere men were ware of it.

25   And his tongue I ween was heard again
      As they rode 'neath greenwood tree:
      "Magnus the Mighty, thou'lt see us no more,
      And so goodnight to thee!"

26   So fast and free by greenwood tree
      And blowing mead he sped,
      Till to his mother's home he came
      Ere they were boun for bed.

27    *Up stood she, proud Dame Mettelil,*
      *Wrapped well in cloak of vair,*
      *She kissed her son, Svend Dyre,*
      *And kissed his bride so fair.*

28    *Now hath the damsel Ellensborg*
      *Forgot all hurt and harm,*
      *For soft and sweet she sleepeth*
      *All on his lily-white arm.*

NOTE: Among the many ballads describing the rescue of a lady from an unwelcome marriage, this is remarkable for the mixture of force and polished impudence with which the hero gains access to the bride. It makes, moreover, its own little contribution to the history of manners, inasmuch as Svend Dyre, it seems, learnt his powers of repartee and his general savoir faire in Paris, "where many folk there be"—one of the few testimonies found in the ballads to the cultural influence of foreign towns and foreign chivalry.

## 28

## SIR PALLE'S BRIDAL

1    *And now the lady Gundelil*
      *Went in the kirk to pray,*
      *'Twas she the proud Sir Palle*
      *By force would bear away.*
      *Now spring the leaves on greenwood tree.*

2    *'Twas the proud knight Sir Palle*
      *Her litter straight did seek,*
      *All in his arms he seized the maid*
      *And kissed her rosy cheek.*

3    *"Ride hence, thou proud Sir Palle,*
      *And be not overbold!*
      *When bells are rung and Mass is sung*
      *I'll follow thee home to hold."*

4   'Twas the proud knight Sir Palle
     To kirk rode on eftsoon,
     His spurs were all of the red, red gold,
     And gilt his courser's shoon.

5   It was the lady Gundelil
     Stole off 'neath greenwood tree,
     And clad the swain that drove her steeds
     In guise of gay ladye.

6   She clad the swain that drove her steeds
     In silk and samite gay,
     And after him followed Gundelil
     All in the wadmal grey.

7   When Mass was done and folk were gone
     Homeward by wood and wold,
     It was the lady Gundelil
     That sought Sir Palle's hold.

8   And for to greet his beauteous bride
     His friends and kinsfolk fared,
     The silver white and gold so red
     Were spent and never spared.

9   They seated her on the bridal bench,
     That bride so fair and fine,
     And they pledged her in the mead so brown,
     And in the good red wine.

10  So fast when dew was falling
     Within the midnight hour,
     The bonnie bride and bridegroom
     Must go to bridal bower.

11 The bride they led to bridal bower
All at the mirk midnight,
Before went knights and pages
To bear the torches bright.

12 'Twas the proud knight Sir Palle
In bridal bed that lay,
It was the bride that moved aside
And turned her face away.

13 It was the proud Sir Palle
That kissed her cheek so red:
"Now turn not from me, mine own true-love,
Here in our bridal bed!"

14 "Shalt get no kiss from me, I wis,
Scathe shall be thine and scorn,
For I that am Gundelil's horse-boy
Was never a maiden born!"

15 "And art thou Gundelil's horse-boy
Hast done me this despite,
Ne'er shalt thou live to see the day
After this bridal night!"

16 'Twas the proud knight Sir Palle
For sword and spear did cry,
It was the lady's serving-lad
Sprang from the window high.

17 Great praise won that little horse-boy
That was to his lady true,
He forgot not her headgear of gold to bring,
Nor yet her silver shoe.

18    *It was the lady Gundelil*
      *Asked all the countryside:*
      *"What magic hath proud Sir Palle*
      *That could turn a swain to bride?"*

19    *It was the lady Gundelil*
      *That did him great annoy:*
      *She sent him cradle and swaddling-bands*
      *For the babe of the serving-boy!*

## 29
## TWO BRIDES AND ONE GROOM

1    *Sir Jens he sat with cup in hand,*
      *(So will we tread)*
      *And saw his sister before him stand.*
      *Sir Lovel's sweet flowers.*

2    *"Speak now, my sister, and rede me aright,*
      *Why is thy cheek so wan and white?"*

3    *Up spake young Kirsteen with many a tear:*
      *"Sir Lovel's babe I soon must bear."*

4    *Sir Jens sprang over the rocking board,*
      *Mead and wine at his feet were poured.*

5    *Sir Jens bade saddle his good grey steed:*
      *"I'll seek Sir Lovel, and that with speed!"*

6    *Unto his homestead they rode so straight,*
      *And there stood Sir Lovel beside the gate.*

7    *"Sir Lovel, my comrade, God give thee good cheer!*
      *Why hast thou beguiled my sister dear?"*

8  "May Christ forsake me in my need,
   If e'er I did so foul a deed!

9  "A love have I so fair and fine,
   Kirsteen shall never be bride of mine."

10 From the garth he rode away,
   Fast he spurred his courser grey.

11 The ladies decked Sir Lovel's maid,
   Sir Jens his sister fair arrayed.

12 Sir Jens rode forth from home again
   O'er the swart moorland with bridal train.

13 Two brides were led to the old kirk door,
   Sir Jens and his sister went before.

14 Up stood Sir Jens and spake and said:
   "Now first to my sister shalt thou be wed!"

15 Right merry it was for the folk to see
   How the priest held bridal for all the three.

16 Two brides were led to Sir Lovel's door,
   Sir Jens and his sister they went before.

17 Two brides on bridal bench they seated,
   And first Sir Jens his sister greeted.

18 When dew fell fast in the evening hour,
   Two brides must go to the bridal bower.

19 They kindled up the torches tall,
   And lighted the brides to the door withal.

20  Sir Jens did his sister in bride-bed lay,
    And to seek Sir Lovel he took his way.

21  "Now wilt thou sleep with the ravished bride,
    Or die by my hand this eventide?"

22  "Nay, rather I'll sleep with the ravished bride
    Than die by thy hand this eventide!"

23  Sir Jens he locked the door aright:
    "Stand out, bride the second, I bid thee goodnight!"

NOTE: The burden refers to the flowers and sweet herbs, with which the floors were strewn on festive occasions.

30

## SIR DAVID AND HIS STEPSONS

1  The lady Inger is fair as a rose,
   (By Brunby do the lordlings lie)
   Sir David to her a-wooing goes.
   So sore did the lady Inger weep.

2  "My sons are o'er young, my sons are o'er small
   For a stepfather's rule in bower and hall."

3  He swore by all on earth that grew
   He would be to her sons a father true.

4  "A tender father I'll be, and more,
   Till they can wear weapons and go to war."

5  Fair Ingerlil wrapped her in cloak of vair,
   And all to speak with her sons did fare.

6    "Now lithe and listen, my children twain,
      Would it please ye or no if I wed again?"

7    Her elder son he up and said:
      "I beg thee, dear mother, to bide unwed."

8    Up spake her younger that thought no ill:
      "Now let our dear mother do what she will!"

9    Or ever Sir David wended and went
      He won fair Inger to give consent.

10    When a month was gone and two and three
      Her sons he would neither hear nor see.

11    Their mother nurtured them tenderly,
      But the kinder she was the harsher waxed he.

12    Sir David wrapped him in cloak of vair,
      And went to speak with his lady fair.

13    "Harken, my lady so fair and fine,
      Shall they not be chieftains, those sons of thine?"

14    "So young they are, they still would fail
      To bear the heavy coat of mail."

15    "And if they may not warriors be,
      They shall be seamen and sail the sea."

16    He built him a ship, that knight so bold,
      With burning charcoal he laded her hold.

17    Aloft she was laden with mead so sweet,
      But the burning fire was under their feet.

18  Sir David thrust them out from land,
    Fair Ingerlil wept on the snow-white strand.

19  The mead was sweet, the day was fair,
    Fast they slept and slumbered there.

20  Sir Arild woke to a sight of dread,
    For his brother in burning fire lay dead.

21  "Now will I drown in the deep, I wis,
    Rather than die a death like his!"

22  Sir David went down to the snow-white strand,
    And saw where her sons had drifted to land.

23  The rings he took from their hands so white,
    And he buried them deep out of all men's sight.

24  Now five long months were past and o'er,
    But fair Ingerlil's sons returned no more.

25  All on the Sabbath when eve drew on
    The knight and his lady to bathe were gone.

26  And when fair Ingerlil looked aside
    She saw on his hands those rings of pride.

27  "What sight is this mine eyes behold?
    Sir Arild wore those rings of gold!"

28  "Now cease thy prating, and let be!
    One ring like another is fair to see."

29  Fair Ingerlil took her maidens three,
    And went to gaze o'er the salt blue sea.

30   Lo, there sang a bird all shining and white:
     "Now weep no more for thy sons tonight!

31   "On the spot where thou sittest they lie and sleep,
     And ne'er wilt thou wake them from slumber deep."

32   Fair Ingerlil dug with her lily-white hands
     Till she found her sons in the shifting sands.

33   With linen fine in fair array
     She decked their bodies where they lay.

34   "Now since my sons no longer live
     Their heritage for their souls I'll give.

35   "Here shall the bells of a minster ring,
     And priests the Holy Mass shall sing.

36   "What ill did they do thee, thou cruel knight,
     Those that I weep for in woeful plight?

37   "Love I gave them and kisses sweet,
     But thou didst grudge them dry bread to eat.

38   "God pity the widow with babes at her knee
     If she give them a stepsire like unto thee!

39   "God grant us a better life than this
     Before His throne in heaven's bliss!"

NOTE: At the fishing village of Arildsleje in the parish of Brunby, stands a chapel where services were held only during the fishing season, and where no bodies were buried except those which were washed ashore. Popularly known as Saint Arild's chapel, it was said to have been erected over the body of an unfortunate boy who was drowned by his wicked stepfather.

There are various versions of the ballad. One, current in Skaane during the eighteenth century, concludes with the building of the church. Another, preserved in the M.S. albums of the sixteenth and seventeenth centuries, ends with the story of the stepfather's punishment.

# 31

# SIR KAREL'S LYKEWAKE

1  *It was young Sir Karel*
   *His mother's rede did pray*
   *If he should to the convent ride*
   *And bear his love away.*
   *The roses and the lilies all a-blowing.*

2  "Now feign that thou art sick to death,
   And lie the bier upon,
   And heed lest any ask of thee
   If thou art living man."

3  Late, so late at even
   Sore sickness on him fell,
   So early in the morning
   They tolled for him the bell.

4  They took the young Sir Karel
   And streeked him for a corse,
   While all to bear the tidings round
   His page hath taken horse.

5  Unto the door of the cloister
   All with the bier they hied,
   The Prior came forth to meet them
   With mickle pomp and pride.

6  Forth fared the little pages,
   Clad in the scarlet red,
   They bade the damsels come to watch,
   "For young Sir Karel is dead."

7   *It was little Kirsteen*
    *Spake with her mother dear:*
    *"And may I wend to the watching*
    *Over Sir Karel's bier?"*

8   *"Yea, do thou on thy scarlet weed,*
    *And deck thy head with gold,*
    *But be thou ware of Sir Karel,*
    *His wiles are manifold!"*

9   *She entered in, the little maid,*
    *Amid the tapers' shine,*
    *She could not see them burning*
    *So tearful were her eyne.*

10   *Beside his head she sat her down,*
    *And for his soul she prayed:*
    *"Alas, thou wert my dearest love*
    *In the days ere thou wert dead!"*

11   *Beside his feet she sat her down,*
    *And smoothed the linen white:*
    *"Oh, in the days ere thou wert dead*
    *I called thee heart's delight!"*

12   *Right softly then he up and spake:*
    *"Now cease from tene and tear,*
    *Behold, 'tis all for love of thee*
    *I lie upon the bier!*

13   *"My steed stands in the cloister-garth*
    *A-tarrying all for thee,*
    *Then ho for the woods and waters,*
    *And a home in the wilds with me!"*

14   *It was young Sir Karel*
     *Rose straightway from the dead,*
     *And a gay goodnight to the cloister,*
     *And its bells and its books they bade.*

15   *The nuns they all sat silent,*
     *And on their books read they,*
     *They thought 'twas God's good angel*
     *That bore the maid away.*

16   *The nuns they all sat silent,*
     *Each to herself said she:*
     *"God grant that His good angel*
     *May speedily come for me!"*